Cloud Infrastructure Deep Dive: Azure the Pro Way

Kameron Hussain and Frahaan Hussain

Published by Sonar Publishing, 2025.

CLOUD INFRASTRUCTURE DEEP DIVE: AZURE THE PRO WAY

First edition. April 25, 2025.

ISBN: 979-8231133185

Written by Kameron Hussain and Frahaan Hussain.

Azure 101: The No-Fluff Beginner's Guide

First Edition

Preface

Welcome to the **first edition** of *Azure 101: The No-Fluff Beginner's Guide*. This book is designed for readers who are new to Microsoft Azure or cloud computing in general, and want a clear, practical, and structured introduction to the platform. Whether you're a student, developer, IT professional, or cloud enthusiast, this book aims to give you the foundation you need to start building, deploying, and managing cloud solutions using Azure.

The cloud can be an overwhelming domain to enter, especially with its fast-changing services and expansive documentation. Our approach with this book is to cut through the noise and provide you with a learning journey that gradually builds up your knowledge—from understanding basic infrastructure components to deploying advanced multi-cloud architectures.

We start with an introduction to cloud computing and Microsoft Azure's core offerings, before diving into resource management with Azure Resource Manager. Compute services, including virtual machines, containers, and serverless solutions, are covered in depth to give you multiple paths for hosting applications. Networking and storage are explored in technical and practical terms so that you can architect robust, scalable systems.

Security is a critical part of working in the cloud, and we devote dedicated chapters to identity, access management, and compliance. You'll also learn how to monitor your resources and optimize their performance with Azure-native tools. High availability and resiliency are essential for modern systems, so we walk you through planning for redundancy and disaster recovery.

We also explore hybrid and multi-cloud solutions, showing how Azure integrates with on-premises environments and other major cloud providers. Finally, real-world case studies help contextualize what you've learned and demonstrate how large-scale Azure solutions are built in industries such as healthcare, fintech, and government.

Throughout the book, we emphasize practical examples, command-line tools, architectural best practices, and security guidelines. The appendices provide reference material, further learning resources, and code snippets to extend your skills even after you've finished the core content.

We hope this guide empowers you to start your Azure journey confidently and inspires you to explore deeper into the possibilities of cloud computing.

Table of Contents

Data Lake

Defender for Cloud

Disaster Recovery (DR)

Elasticity

Event Grid

ExpressRoute

High Availability (HA)

Hybrid Cloud

Infrastructure as Code (IaC)

Key Vault

Load Balancer

Managed Identity

Microservices

Network Security Group (NSG)

PaaS (Platform as a Service)

RBAC (Role-Based Access Control)

Resource Group

Serverless

Site-to-Site VPN

Virtual Network (VNet)

Chapter 1: Introduction to Azure Cloud Infrastructure

Overview of Cloud Computing Models

Cloud computing has revolutionized how businesses and individuals build, deploy, and scale applications and services. Before diving into Azure specifically, it's important to understand the foundational cloud computing models that Azure—and all major cloud platforms—operate on. These models dictate how resources are provisioned, maintained, and consumed by end-users and enterprises.

The Three Service Models

There are three primary service models in cloud computing:

---

1. Infrastructure as a Service (IaaS)

IaaS provides virtualized computing resources over the internet. It allows you to rent servers, storage, and networking hardware on demand. You are responsible for managing the OS, applications, and runtime, while the provider manages the physical infrastructure.

Key Characteristics:

- Virtual Machines (VMs) for full control
- Networking configuration
- Storage management
- Load balancing and IP allocation

Examples in Azure:

- Azure Virtual Machines
- Azure Virtual Network
- Azure Load Balancer

---

2. Platform as a Service (PaaS)

PaaS abstracts much of the infrastructure layer and focuses on the application logic. Developers can deploy applications without worrying about hardware provisioning, OS maintenance, or server configuration.

Key Characteristics:

- Application hosting
- Integrated development tools
- Database services
- Built-in scalability and load balancing

Examples in Azure:

- Azure App Services
- Azure Functions
- Azure SQL Database

---

3. Software as a Service (SaaS)

SaaS delivers complete applications via the internet. Users access the software through a web browser, while everything from infrastructure to application maintenance is handled by the provider.

Key Characteristics:

- No local installation required
- Subscription or usage-based pricing
- Accessible across devices

Examples in Azure Ecosystem:

- Microsoft 365
- Dynamics 365
- Power BI (in SaaS form)

Cloud Deployment Models

Besides service models, cloud deployments fall into three major categories, each with its use cases and constraints.

Public Cloud

All hardware, software, and supporting infrastructure are owned and managed by a third-party cloud provider and delivered over the internet.

- Resources shared across multiple users (multi-tenant)
- Cost-effective for most use cases
- High scalability and redundancy

Example: Azure's public cloud offering.

Private Cloud

Resources are exclusively used by a single organization. This infrastructure can be located on-premises or hosted by a third-party provider.

- Enhanced security and control
- Suitable for compliance-heavy industries (e.g., finance, healthcare)
- Higher cost due to dedicated infrastructure

Example: Azure Stack HCI, used for on-premises Azure services.

Hybrid Cloud

A combination of public and private cloud, often used to support legacy workloads while modernizing with public cloud services.

- Balanced approach between control and scalability
- Supports gradual migration to the cloud
- Complex integration required

Example: Azure Arc, which allows unified operations across environments.

The Shared Responsibility Model

In any cloud model, security and compliance responsibilities are divided between the cloud provider and the customer. This concept is known as the Shared Responsibility Model.

For IaaS:

- Azure secures the physical layer, virtualization, and networking
- You are responsible for OS patching, data, applications, firewalls

For PaaS:

- Azure handles OS and platform maintenance
- You manage your code, configurations, and identity controls

For SaaS:

- Azure manages the entire stack
- You are mainly responsible for identity and access controls

Understanding this model is critical for ensuring security best practices and compliance.

Benefits of Cloud Computing

Some of the major benefits of cloud adoption include:

- **Scalability**: Rapidly scale up or down based on demand
- **Cost-Efficiency**: Pay-as-you-go pricing and no capital expenditure

- **Agility**: Faster provisioning of resources to support innovation
- **Global Reach**: Deploy applications closer to users around the world
- **Resiliency**: Built-in failover and redundancy capabilities

---

Challenges and Considerations

While cloud computing brings many benefits, it also introduces new complexities:

- **Vendor Lock-in**: Reliance on specific cloud tools can hinder portability
- **Security and Compliance**: Must ensure encryption, access controls, and auditability
- **Cost Overruns**: Mismanaged resources can lead to unexpected bills
- **Performance**: Multi-tenancy can affect resource availability
- **Data Governance**: You must know where your data resides and who has access

---

Example: Deploying a Web App on Azure

Here's a basic example using Azure CLI to deploy a PaaS web app:

```
# Login to Azure
```

az login

Create a resource group

az group create—name MyResourceGroup—location eastus

Create an App Service plan

az appservice plan create—name MyPlan—resource-group MyResourceGroup—sku FREE

Create a web app

az webapp create—name MyWebApp123—resource-group MyResourceGroup—plan MyPlan

This simple set of commands sets up an environment where you can deploy and host your website in minutes.

Conclusion

Understanding the fundamental models of cloud computing is essential before diving into Azure-specific services. Whether you're building applications or designing enterprise architectures, the choice between IaaS, PaaS, and SaaS—and between public, private, or hybrid deployments—will significantly affect your architecture, security posture, and operational model.

With this foundational knowledge, you're now ready to explore the Microsoft Azure platform in more depth, beginning with how to manage resources effectively using the Azure Resource Manager.

Introduction to Microsoft Azure

Microsoft Azure is one of the leading public cloud platforms in the world, offering a comprehensive set of tools and services to build, deploy, and manage applications through Microsoft-managed data centers. Azure provides solutions that span infrastructure (IaaS), platform (PaaS), and software (SaaS) services, catering to developers, IT professionals, and businesses of all sizes.

Understanding Azure requires not only knowledge of its individual services, but also of how they fit into real-world business and technical contexts. This section dives deep into the origins, architecture, service categories, and usage of Microsoft Azure, laying the groundwork for mastering the platform.

Origins and Evolution

Microsoft Azure was launched in 2010 under the name "Windows Azure," initially focusing on providing Windows-based PaaS offerings. Over time, it evolved to support a wide range of operating systems, programming languages, frameworks, databases, and devices. In 2014, Microsoft rebranded it to "Microsoft Azure" to reflect its broader scope and cross-platform support.

Azure has grown to become one of the top three global cloud providers, alongside Amazon Web Services (AWS) and Google Cloud Platform (GCP). With continual investments in regions, services, AI, hybrid cloud, and multi-cloud capabilities, Azure has positioned itself as a platform of choice for enterprises and startups alike.

Key Characteristics

Some defining attributes of Microsoft Azure include:

- **Global Presence**: Dozens of regions and availability zones worldwide.

- **Enterprise Integration**: Tight integration with Microsoft services like Active Directory, Windows Server, and Microsoft 365.

- **Hybrid Capabilities**: Tools like Azure Arc and Azure Stack enable hybrid and on-premises scenarios.

- **Open Source Support**: Native support for Linux, Kubernetes, PostgreSQL, and other open-source technologies.

- **Security and Compliance**: Advanced tools for identity, encryption, and governance with support for compliance standards (HIPAA, GDPR, ISO 27001).

Azure Account Structure

To use Azure effectively, it's essential to understand how accounts, subscriptions, and resources are organized.

Azure Account

Your Azure account is tied to a Microsoft identity (e.g., a Microsoft 365 or Outlook account). It is the foundation for billing and identity management.

Subscription

A subscription is a container for resources and serves as the billing boundary. You can have multiple subscriptions under one account to separate projects, environments, or departments.

Management Groups

For organizations with multiple subscriptions, management groups allow you to organize and apply governance policies at scale.

Tenants and Azure Active Directory (AAD)

Every Azure account belongs to a tenant—a dedicated and trusted instance of Azure Active Directory. This is where identities and directory data are managed.

View your current tenant ID using Azure CLI

az account show—query tenantId—output tsv

Azure Portal

The **Azure Portal** is the web-based UI where users can manage resources, create services, monitor performance, configure policies, and much more. It's intuitive and supports advanced features such as dashboards, role-based access control, and cost analysis tools.

Key Features:

- Resource search and creation
- Blade-based UI navigation
- Access to Azure Marketplace
- Integration with documentation and support
- Customizable dashboards

For example, to create a new virtual machine from the portal:

1. Navigate to "Virtual Machines"
2. Click "Create"
3. Choose an image, size, and region
4. Configure networking and security
5. Review and create

Azure CLI and PowerShell

For automation and scripting, Azure supports both a cross-platform command-line interface (Azure CLI) and Azure PowerShell.

Example: Creating a resource group with Azure CLI

az group create—name MyGroup—location westus

Example: Creating the same with Azure PowerShell

New-AzResourceGroup -Name "MyGroup" -Location "West US"

CLI tools are vital for CI/CD, infrastructure as code, and DevOps practices, and are explored in greater detail in later chapters.

Azure Marketplace

Azure Marketplace is a hub for third-party solutions and preconfigured services that can be deployed with a few clicks. This includes:

- Virtual machine images
- Application stacks
- Security solutions
- SaaS integrations

You can use the marketplace to deploy common solutions like WordPress, Ubuntu, Barracuda firewalls, or Splunk in seconds.

Categories of Azure Services

Azure is organized into numerous service categories. Here are some of the most critical:

Compute

Services to run applications and workloads:

- **Azure Virtual Machines**: Windows and Linux VMs
- **Azure App Service**: Managed web apps and APIs
- **Azure Functions**: Serverless computing
- **Azure Kubernetes Service (AKS)**: Managed Kubernetes

Storage

Durable and scalable storage for any kind of data:

- **Blob Storage**: Object storage for unstructured data
- **Azure Files**: SMB file shares
- **Queues, Tables, and Disks**: Messaging, NoSQL, and block storage

Networking

Connect and secure applications:

- **Virtual Network (VNet)**: Logical network isolation
- **Application Gateway**: Load balancing and web app firewall
- **Azure Front Door**: Global routing and CDN
- **ExpressRoute**: Private connection to on-premises environments

Databases

Fully managed database services:

- **Azure SQL Database**
- **Cosmos DB** (globally distributed NoSQL)
- **Azure Database for MySQL/PostgreSQL**

AI & Machine Learning

Cloud-based AI capabilities:

- **Azure Machine Learning**: Model training and deployment
- **Cognitive Services**: Vision, speech, and language APIs

- **Azure OpenAI Service**: Access to GPT-based models

Identity

Access management and security:

- **Azure Active Directory**
- **Multi-Factor Authentication (MFA)**
- **Conditional Access Policies**

DevOps

Tools for continuous integration and delivery:

- **Azure DevOps Services**: Boards, Pipelines, Repos, Artifacts
- **GitHub Actions**: Native integration with GitHub for automation
- **Azure Container Registry**: Docker image storage

Analytics

Data pipelines and real-time insights:

- **Azure Synapse Analytics**
- **Azure Data Factory**
- **Azure Stream Analytics**

- **Log Analytics**

IoT

Support for internet-connected devices:

- **IoT Hub**
- **Azure Digital Twins**
- **Azure Sphere**

Each of these service categories is covered in more depth in later chapters, with walkthroughs and architecture diagrams.

Regional Availability

Azure services are available across multiple geographic regions and availability zones. A region is a set of data centers deployed within a specific geographical area, and each region is isolated and contains one or more availability zones.

To deploy a service in a specific region:

```
az vm create \
—resource-group MyGroup \
—name MyVM \
—image UbuntuLTS \
—location eastus
```

Azure regions include:

- East US, West US, Central US

- North Europe, West Europe
- Southeast Asia, Japan East
- Australia East, South India
- Brazil South, Canada Central

Azure's global footprint is continuously expanding to meet data residency, redundancy, and performance needs.

Azure Support and SLAs

Azure offers multiple levels of support—from community-based forums to enterprise-grade support with guaranteed response times. It also provides service-level agreements (SLAs) that guarantee uptime (e.g., 99.9% or higher for most services), which is critical for planning high-availability solutions.

Cost Management and Free Tier

Azure's pay-as-you-go pricing means you are charged based on your actual usage. Tools such as the **Azure Pricing Calculator** and **Cost Management + Billing** help you estimate and track your spending.

New users often start with the **Azure Free Account**, which includes:

- $200 credit for 30 days
- Free tier services for 12 months (e.g., Linux/Windows VMs, SQL DB)
- Always-free services (e.g., Functions, DevTest Labs, App Services)

Example: Provisioning a Web App via CLI

```
# Login

az login

# Create a resource group

az group create—name WebAppGroup—location centralus

# Create an App Service Plan

az appservice plan create—name WebPlan—resource-group WebAppGroup—sku B1—is-linux

# Create a Web App

az webapp create \

—resource-group WebAppGroup \

—plan WebPlan \

—name MyUniqueWebAppName \

—runtime "NODE|16-lts"
```

Conclusion

Microsoft Azure is a powerful and versatile cloud platform that offers solutions for almost every type of modern workload—from small developer projects to large-scale enterprise systems. Its hybrid-friendly architecture, expansive global infrastructure, deep integrations with Microsoft products, and commitment to security and compliance make it an ideal choice for both new learners and seasoned professionals.

In the upcoming chapters, we'll take a hands-on approach to managing resources, deploying compute services, configuring networks, securing data, and building resilient systems. With a solid understanding of Azure's capabilities and ecosystem, you are well-prepared to start building in the cloud.

Key Components of Azure Infrastructure

Microsoft Azure offers a vast and interconnected ecosystem of services and resources that form the backbone of its cloud infrastructure. At the heart of Azure's functionality lies a well-orchestrated infrastructure stack, built to support global availability, resilience, security, and performance for workloads of any scale. In this section, we will explore the core components that underpin Azure's infrastructure, from resource hierarchies and compute layers to storage architecture, networking fabric, and identity models.

Understanding these components is crucial for architects, developers, and IT professionals as they design and operate applications in the cloud.

Resource Hierarchy in Azure

Azure organizes its infrastructure using a logical hierarchy to help manage, secure, and govern cloud resources effectively.

1. Management Groups

These are containers for organizing multiple subscriptions. Policies and access controls can be applied at this level and inherited down the hierarchy.

2. Subscriptions

Subscriptions define billing boundaries and serve as containers for resources. Each subscription has its own resource quotas and access controls.

3. Resource Groups

A resource group is a logical container for related resources. You can deploy, manage, and monitor resources collectively. It's best practice to group resources with the same lifecycle into a single resource group.

```
# Creating a resource group using Azure CLI

az group create—name MyResourceGroup—location eastus
```

4. Resources

Resources are the actual services like virtual machines, storage accounts, databases, etc. Each resource belongs to one resource group.

This hierarchical model ensures scalability in management and the application of policies and role-based access control (RBAC).

Compute Infrastructure

Compute is a fundamental building block in Azure. It encompasses all resources that perform processing tasks, whether in the form of virtual machines, containers, or serverless functions.

Virtual Machines (VMs)

Azure VMs allow users to deploy scalable, on-demand Windows or Linux machines. These VMs run on physical servers in Azure's data centers and are managed via Azure Resource Manager (ARM).

Key elements of VMs:

- **VM Sizes**: Optimized for general, compute, memory, GPU, or storage workloads.
- **Disks**: OS disk, data disks, and temporary disks.
- **Availability**: Availability Sets and Availability Zones for redundancy.

```
# Provision a basic VM

az vm create \

—resource-group MyResourceGroup \

—name MyVM \

—image UbuntuLTS \

—admin-username azureuser \

—generate-ssh-keys
```

Azure App Services

A PaaS offering that simplifies web app and API hosting. It abstracts the OS layer and provides automatic scaling, load balancing, custom domains, and CI/CD integration.

Containers and Kubernetes

Azure supports containerized applications via:

- **Azure Kubernetes Service (AKS)**: Managed Kubernetes
- **Azure Container Instances (ACI)**: Lightweight container deployment
- **Azure Container Apps**: Managed environment for microservices

```
# Deploy a container instance
az container create \
—name mycontainer \
—image nginx \
—resource-group MyResourceGroup \
—dns-name-label mynginxtest \
—ports 80
```

Serverless Functions

Azure Functions allow you to execute code without provisioning servers. Ideal for event-driven applications.

```
# Create a function app (requires storage and app service plan)
az functionapp create \
—name myfunctionapp \
```

```
—storage-account mystorage \
—resource-group MyResourceGroup \
—consumption-plan-location eastus \
—runtime node
```

Networking Infrastructure

Networking is critical for communication within and between resources, as well as for user access from external systems.

Virtual Network (VNet)

A VNet is an isolated network within Azure that allows resources to securely communicate. It supports subnets, routing tables, and network security groups (NSGs).

```
# Create a virtual network
az network vnet create \
—name MyVNet \
—resource-group MyResourceGroup \
—subnet-name MySubnet
```

Network Security Groups (NSGs)

NSGs act as virtual firewalls, allowing or denying traffic based on source IP, destination IP, protocol, and port.

```
# Create NSG and add rule
```

az network nsg create—resource-group MyResourceGroup—name MyNSG

az network nsg rule create \

—resource-group MyResourceGroup \

—nsg-name MyNSG \

—name AllowSSH \

—protocol Tcp \

—direction Inbound \

—priority 1000 \

—source-address-prefix '*' \

—source-port-range '*' \

—destination-address-prefix '*' \

—destination-port-range 22 \

—access Allow

Load Balancers and Gateways

Azure provides several load balancing options:

- **Basic Load Balancer**: Layer 4 (TCP/UDP) traffic distribution
- **Application Gateway**: Layer 7 routing, SSL termination, Web Application Firewall (WAF)

- **Azure Front Door**: Global HTTP/HTTPS routing and CDN
- **Traffic Manager**: DNS-based traffic distribution

ExpressRoute and VPN Gateway

For private or hybrid connectivity, use:

- **VPN Gateway**: Secure tunnels over the internet
- **ExpressRoute**: Dedicated private connections with high bandwidth and low latency

---

Storage Infrastructure

Azure offers highly durable, scalable storage for every data need—from unstructured objects to structured relational databases.

Storage Types

- **Blob Storage**: For massive unstructured data (videos, backups, logs)
- **File Storage**: Managed SMB file shares
- **Queue Storage**: Messaging between distributed components
- **Table Storage**: Key-value NoSQL data
- **Disk Storage**: Used for VM OS and data disks

```
# Create a storage account

az storage account create \

—name mystorageaccount \

—resource-group MyResourceGroup \

—location eastus \

—sku Standard_LRS
```

Storage Tiers

Azure Blob Storage supports access tiers:

- **Hot**: Frequent access
- **Cool**: Infrequent access
- **Archive**: Rare access, archival only

You can change tiers programmatically or automatically using lifecycle management policies.

Redundancy Options

- **LRS (Locally Redundant Storage)**: 3 copies in a single datacenter
- **GRS (Geo-Redundant Storage)**: Replication to a secondary region
- **RA-GRS (Read-Access GRS)**: GRS with read access to the secondary

Identity and Access Infrastructure

Azure uses a robust identity framework to manage authentication and authorization.

Azure Active Directory (AAD)

AAD is Microsoft's cloud-based identity and access management service. It handles user identities, single sign-on, MFA, and directory federation.

AAD components:

- **Users & Groups**
- **Service Principals**: Used for applications and automation
- **Managed Identities**: Auto-managed credentials for Azure services
- **Enterprise Applications**: Pre-integrated SaaS apps with SSO

```
# Create a service principal
az ad sp create-for-rbac—name "myapp"
```

Role-Based Access Control (RBAC)

RBAC lets you assign specific permissions to users, groups, and services.

Built-in roles include:

- **Owner**
- **Contributor**
- **Reader**
- **Storage Blob Data Contributor**

```
# Assign Contributor role
az role assignment create \
—assignee <userPrincipalName> \
—role Contributor \
—scope /subscriptions/<subscription-id>/resourceGroups/MyResourceGroup
```

Monitoring and Telemetry

Every Azure resource can emit logs and metrics, which can be captured and analyzed through:

- **Azure Monitor**: Unified monitoring solution
- **Log Analytics**: Query and analyze logs
- **Application Insights**: App-level performance monitoring
- **Activity Logs**: Track subscription-level events

```
# Enable diagnostics on a VM
az monitor diagnostic-settings create \
```

—name vmDiagnostics \

—resource /subscriptions/<sub-id>/resourceGroups/MyResourceGroup/providers/Microsoft.Compute/virtualMachines/MyVM \

—workspace <log-analytics-workspace-id>

Security and Compliance Infrastructure

Security is a first-class citizen in Azure's infrastructure:

- **Azure Security Center**: Centralized view of security posture
- **Microsoft Defender for Cloud**: Threat protection for workloads
- **Key Vault**: Secure storage of secrets, certificates, and keys
- **Policy & Blueprints**: Enforce compliance and governance

Integration and Extensibility

Azure resources can be integrated with:

- **DevOps pipelines** using GitHub Actions or Azure DevOps
- **Infrastructure as Code (IaC)** using ARM templates, Bicep, Terraform

- **Event-driven automation** using Event Grid, Logic Apps, or Functions
- **Third-party tools** like Datadog, Splunk, and ServiceNow

Example: Deploying with a Bicep template

```
resource stg 'Microsoft.Storage/storageAccounts@2022-09-01' =
{
name: 'mystoragebicep'
location: 'eastus'
sku: {
name: 'Standard_LRS'
}
kind: 'StorageV2'
properties: {}
}
```

Conclusion

The components of Azure infrastructure form a powerful and flexible foundation for building virtually any type of cloud solution. From organizing resources using subscriptions and groups, to deploying compute and storage, to securing access and configuring global networking, Azure equips users with all the tools needed to operate at scale.

Each layer—from compute to storage to identity—is deeply integrated and can be managed through portals, APIs, command-line tools, or code. As we continue through this book, we'll explore how to architect these components effectively and automate their deployment using modern DevOps practices. With this knowledge, you can confidently begin architecting real-world systems on Azure.

Azure's Global Infrastructure Footprint

Microsoft Azure operates one of the largest, most secure, and resilient cloud infrastructures in the world. Its global architecture is strategically built to support massive scale, low latency, geographic compliance, fault tolerance, and business continuity. Understanding Azure's global infrastructure footprint is essential for deploying applications that need to be high-performing, reliable, and available across regions and markets.

This section explores how Azure's data centers, regions, availability zones, geographies, edge nodes, and network fabric contribute to its cloud infrastructure strategy. It also examines the implications of these elements for developers, architects, and organizations seeking to optimize for performance, compliance, and disaster recovery.

Global Reach and Data Centers

Azure spans a vast network of **physical data centers** distributed across the world. These data centers are the foundational layer upon which all other Azure services operate.

- Each data center houses physical servers, storage arrays, networking equipment, and other critical infrastructure.

- Data centers are operated and maintained by Microsoft and are secured using advanced physical and logical protection.
- Microsoft continually adds new data centers to meet global demand and ensure data sovereignty.

The goal of this physical footprint is to provide **global coverage with local presence**—allowing customers to deploy workloads close to their users for optimal performance and to comply with regional regulations.

Azure Regions

A **region** in Azure is a set of data centers deployed within a defined geographic area, interconnected through a dedicated low-latency network.

Key facts:

- As of writing, Azure has **60+ regions** available and announced, covering more global markets than any other cloud provider.
- Each region is designed to be **independent and isolated**, with its own power, cooling, and networking resources.
- Regions typically contain **multiple data centers** to support redundancy and scaling.

Example regions:

- East US

- West Europe
- Southeast Asia
- Australia East
- Brazil South
- South Africa North
- UAE Central
- Norway East

When creating a resource, you must choose a region. It impacts performance, latency, availability, and compliance.

List available regions in your subscription

az account list-locations—output table

Choosing a Region

When selecting a region, consider the following factors:

- **Proximity to end users**
- **Regulatory requirements** (e.g., GDPR, HIPAA)
- **Service availability** (not all services are available in all regions)
- **Pricing differences** between regions
- **Disaster recovery planning** (using paired or distant regions)

Availability Zones

Azure provides **Availability Zones** within certain regions to ensure high availability and fault tolerance for mission-critical applications.

An Availability Zone (AZ) is:

- A **physically separate zone** within a region, with its own power, cooling, and networking.
- Connected to other zones via **high-speed, low-latency links**.
- Designed to support **99.99% uptime SLA** when services are deployed across multiple zones.

Regions with Availability Zones are referred to as **zone-redundant regions**.

Example: East US 2, West Europe, Southeast Asia

You can explicitly deploy resources across zones. For example, when creating a virtual machine or a managed disk, you can specify the zone:

```
az vm create \

—resource-group MyResourceGroup \

—name MyZoneVM \

—image UbuntuLTS \

—zone 1 \

—admin-username azureuser \
```

—generate-ssh-keys

Zone-Redundant Services

Some Azure services are **zone-redundant** by default:

- Azure SQL Database (Premium/Business Critical tiers)
- Azure Kubernetes Service (AKS)
- Azure Load Balancer (Standard SKU)
- Azure Storage (ZRS—Zone-Redundant Storage)

Benefits of Zones

- **Fault Isolation**: Failure in one zone doesn't affect others.
- **Higher Availability**: Deploying across multiple zones minimizes downtime.
- **Resilience**: Supports recovery from power, cooling, or networking failures.

Paired Regions

Every Azure region is paired with another region within the same geography to support **business continuity and disaster recovery** (BCDR).

- Region pairs are typically **separated by at least 300 miles.**

- Microsoft schedules updates so that paired regions aren't updated simultaneously.
- Data replication between services (e.g., GRS storage) happens between paired regions.

Examples:

- East US ↔ West US
- North Europe ↔ West Europe
- Southeast Asia ↔ East Asia

These pairs are especially important when designing **geo-redundant solutions**, as they ensure that failover can occur across geographically distinct but logically linked regions.

Azure Geographies

Azure geographies are **defined markets** that contain multiple regions. Each geography aligns with **legal and regulatory boundaries**, ensuring compliance with local laws and standards.

Examples:

- **United States**
- **European Union**
- **United Kingdom**
- **Canada**
- **India**

- **China (operated by 21Vianet)**
- **Germany (Sovereign region)**

Geographies allow customers to ensure that data residency and sovereignty requirements are met. For instance, German customer data may never leave German soil if stored in Germany's sovereign cloud.

Edge Nodes and CDN Integration

Beyond core data centers, Azure includes **edge nodes**, which are distributed points of presence (PoPs) around the world. These nodes support services like:

- **Azure Content Delivery Network (CDN)**
- **Azure Front Door**
- **Traffic Manager**
- **ExpressRoute peering points**

Edge nodes help improve performance and reduce latency by bringing content closer to users.

Azure CDN, for instance, caches static content like images and scripts at these edge locations:

```
az cdn endpoint create \
—resource-group MyResourceGroup \
—profile-name MyCDNProfile \
—name MyCDNEndpoint \
```

—origin mywebsite.azurewebsites.net

These edge services work in tandem with Azure's global infrastructure to deliver content efficiently and securely across continents.

Azure Network Backbone

Azure's regions and services are connected by a **dedicated fiber-optic network** that spans the globe:

- Over **175,000 miles** of terrestrial and subsea fiber
- Private interconnects with ISPs and partners
- Global reach for **high-performance, low-latency** routing

This network underpins services like Azure Virtual WAN, ExpressRoute, and Azure Front Door, and allows organizations to securely and reliably build **cross-region** or **multi-region** architectures.

Compliance and Data Residency

Azure's infrastructure is designed with **compliance in mind.** Microsoft adheres to **more than 100 compliance certifications**, including:

- ISO 27001, 27017, 27018
- SOC 1, 2, 3
- HIPAA
- FedRAMP

- GDPR
- IRAP (Australia)
- MTCS (Singapore)

Azure enables customers to **control where their data resides**, a crucial capability for regulated industries like finance, government, and healthcare. This is achieved through:

- Choosing specific regions for storage and compute
- Using data residency tools
- Employing encryption and key management (e.g., Azure Key Vault, Customer Managed Keys)

Service Availability by Region

Not all services are immediately available in all regions. Azure maintains a **region service availability matrix**, which helps determine where you can deploy certain SKUs.

Use the Azure CLI to check service availability:

az vm list-skus—location eastus—output table

When designing for global reach, always validate service support in target regions to avoid deployment issues or feature gaps.

Designing for Global Scale

Leveraging Azure's global footprint effectively means:

- **Distributing workloads** across regions and zones

- Using **zone- and geo-redundant storage**
- Implementing **failover and DR strategies**
- Optimizing **latency-sensitive workloads** with edge services
- Planning for **compliance and governance**

Common architectural patterns include:

- Active-Active deployments across multiple regions
- Active-Passive with automated failover
- Regional sharding of services for locality

Azure provides reference architectures and blueprints to guide implementation of these patterns in alignment with best practices.

Conclusion

Azure's global infrastructure is one of its greatest strengths. With hundreds of data centers, dozens of regions, availability zones, edge nodes, and a dedicated network backbone, Azure enables organizations to deploy highly available, resilient, and compliant applications anywhere in the world.

By understanding the structure and strategic layout of Azure's infrastructure footprint, architects and developers can design cloud-native solutions that meet enterprise requirements for uptime, data residency, performance, and disaster recovery. As global digital transformation accelerates, Azure's infrastructure is ready to support the most demanding workloads across every industry and geography.

Chapter 2: Azure Resource Management Essentials

Azure Resource Manager (ARM) Overview

Azure Resource Manager (ARM) is the unified management layer for deploying, managing, and organizing Azure resources. Introduced to simplify and modernize resource management in Azure, ARM provides a consistent way to work with infrastructure and services using declarative templates, security principles, tagging, grouping, and automation tooling.

ARM sits at the core of how Azure operates. Everything you deploy in Azure—virtual machines, storage accounts, web apps, databases—is considered a "resource," and all resources are deployed and managed through ARM. This logical approach to management is a major shift from traditional IT, promoting efficiency, consistency, and automation at scale.

Key Features of ARM

Declarative Deployment with ARM Templates

Rather than deploying resources manually, ARM enables you to describe the desired infrastructure in a JSON or Bicep template. This declarative syntax allows repeatable deployments that are version-controlled and easily shared.

Example (JSON-based ARM Template snippet):

{

"$schema": "https://schema.management.azure.com/schemas/2019-04-01/deploymentTemplate.json#",

```
"contentVersion": "1.0.0.0",
"resources": [
{
"type": "Microsoft.Storage/storageAccounts",
"apiVersion": "2021-02-01",
"name": "[parameters('storageAccountName')]",
"location": "[resourceGroup().location]",
"sku": {
"name": "Standard_LRS"
},
"kind": "StorageV2",
"properties": {}
}
]
}
```

1.

2. **Resource Grouping**
   Every resource in Azure must belong to a resource group. These groups act as containers that hold related resources for an application or workload. Grouping resources provides logical separation and aids in permission control, cost tracking, and lifecycle management.
3. **Role-Based Access Control (RBAC)**

ARM enforces security through RBAC, which allows you to assign fine-grained permissions to users, groups, or service principals. This ensures that only authorized individuals can perform certain actions on resources.

4. **Tagging and Cost Management**
   Tags are metadata key-value pairs assigned to resources. Tags support governance, cost tracking, automation, and reporting. For example, you might use tags like Environment: Production or Department: Finance.
5. **Consistency Across Tools**
   ARM provides a unified API across the Azure Portal, Azure CLI, Azure PowerShell, SDKs, and REST APIs. This consistency simplifies automation and enables DevOps and Infrastructure as Code (IaC) practices.

The Lifecycle of a Resource Deployment

Understanding how ARM processes deployments is key to working efficiently in Azure:

1. **Template Definition**
   Define what you want using a template (JSON or Bicep). Specify resources, parameters, and outputs.
2. **Validation**
   Azure validates your template for syntax and internal logic. This step helps catch mistakes early.
3. **Execution**
   Azure provisions resources in the correct order based on dependencies defined in the template.
4. **State Management**
   ARM keeps a record of deployed resources. Changes are tracked over time, and incremental deployments only

apply updates, not full replacements.

ARM Template vs Bicep

While JSON has traditionally been used, **Bicep** is a domain-specific language introduced to make template writing easier and more readable. It transpiles into standard ARM JSON templates but offers cleaner syntax.

Example of a Bicep template for a storage account:

resource storageAccount 'Microsoft.Storage/storageAccounts@2021-02-01' = {

name: 'myuniquestorageacct'

location: resourceGroup().location

sku: {

name: 'Standard_LRS'

}

kind: 'StorageV2'

}

Advantages of Bicep:

- Simpler syntax
- Easier parameterization
- Better tooling and error messages

Resource Scope Hierarchy

ARM operates within a defined **scope**:

- **Management Group** – Highest level for organization-wide policies
- **Subscription** – Billing and resource isolation
- **Resource Group** – Logical grouping of related resources
- **Resource** – Individual Azure service or instance

Each scope level supports its own RBAC, policies, and compliance rules. Understanding this hierarchy is essential for governance and scaling operations.

Deployment Modes: Incremental vs Complete

When deploying with ARM, you can specify a deployment mode:

- **Incremental**: Adds or updates resources without affecting others.
- **Complete**: Replaces the entire resource group to match the template—resources not in the template are deleted.

Use complete mode cautiously, especially in shared resource groups.

Best Practices for Working with ARM

1. **Use Templates for Everything**

Avoid "click-ops" in the Azure Portal for production deployments. Templates ensure repeatability and traceability.

2. **Modularize Templates**
Break down large templates into modular components (e.g., separate templates for networking, compute, storage).
3. **Version Control Templates**
Store your templates in Git or another source control system. This enables rollback and collaboration.
4. **Automate with Pipelines**
Integrate ARM templates into CI/CD pipelines using Azure DevOps or GitHub Actions to automate infrastructure deployments.
5. **Apply Tags and Naming Conventions**
Consistent tagging and naming conventions enhance visibility, compliance, and cost management.

Access Control and Governance with ARM

ARM provides fine-grained governance tools:

- **RBAC**: Assign roles like Reader, Contributor, Owner, or custom roles.

- **Management Locks**: Prevent accidental deletion or modification.

- **Policies**: Define rules such as allowed locations, SKU types, or tag requirements.

- **Blueprints**: Package policies, roles, and templates for repeatable governance enforcement.

Real-World Example: ARM Deployment for a Web App

Using Azure CLI and a Bicep template:

webapp.bicep

```
param appName string

param location string = resourceGroup().location

resource appServicePlan 'Microsoft.Web/serverfarms@2021-03-01' = {

name: '${appName}-plan'

location: location

sku: {

name: 'B1'

tier: 'Basic'

}

}

resource webApp 'Microsoft.Web/sites@2021-03-01' = {

name: appName

location: location

properties: {

serverFarmId: appServicePlan.id
```

```
}
}
```

Deploy via CLI:

```
az deployment group create \
—resource-group MyResourceGroup \
—template-file webapp.bicep \
—parameters appName=myapp123
```

Summary

Azure Resource Manager is the backbone of the Azure ecosystem, enabling consistent, secure, and automated resource management. Through ARM templates or Bicep, you gain the power to define infrastructure as code, enforce governance, and ensure repeatable deployments. Whether deploying a simple storage account or orchestrating a complex hybrid environment, mastering ARM is essential for any Azure practitioner.

Understanding ARM not only improves your operational efficiency but also lays the groundwork for DevOps, automation, and scalable cloud architectures. As we move further into Azure's ecosystem, this knowledge will serve as the bedrock for everything you build.

Subscription and Resource Group Strategy

Effectively organizing Azure resources is critical to managing cost, access, compliance, and operational efficiency. A sound strategy for subscriptions and resource groups serves as the foundation for successful cloud adoption. While it's easy to create resources ad hoc in the Azure Portal, this approach doesn't scale well. Enterprises—small and large—must approach their Azure architecture with foresight, structure, and discipline.

This section focuses on designing a scalable and secure strategy for managing subscriptions and resource groups, exploring best practices, governance models, billing considerations, lifecycle alignment, and automation techniques.

Understanding Azure Subscriptions

An **Azure subscription** is a logical container used to provision resources and associate them with billing and access management policies. Every resource deployed in Azure must belong to one—and only one—subscription.

Key Characteristics of Subscriptions:

- **Billing Boundary**: Each subscription is linked to a specific billing account. This enables detailed cost tracking.
- **Quota Management**: Azure imposes resource limits (e.g., number of cores, storage, etc.) per subscription.
- **Isolation and Governance**: Permissions, policies, and role assignments are scoped at the subscription level.

Organizations often use multiple subscriptions to:

- Separate environments (e.g., dev/test/prod)
- Isolate workloads or business units

- Manage cost centers and chargebacks
- Apply differing compliance policies

Subscription Design Models

Choosing the right subscription model depends on your organization's size, regulatory needs, budget structure, and operational models. Below are common subscription design strategies:

1. Environment-Based Subscriptions

- **Example**: One subscription each for Development, Testing, Staging, and Production.
- **Use Case**: Prevents dev/test work from affecting production systems. Enables strict access controls per environment.
- **Pros**: Clear separation; simplified policy management.
- **Cons**: May lead to sprawl if not governed properly.

2. Business Unit or Department-Based Subscriptions

- **Example**: Separate subscriptions for Finance, HR, IT, Sales.
- **Use Case**: Aligns to organizational structure for accountability and chargebacks.

- **Pros**: Easy cost attribution; aligns with business goals.
- **Cons**: Requires robust central governance to avoid inconsistent configurations.

3. Application or Workload-Based Subscriptions

- **Example**: CRM application in its own subscription.
- **Use Case**: Large or critical workloads that require resource and policy isolation.
- **Pros**: Scoped policies; better performance visibility.
- **Cons**: Management overhead increases with many subscriptions.

4. Hybrid Model

- Combine environment, business unit, and workload strategies.
- Typically used by large enterprises to balance control and flexibility.

Subscription Management Best Practices

Use Azure Management Groups Organize subscriptions into a hierarchy using management groups. Apply policies and RBAC at the management group level for consistent governance.

Example:

Root Management Group

```
├── Enterprise
│ ├── Finance
│ │ ├── Finance-Prod (Subscription)
│ │ └── Finance-Dev
│ └── IT
│ ├── IT-Prod
│ └── IT-Test
```

1.

2. **Implement Naming Conventions** Use consistent naming like sub-{org}-{env}-{dept}, e.g., sub-contoso-prod-finance.

3. **Tag Subscriptions with Metadata** Example:

   ○ Owner = john.doe@company.com

   ○ CostCenter = 12345

   ○ Environment = Production

4. **Assign Billing Profiles** Link subscriptions to billing accounts and profiles in Cost Management + Billing for chargeback and showback reporting.

Understanding Resource Groups

A **Resource Group (RG)** is a container that holds related Azure resources. Every resource (VM, storage, DB, etc.) must belong to exactly one RG.

Key Characteristics of Resource Groups:

- **Lifecycle Management**: Deleting a RG deletes all resources within it.
- **Access Control**: RBAC roles can be applied at the RG level.
- **Tagging and Organization**: RGs can be tagged like individual resources.
- **Deployment Scope**: ARM templates and Bicep deployments often target a specific RG.

Resource Group Design Patterns

Designing RGs properly ensures easier operations, lower costs, and better security posture. Below are common strategies:

1. Environment-Based RGs

- Example: rg-webapp-dev, rg-webapp-prod
- Keeps development resources separate from production.

2. Service-Based RGs

- Example: rg-storage, rg-networking, rg-compute
- Useful for shared service models.

3. Application or Workload-Based RGs

- Example: rg-crm-frontend, rg-crm-backend
- Allows easier deployments and teardown.

4. Per-Project RGs

- Example: rg-2025cloudmigration, rg-ai-data-pipeline
- Ideal for temporary or time-boxed initiatives.

Guidelines for Resource Group Design

1. **Group Resources with Shared Lifecycle** Place resources that get deployed, updated, and deleted together in the same RG.
2. **Avoid Overloading Resource Groups** Don't treat RGs like folders—cramming unrelated resources together leads to chaos and governance problems.
3. **Minimize Cross-RG Dependencies** Resources within a single RG are easier to manage and deploy. While cross-RG dependencies are possible, they complicate automation.
4. **Use Meaningful Names** Use names like rg-{project}-{env} or rg-{app}-{tier}, e.g., rg-erp-prod-web.

5. **Apply Tags Consistently** Tags help you report and control resources. Enforce tag policies using Azure Policy.

Lifecycle and Automation Considerations

Managing lifecycle is easier when subscription and RG strategies align with automation tools.

Example ARM/Bicep Resource Group Deployment

Bicep Template to Create a Resource Group (when using a deployment script):

```
param location string = 'eastus'

param rgName string

resource newRG 'Microsoft.Resources/resourceGroups@2021-04-01' = {

name: rgName

location: location

}
```

Deploy via CLI:

```
az deployment sub create \

—location eastus \

—template-file create-rg.bicep \

—parameters rgName='rg-cloudapp-prod'
```

Security and Access Management Across Subscriptions and RGs

Both subscriptions and RGs support Azure RBAC:

- **Subscription Level**: Use for broad roles (e.g., Network Admin across all RGs).
- **Resource Group Level**: Assign specific roles (e.g., Developer can manage only resources in rg-webapp-dev).

Example:

```
az role assignment create \
—assignee john.doe@company.com \
—role "Contributor" \
—scope /subscriptions/{sub-id}/resourceGroups/rg-webapp-dev
```

Use **Management Locks** to protect critical RGs:

```
az lock create \
—name "PreventDeletion" \
—lock-type CanNotDelete \
—resource-group rg-prod-app
```

Cost Management by Subscription and RG

- Use **Cost Management + Billing** in Azure Portal.
- Set **budgets** at subscription or RG level.

- Define **alerts** when cost thresholds are exceeded.

Tagging can provide enhanced cost granularity:

az tag create—resource-id /subscriptions/{sub-id}/resourceGroups/rg-data-pipeline—tags CostCenter=456 Environment=Production

---

Subscription and RG Governance with Azure Policy

Use **Azure Policy** to enforce organizational standards, such as:

- Required tags on RGs
- Allowed VM SKUs
- Approved Azure regions

Example policy to enforce tagging:

```
{
"if": {
"not": {
"field": "tags['Environment']",
"exists": true
}
},
"then": {
"effect": "deny"
```

```
}
}
```

Assign policies at the **Management Group**, **Subscription**, or **RG** level.

Summary

Crafting a solid subscription and resource group strategy is not optional—it's foundational. Subscriptions provide isolation for cost, governance, and compliance. Resource groups enable you to manage application components as units. Together, they determine how your Azure environment scales, how secure it is, how much it costs, and how easily you can automate operations.

Follow a principle of **logical isolation + governance + automation**. Use Azure's native tools—like ARM templates, Bicep, Azure Policy, RBAC, and Cost Management—to enforce these strategies in a repeatable and scalable way.

Adopt the mindset of "structure first, deployment second." With a well-thought-out subscription and resource group strategy, you set the stage for cloud success.

Tags, Policies, and Role-Based Access Control (RBAC)

In cloud environments, managing sprawl, controlling access, and ensuring compliance are essential tasks. Azure provides a set of powerful tools to address these concerns: **Tags**, **Azure Policy**, and **Role-Based Access Control** (**RBAC**). When used together, they create a framework for secure, organized, and governable cloud environments.

This section covers how each mechanism works, when and how to use them, and best practices for combining them into a unified cloud governance strategy.

Tags: Metadata That Powers Organization and Reporting

Tags are name-value pairs that can be applied to Azure resources, resource groups, and subscriptions. They are crucial for categorizing and organizing resources, enabling cost tracking, automation, and policy enforcement.

Common Use Cases for Tags

- **Cost Allocation**: Tag resources by CostCenter, Department, or Project to track spending.
- **Environment Classification**: Apply Environment=Production or Environment=Dev for lifecycle management.
- **Ownership**: Use Owner=email@domain.com to assign responsibility.
- **Automation**: Trigger scripts or policies based on tag values.

Example: Applying Tags via Azure CLI

az tag create—resource-id /subscriptions/abc123/resourceGroups/rg-crm-prod \

—tags Environment=Production Owner=jane.doe@company.com Project=CRM

Tag Inheritance and Limitations

- Tags are **not automatically inherited** from resource groups to individual resources.
- Maximum of **50 tags** per resource.
- Tags support **string values only**.

Use scripts or Azure Policy to ensure consistent tagging across all assets.

Enforcing Tagging Standards with Azure Policy

You can enforce tagging standards using **Azure Policy**, a governance engine that evaluates resource compliance.

Example: Deny Deployment Without Required Tags

This policy prevents resources from being created unless they include an Environment tag.

```
{
"mode": "All",
"policyRule": {
"if": {
"not": {
"field": "tags['Environment']",
"exists": true
```

```
}
},
"then": {
"effect": "deny"
}
},
"parameters": {},
"displayName": "Require Environment Tag"
}
```

Assign Policy via Azure CLI

```
az policy definition create \
—name 'require-env-tag' \
—rules policy.json \
—display-name 'Require Environment Tag' \
—mode All
az policy assignment create \
—name 'require-env-tag-assignment' \
—policy require-env-tag \
—scope /subscriptions/abc123
```

Azure Policy: Control, Audit, and Enforce

Azure Policy helps ensure your Azure environment remains compliant with corporate or regulatory requirements by evaluating resource configurations against rules you define.

Types of Azure Policy Effects

- **Deny** – Blocks resource creation/modification if policy isn't met.
- **Audit** – Flags non-compliant resources.
- **Append** – Adds specified fields during resource creation.
- **Modify** – Alters the request payload (e.g., auto-adding tags).
- **DeployIfNotExists** – Deploys supporting resources if conditions are unmet.

Example: Restrict Locations

Prevent resources from being deployed outside approved Azure regions:

```
{
"if": {
"not": {
"field": "location",
```

```
"in": ["eastus", "westeurope"]
}
},
"then": {
"effect": "deny"
}
}
```

Built-In Policies vs. Custom Policies

Azure includes hundreds of **built-in policies**, such as:

- Allowed Resource Types
- Allowed Storage Account SKUs
- Enable Monitoring in VMs

For custom requirements, define your own policy definitions in JSON.

Policy Initiatives (Policy Sets)

Group multiple related policies into an **initiative**. For example, a "Production Compliance" initiative might include policies for:

- Allowed locations
- Tag requirements

- Disk encryption enforcement
- Monitoring configuration

Managing Policies at Scale

Policies can be assigned at:

- **Management Group** – Apply to multiple subscriptions
- **Subscription** – Enforce org-wide standards
- **Resource Group** – Local governance

Policy Lifecycle

1. **Definition** – Create a policy rule
2. **Assignment** – Apply it to a scope
3. **Evaluation** – Azure scans and reports compliance
4. **Remediation** – Fix non-compliant resources via automation or manual correction

Example CLI Workflow

```
# Create definition

az policy definition create \

—name restrict-location \

—rules restrict-location.json \

—display-name 'Restrict Location' \
```

```
—mode All

# Assign to subscription

az policy assignment create \

—name restrict-location-assignment \

—policy restrict-location \

—scope /subscriptions/abc123
```

Role-Based Access Control (RBAC)

RBAC is Azure's built-in authorization system. It allows you to assign roles to users, groups, or applications at different scopes to control their actions on resources.

Key Concepts

- **Security Principal** – User, group, service principal, or managed identity.
- **Role Definition** – Collection of permissions, such as "Reader", "Contributor", or custom roles.
- **Scope** – Level at which access is granted (management group, subscription, RG, or resource).

Built-in Roles

- **Owner** – Full access, including RBAC.
- **Contributor** – Full resource access, no RBAC changes.

- **Reader** – View-only.
- **User Access Administrator** – Manage role assignments only.

Assigning a Role

az role assignment create \

—assignee jane.doe@company.com \

—role "Contributor" \

—scope /subscriptions/abc123/resourceGroups/rg-webapp-prod

Scope Inheritance

Roles assigned at higher scopes (like a subscription) are inherited by all children (RGs and resources).

Custom Roles

When built-in roles don't meet specific requirements, create **custom roles** using JSON definitions.

Example: Custom Role to Restart VMs Only

{

"Name": "VM Restart Operator",

"IsCustom": true,

"Description": "Can restart virtual machines only",

```
"Actions": [
"Microsoft.Compute/virtualMachines/start/action",
"Microsoft.Compute/virtualMachines/restart/action"
],
"NotActions": [],
"AssignableScopes": ["/subscriptions/abc123"]
}
```

Create via CLI

```
az role definition create—role-definition vm-restart-role.json
```

Combining Tags, Policy, and RBAC

These three systems work together to enforce a secure, well-managed environment.

Scenario: Deploying a Secure Web Application

- **Tags**: Each resource is tagged with Environment=Production and Project=WebPortal
- **Policy**:
  - Deny deployments outside eastus
  - Require encryption on storage accounts
  - Auto-add CostCenter tag

- **RBAC**:
  - Developers get Contributor access only to the dev resource group
  - Security team has Reader access org-wide
  - Ops has Owner rights in production

This layered approach ensures:

- Resources are traceable and organized
- Compliance is automated and visible
- Least-privilege access is maintained

Auditing and Monitoring Access

Use **Azure Activity Logs** and **Azure Monitor** to track RBAC changes and policy compliance.

Query activity logs via CLI:

az monitor activity-log list—resource-group rg-webapp-prod—output table

Enable diagnostic settings to stream logs to a Log Analytics workspace or SIEM tool for audit trails.

Best Practices

1. **Define Governance Early** Don't retrofit tagging and policy—define standards at the start of your cloud journey.

2. **Start with Audit Policies** Before enforcing deny effects, begin with audit policies to evaluate impact.
3. **Use Initiatives for Organization-Wide Rules** Simplify management by grouping related policies.
4. **Implement Least Privilege Access** Regularly review RBAC assignments. Use custom roles only when necessary.
5. **Automate Tagging and Remediation** Use Azure Automation, Logic Apps, or Functions to auto-correct non-compliant resources.
6. **Monitor and Improve** Continuously monitor compliance scores and iterate on your governance model.

Summary

Tags, Policies, and RBAC form the governance and security triangle in Azure. Tags provide metadata for organizing and tracking resources. Azure Policy enforces compliance by evaluating and controlling resource configurations. RBAC defines who can access what and at which scope.

Together, they enable enterprise-scale cloud governance, helping organizations control complexity, reduce risk, and increase operational efficiency. When thoughtfully implemented, these mechanisms allow Azure environments to scale securely, sustainably, and in alignment with organizational goals.

Using Azure Portal, CLI, PowerShell, and REST APIs

Azure offers a broad range of management interfaces to deploy, configure, and operate resources. These interfaces cater to users of all technical backgrounds—GUI users, DevOps engineers, sysadmins, and developers. Each interface—Azure Portal, Azure CLI, Azure PowerShell, and Azure REST APIs—serves distinct needs, but all interoperate with the same underlying infrastructure: Azure Resource Manager (ARM).

This section explores these interfaces in depth, examining their strengths, appropriate use cases, and how to use each of them effectively for provisioning and managing Azure resources.

Azure Portal: Graphical Web-Based Interface

The **Azure Portal** is the web-based graphical interface most users encounter first. Accessible athttps://portal.azure.com[1], it provides a rich user experience for creating, configuring, and monitoring resources.

Key Features of Azure Portal

- Intuitive visual dashboards
- Resource browsing, searching, filtering
- Integration with monitoring (charts, logs)
- Role-based access controls
- Interactive walkthroughs and templates
- Resource blade navigation structure

1. https://portal.azure.com/

When to Use

- Ideal for initial exploration and prototyping
- Ad-hoc configurations or changes
- Visualizing architecture using Resource Graph Explorer or Diagrams
- Role assignments, tagging, and policy browsing
- Reviewing billing and usage metrics

Best Practices

- Use favorites and dashboards to organize commonly used resources
- Enable **Activity Log Alerts** for audit tracking
- Leverage **Cloud Shell** (embedded Bash or PowerShell shell) for automation without leaving the portal
- Always copy Portal-generated ARM templates for repeatability

---

Azure CLI: Cross-Platform Command-Line Interface

The **Azure Command-Line Interface (CLI)** is a fast, scriptable, and cross-platform tool (Windows, macOS, Linux) for managing Azure services via commands. Built with a Python core, it is designed to simplify the scripting of Azure operations.

Installing Azure CLI

Windows:

winget install Microsoft.AzureCLI

•

macOS (Homebrew):

brew install azure-cli

•

Linux (Debian/Ubuntu):

curl -sL https://aka.ms/InstallAzureCLIDeb | sudo bash

•

Authentication and Configuration

az login

az account list—output table

az account set—subscription "My Azure Subscription"

Creating a Resource Group with CLI

az group create \

—name rg-myapp-prod \

—location eastus

Creating a Storage Account

az storage account create \

—name mystorageacct123 \

—resource-group rg-myapp-prod \

—location eastus \

—sku Standard_LRS

When to Use

- CI/CD pipelines and DevOps tasks
- Scripting and bulk operations
- Cross-platform, developer-friendly tooling
- Lightweight alternative to the Portal

Best Practices

- Use—output table or—output json for better parsing
- Combine with shell scripting for automation
- Use environment variables or configuration files for consistency
- Integrate with GitHub Actions or Azure Pipelines

Azure PowerShell: Admin-Centric Scripting

Azure PowerShell is a set of cmdlets for managing Azure resources directly from PowerShell. It is favored by Windows system administrators and organizations with a strong Microsoft tooling preference.

Installing Azure PowerShell

In PowerShell 7+:

Install-Module -Name Az -AllowClobber -Scope CurrentUser

-

Logging In and Setting Context

Connect-AzAccount

Get-AzSubscription

Set-AzContext -Subscription "My Azure Subscription"

Creating a Resource Group

New-AzResourceGroup -Name rg-app-prod -Location "East US"

Creating a Virtual Machine

New-AzVM `

-ResourceGroupName "rg-app-prod" `

-Name "myVM" `

-Location "East US" `

-Image "Win2019Datacenter"

When to Use

- Windows-heavy environments
- Infrastructure scripting and configuration tasks
- Admin-focused automation scenarios

Best Practices

- Use Az.Accounts and Az.Resources modules in isolated scripts
- Log all operations using $VerbosePreference = "Continue"
- Modularize scripts using functions and reusable modules

Azure REST APIs: Programmatic and Scalable Access

The **Azure REST APIs** provide low-level access to every operation available in Azure. These are ideal for developers building custom applications, integrations, or tooling on top of Azure.

API Structure Overview

Base URL:

https://management.azure.com/

-

Typical Endpoint:

https://management.azure.com/
subscriptions/{subscriptionId}/resourcegroups/{resourceGroupName}?a

-

- All requests require a valid **Azure Active Directory (AAD)** access token.

Acquiring an AAD Token

Using Azure CLI:

az account get-access-token—resource=https://management.azure.com

Use the returned token as a Bearer token in HTTP headers.

Example: Create Resource Group (POST Request)

POST https://management.azure.com/subscriptions/abc123/resourcegroups/rg-api-test?api-version=2021-04-01

Authorization: Bearer <token>

Content-Type: application/json

{

"location": "eastus",

```
"tags": {
"Environment": "Test",
"Project": "API"
}
}
```

When to Use

- Custom platforms, dashboards, or control planes
- Advanced automation scenarios
- Server-side integration with other cloud services
- Direct access where SDKs are unavailable or unnecessary

Choosing the Right Interface

Task	Azure Portal	Azure CLI	PowerShell	REST API
Quick visual inspection	�	�	�	�
DevOps scripting	�	�	�	�
Automation in CI/CD	�	�	�	�
Admin tasks (e.g., bulk RBAC)	�	�	�	�
Deep customization or integration	�	�	�	�
Resource visualization	�	�	�	�

Each interface complements the others. For example, you might prototype in the Portal, extract the equivalent ARM/Bicep template, and automate future deployments with CLI or PowerShell.

Integration with Automation Tools

Azure management interfaces integrate with:

- **Azure DevOps**: Pipelines can use CLI/PowerShell tasks
- **GitHub Actions**: CLI commands automate deployments and governance
- **Terraform and Pulumi**: Leverage REST APIs under the hood
- **Azure SDKs**: Use CLI/REST within Node.js, Python, Java applications

---

Advanced Scenarios

Scenario 1: Tagging Resources with CLI in CI/CD

az resource tag \

—ids $(az resource show—name myvm—resource-group rg-prod—query id -o tsv) \

—tags Environment=Prod Owner=admin@company.com

Scenario 2: Auto-Remediation with PowerShell

```
$resources = Get-AzResource -Tag @{ "Environment" = "Test" }

foreach ($res in $resources) {

Remove-AzResource -ResourceId $res.ResourceId -Force

}
```

Scenario 3: Programmatic Dashboard Builder with REST

- Use REST to pull metrics, create resource groups, and manage alert rules dynamically based on workload changes.

Summary

Azure provides four main interfaces for managing its vast set of services—Azure Portal, CLI, PowerShell, and REST APIs. Each has unique advantages and is tailored to different personas and tasks:

- Use **Azure Portal** for visual, ad-hoc, and discovery-based operations.
- Use **Azure CLI** for fast, repeatable command-line automation.
- Use **PowerShell** for rich administrative tasks and complex scripts.
- Use **REST APIs** for programmatic, scalable integration in software and custom platforms.

Mastering all four interfaces is not required, but knowing when and how to use each is a vital skill for any cloud practitioner. Combining these tools with infrastructure-as-code practices and automation strategies ensures that your Azure environment remains robust, scalable, and maintainable across its lifecycle.

Chapter 3: Compute Services in Depth

Virtual Machines: Planning, Deployment, and Scaling

Virtual Machines (VMs) are a foundational element in Azure's Infrastructure-as-a-Service (IaaS) offerings. While the cloud provides various abstracted compute options like containers and serverless functions, VMs continue to be essential for workloads requiring full control over the operating system, specialized software environments, or traditional enterprise applications. In this section, we'll explore the lifecycle of Azure VMs—starting from planning and deployment to optimization and scaling.

Planning Virtual Machine Deployments

Before deploying a VM, it's essential to plan key aspects of the configuration to ensure performance, cost-efficiency, and compliance. Planning includes decisions around size, region, availability, image selection, storage type, and networking.

Key Planning Factors

1. **Workload Requirements**

   ○ Is the workload CPU-bound, memory-intensive, or storage-heavy?

   ○ Will the VM run 24/7, or is it needed only during business hours?

2. **VM Size and Series**

- Azure offers multiple VM series: D, E, F, M, L, B, etc.
- Choose the VM SKU based on workload:
  - **D-series**: General-purpose
  - **E-series**: Memory-optimized
  - **F-series**: Compute-optimized
  - **M-series**: High-memory workloads like SAP
  - **L-series**: Storage-optimized
  - **B-series**: Burstable workloads

3. **Operating System**

- Windows Server or Linux distributions (Ubuntu, CentOS, RHEL, SUSE, etc.)
- Bring-your-own-license (BYOL) scenarios supported

4. **Availability Requirements**

- Use **Availability Zones** for zone-level redundancy
- Use **Availability Sets** for fault domain and update domain separation

5. **Networking**

- Plan for Virtual Network (VNet), subnets, NSGs (Network Security Groups), and IP assignments

○ Consider VPN, ExpressRoute, or VNet peering if connecting to on-prem

6. **Storage**

○ OS disk: Standard HDD, Standard SSD, Premium SSD

○ Data disks: Up to 32 TB depending on VM size

○ Use Managed Disks for better performance and reliability

Deploying Virtual Machines via Azure Portal

1. Go to **Virtual Machines > Create**

2. Choose:

○ Subscription and Resource Group

○ VM name

○ Region

○ Availability options (zone or set)

○ Image (e.g., Ubuntu 20.04 LTS)

○ Size (e.g., D2s_v3)

○ Authentication type (password or SSH)

3. Configure:

  - Disks (Standard SSD, Premium SSD, etc.)
  - Networking (VNet, subnet, public IP, NSG)
  - Management settings (monitoring, auto-shutdown)

4. Review and deploy

Once deployed, you can access the VM using:

- **SSH** (for Linux VMs)
- **RDP** (for Windows VMs)

Deploying Virtual Machines via CLI

az vm create \

—resource-group rg-prod \

—name myvm001 \

—image UbuntuLTS \

—admin-username azureuser \

—generate-ssh-keys \

—size Standard_D2s_v3 \

—public-ip-sku Standard

Additional options include specifying:

- —availability-set or—zone
- —data-disk-sizes-gb

- —custom-data (for cloud-init scripts)

Deploying Virtual Machines via ARM or Bicep

Bicep Example:

```
param adminUsername string

param adminPassword string

resource vm 'Microsoft.Compute/virtualMachines@2022-08-01' = {

name: 'vmAppServer'

location: resourceGroup().location

properties: {

hardwareProfile: {

vmSize: 'Standard_D2s_v3'

}

storageProfile: {

imageReference: {

publisher: 'Canonical'

offer: 'UbuntuServer'

sku: '18.04-LTS'

version: 'latest'

}
```

```
osDisk: {
createOption: 'FromImage'
managedDisk: {
storageAccountType: 'StandardSSD_LRS'
}
}
}
osProfile: {
computerName: 'vmAppServer'
adminUsername: adminUsername
adminPassword: adminPassword
}
networkProfile: {
networkInterfaces: [
{
id: resourceId('Microsoft.Network/networkInterfaces', 'nicAppServer')
}
]
}
}
```

}

Scaling Virtual Machines

Scaling VMs involves either **vertical scaling** (changing the VM size) or **horizontal scaling** (adding more VMs). Azure supports both.

Vertical Scaling

- Change the size of a VM:

az vm resize \

—resource-group rg-prod \

—name myvm001 \

—size Standard_D4s_v3

Requires the VM to be deallocated first:

az vm deallocate—resource-group rg-prod—name myvm001

az vm resize—resource-group rg-prod—name myvm001—size Standard_D4s_v3

az vm start—resource-group rg-prod—name myvm001

Horizontal Scaling

- Use **Virtual Machine Scale Sets (VMSS)** to manage and auto-scale VMs:
    - Supports autoscaling based on metrics (CPU, RAM, custom metrics)

○ Integrated with Azure Load Balancer and Application Gateway

Create a scale set:

az vmss create \

—resource-group rg-prod \

—name myScaleSet \

—image UbuntuLTS \

—upgrade-policy-mode automatic \

—admin-username azureuser \

—generate-ssh-keys \

—instance-count 2 \

—vm-sku Standard_D2s_v3

Set scaling rules:

az monitor autoscale create \

—resource-group rg-prod \

—resource myScaleSet \

—resource-type Microsoft.Compute/virtualMachineScaleSets \

—name autoscaleRule \

—min-count 2 \

—max-count 10 \

—count 2

Availability and Resilience

Azure offers multiple options to ensure VM availability:

Availability Sets

- Two or more VMs are distributed across fault domains (physical racks) and update domains.
- Helps avoid simultaneous reboots or failures.

Availability Zones

- Data centers in a region separated by physical and logical boundaries.
- Deploy VMs in multiple zones for high resiliency.

az vm create \

—resource-group rg-prod \

—name zoneVm001 \

—zone 1 \

—image UbuntuLTS \

—admin-username azureuser \

—generate-ssh-keys

Azure Site Recovery

- Set up disaster recovery for VMs
- Supports cross-region replication and failover
- Useful for critical workloads

Security and Management

- **OS Patching**: Use **Update Management** in Azure Automation
- **Backup**: Enable Azure Backup for VMs
- **Encryption**: OS and data disks can be encrypted using Azure-managed keys or customer-managed keys (CMKs)
- **Just-In-Time (JIT) Access**: Limit RDP/SSH access to specified IP ranges and time windows

---

Monitoring and Diagnostics

- **Azure Monitor** and **Log Analytics**: Collect performance metrics, logs, and alerts
- **Diagnostic Settings**: Enable boot diagnostics, guest-level metrics
- **Azure Policy**: Enforce monitoring, tagging, and encryption standards

---

Cost Optimization

- **Reserved Instances**: Save up to 72% by committing to 1 or 3 years
- **Spot VMs**: Take advantage of unused capacity at deep discounts; suitable for batch jobs, testing
- **Auto-shutdown**: Automatically shut down VMs at night to save cost
- **Azure Advisor**: Get recommendations for right-sizing VMs

---

Summary

Azure Virtual Machines provide a highly customizable and powerful compute option suitable for a wide range of workloads. Whether you're hosting a simple web application or a critical database server, VMs offer the flexibility and control that some workloads demand. Mastering VM planning, deployment, and scaling ensures your environment is performant, cost-efficient, and resilient.

By using the right tools—Azure CLI, PowerShell, Portal, or Bicep—you can automate and scale your deployments with ease. Combine VMs with other Azure services like Load Balancer, Backup, Policy, and Monitor to build secure, compliant, and observable infrastructure at scale.

Azure App Services and Functions

Azure offers Platform-as-a-Service (PaaS) compute options that significantly reduce the operational overhead associated with virtual machines. Two of the most widely used services in this category are **Azure App Services** and **Azure Functions**. These offerings allow developers to focus on writing code, not managing servers, scaling infrastructure, or configuring operating systems. In this section, we will explore both services in depth—covering their architectures, use cases, deployment strategies, configuration options, scaling models, and best practices.

Azure App Services: Overview

Azure App Service is a fully managed platform for building, deploying, and scaling web apps, RESTful APIs, and mobile backends. App Services support various programming languages including .NET, Java, Node.js, Python, and PHP.

Key Features

- Managed infrastructure
- Built-in CI/CD integration
- Custom domain and SSL support
- Authentication and authorization via Azure AD and other identity providers
- Auto-scaling and high availability
- Staging environments with deployment slots

- Virtual network integration

Common Use Cases

- Hosting web applications and APIs
- Backend services for mobile apps
- Integration endpoints
- eCommerce platforms, portals, and line-of-business apps

Creating an App Service Plan and Web App

An **App Service Plan** defines the region, pricing tier, scaling configuration, and instance count for your app. The **Web App** is the hosted application within the plan.

CLI Example

```
# Create a resource group

az group create—name rg-webapp—location eastus

# Create an App Service Plan

az appservice plan create \

—name myAppPlan \

—resource-group rg-webapp \

—sku B1 \
```

```
—is-linux

# Create the Web App

az webapp create \

—resource-group rg-webapp \

—plan myAppPlan \

—name myuniquewebapp123 \

—runtime "NODE|18-lts"
```

Uploading Code

```
az webapp deployment source config-zip \

—resource-group rg-webapp \

—name myuniquewebapp123 \

—src app.zip
```

Deployment Slots

Deployment slots allow you to create staging environments for testing and validation before swapping into production. Each slot has its own hostname and configuration.

Benefits

- Zero-downtime deployments
- A/B testing and canary releases

- Rollback support

Creating a Slot

```
az webapp deployment slot create \
—name myuniquewebapp123 \
—resource-group rg-webapp \
—slot staging
```

Swapping Slots

```
az webapp deployment slot swap \
—name myuniquewebapp123 \
—resource-group rg-webapp \
—slot staging \
—target-slot production
```

Scaling App Services

Azure App Services support **manual scaling**, **autoscaling**, and **scale-out/in policies** based on metrics.

Manual Scaling

```
az appservice plan update \
—name myAppPlan \
—resource-group rg-webapp \
```

—number-of-workers 3

Autoscaling with Rules

Use Azure Monitor to create scale-out rules based on CPU, memory, or custom metrics.

az monitor autoscale create \

—resource-group rg-webapp \

—resource myAppPlan \

—resource-type Microsoft.Web/serverfarms \

—name autoscaleRule \

—min-count 1 \

—max-count 5 \

—count 2

Authentication and Security

Azure App Service supports built-in authentication via identity providers:

- Azure Active Directory
- Facebook
- Google
- Microsoft
- Twitter

You can also integrate with **Azure Key Vault** to securely manage app secrets, certificates, and connection strings.

Enabling Azure AD Authentication via Portal

1. Navigate to your App Service > Authentication
2. Click "Add Identity Provider"
3. Choose Azure Active Directory
4. Register a new app or use an existing one
5. Configure allowed token audiences and redirect URIs

Monitoring and Diagnostics

Monitoring App Services includes:

- **Application Insights** integration
- **Log streaming**
- **Metrics and alerts**
- **Diagnostic settings** for collecting logs in Log Analytics or a storage account

```
az monitor diagnostic-settings create \
—resource myuniquewebapp123 \
—resource-group rg-webapp \
—resource-type Microsoft.Web/sites \
—name appDiagnostics \
—workspace <log-analytics-workspace-id> \
```

```
—logs '[{"category": "AppServiceHTTPLogs", "enabled": true}]'
```

Azure Functions: Overview

Azure Functions is a serverless compute service that lets you run event-driven code without provisioning or managing servers. It's ideal for lightweight logic, integration, scheduled jobs, and real-time processing.

Characteristics

- Consumption-based billing
- Triggers and bindings for easy integration
- Automatic scaling
- Supports C#, JavaScript, Python, PowerShell, Java, and more
- Supports durable and timer-based workflows

Common Triggers

- HTTP (REST endpoints)
- Timer (CRON expressions)
- Blob storage (file creation or deletion)
- Queue storage
- Cosmos DB change feed
- Event Grid / Event Hub

- Service Bus

Creating an Azure Function App

```
# Create a Function App in the Consumption Plan
az functionapp create \
—resource-group rg-webapp \
—consumption-plan-location eastus \
—name myfuncapp123 \
—storage-account mystorageacct123 \
—runtime node \
—functions-version 4
```

Deploying Functions

Functions can be deployed using:

- Azure CLI
- Visual Studio Code
- GitHub Actions
- Zip deploy
- Azure DevOps

```
func azure functionapp publish myfuncapp123
```

Or, upload a zipped deployment:

```
az functionapp deployment source config-zip \
—resource-group rg-webapp \
—name myfuncapp123 \
—src functionapp.zip
```

Durable Functions

Durable Functions enable you to write long-running workflows in code, using constructs like:

- Orchestrations (chained or parallel steps)
- Activities (units of work)
- Timers (wait operations)
- Sub-orchestrations

Example: Durable Orchestration (C#)

```
[FunctionName("MyOrchestrator")]
public static async Task<List<string>> RunOrchestrator(
[OrchestrationTrigger] IDurableOrchestrationContext context)
{
var outputs = new List<string>();
outputs.Add(await
context.CallActivityAsync<string>("SayHello", "Tokyo"));
```

```
outputs.Add(await
context.CallActivityAsync<string>("SayHello", "Seattle"));

outputs.Add(await
context.CallActivityAsync<string>("SayHello", "London"));

return outputs;

}
```

Monitoring Azure Functions

Functions integrate with **Application Insights** for telemetry and distributed tracing. Use the Azure Portal or Kusto Query Language (KQL) to analyze:

- Invocations
- Failures
- Cold starts
- Latency

Example KQL query:

```
requests

| where cloud_RoleName == "myfuncapp123"

| summarize count() by resultCode
```

Security and Networking

Secure Functions with:

- Function-level or App-level API keys

- OAuth 2.0 / OpenID Connect via App Service Authentication
- VNet integration for accessing private services
- Private endpoints for secure exposure

Pricing Models

App Services

- **Free Tier**: Ideal for dev/test
- **Basic/Standard/Premium Plans**: Add scaling, staging, and custom domains
- **Isolated Plans**: Run in your own virtual network for added security

Functions

- **Consumption Plan**: Pay per execution and memory usage
- **Premium Plan**: Reserved instances, faster startup
- **Dedicated (App Service Plan)**: For functions that must run continuously or under heavy load

---

Best Practices

For App Services:

- Use deployment slots for zero-downtime updates

- Integrate with CI/CD
- Secure with managed identity and Key Vault
- Enable autoscaling and monitor costs with Azure Advisor
- Use staging for safe rollouts

For Azure Functions:

- Choose the right trigger for the job
- Break down logic into small, testable units
- Use durable functions for complex workflows
- Monitor cold starts and optimize for performance
- Store secrets in Key Vault and avoid inline configurations

Summary

Azure App Services and Functions offer powerful platforms for hosting modern cloud applications with minimal operational overhead. App Services provide flexibility for running full-fledged web apps and APIs, while Functions allow rapid development of small, event-driven tasks with virtually unlimited scalability. Both integrate seamlessly with other Azure services, enabling you to build secure, scalable, and resilient applications tailored to your business needs.

By mastering these services and incorporating best practices in deployment, scaling, security, and monitoring, you can significantly accelerate application development and delivery while maintaining operational excellence in the cloud.

Containers with Azure Kubernetes Service (AKS)

Containers have revolutionized software development and deployment by offering lightweight, consistent environments that encapsulate application code and its dependencies. As enterprises adopt microservices and DevOps practices, container orchestration becomes essential—and this is where **Azure Kubernetes Service (AKS)** shines. AKS is a fully managed Kubernetes service that abstracts the complexity of managing a Kubernetes cluster, allowing teams to focus on developing and deploying containerized applications at scale.

In this section, we'll dive deep into AKS—its architecture, provisioning, configuration, deployment strategies, networking, scaling, security, monitoring, and real-world best practices.

Understanding Kubernetes and AKS

Kubernetes (K8s) is an open-source container orchestration platform that automates deployment, scaling, and management of containerized applications. **AKS** simplifies Kubernetes by managing the master nodes and offering features like integrated monitoring, CI/CD support, and advanced networking.

AKS vs. Self-Managed Kubernetes

Feature	AKS	Self-Managed Kubernetes
Control Plane Management	Managed by Azure	Managed by user
Updates & Patching	Automated	Manual
SLA	99.95% uptime (paid tier)	Depends on user setup
Integration	Deep integration with Azure AD, Monitor, DevOps	Manual setup required

AKS Architecture Overview

- **Control Plane**: Azure manages the Kubernetes API server, scheduler, and etcd datastore.
- **Node Pools**: You manage one or more agent node pools (VMs) that run your workloads.
- **Pods**: The smallest deployable units; encapsulate containers and shared resources.
- **Services**: Abstracts access to Pods and provides load balancing.
- **Ingress Controllers**: Handle HTTP routing into the cluster.

Provisioning an AKS Cluster

AKS can be provisioned via the Azure Portal, Azure CLI, Bicep, or Terraform.

CLI Example

az group create—name rg-aks—location eastus

az aks create \

—resource-group rg-aks \

—name myAKSCluster \

—node-count 3 \

—enable-addons monitoring \

—generate-ssh-keys

Retrieve credentials:

az aks get-credentials \

—resource-group rg-aks \

—name myAKSCluster

Verify cluster access:

kubectl get nodes

Deploying a Containerized App

Create a deployment YAML file (app-deployment.yaml):

apiVersion: apps/v1

```
kind: Deployment
metadata:
name: webapp-deployment
spec:
replicas: 2
selector:
matchLabels:
app: webapp
template:
metadata:
labels:
app: webapp
spec:
containers:
- name: webapp
image: myacr.azurecr.io/webapp:latest
ports:
- containerPort: 80
```

Apply the deployment:

```
kubectl apply -f app-deployment.yaml
```

Expose the deployment with a service:

```
apiVersion: v1

kind: Service

metadata:

name: webapp-service

spec:

type: LoadBalancer

selector:

app: webapp

ports:

- protocol: TCP

port: 80

targetPort: 80

kubectl apply -f app-service.yaml
```

Scaling and Auto-Scaling

AKS supports:

Manual Scaling:

kubectl scale deployment webapp-deployment—replicas=5

•

Cluster Autoscaler: Automatically adjusts the number of nodes. Enable during cluster creation:

—enable-cluster-autoscaler—min-count 1—max-count 5

•

Horizontal Pod Autoscaler:

kubectl autoscale deployment webapp-deployment \

—cpu-percent=50 \

—min=1 \

—max=10

•

Integrating Azure Container Registry (ACR)

ACR stores private container images for AKS.

az acr create—name myacr—resource-group rg-aks—sku Basic

az aks update \

—name myAKSCluster \

—resource-group rg-aks \

—attach-acr myacr

Now AKS can pull images from ACR without credentials.

Networking in AKS

AKS supports:

- **Kubenet**: Basic virtual network implementation.
- **Azure CNI**: Each pod gets an IP in the virtual network.
- **Private Clusters**: No public access to the Kubernetes API server.
- **Ingress Controller**: Handles HTTP(S) traffic routing using NGINX, AGIC, or other controllers.

Example: Deploy NGINX Ingress

```
helm repo add ingress-nginx https://kubernetes.github.io/ingress-nginx
helm install nginx-ingress ingress-nginx/ingress-nginx
```

Monitoring and Logging

- **Azure Monitor**: Collects logs and metrics.
- **Container Insights**: Visualizes CPU, memory, and network usage per pod/node.
- **Log Analytics Workspace**: Query logs with Kusto Query Language (KQL).

Example KQL query:

```
ContainerLog
```

```
| where ContainerName == "webapp"
| sort by TimeGenerated desc
```

Securing AKS

Security features include:

- **Azure AD Integration**: Control kubectl access using RBAC tied to Azure AD identities.
- **Pod Security Policies** and **Azure Policy for AKS**
- **Network Policies**: Limit traffic between pods using labels and rules.
- **Managed Identity**: Use MSI to access Azure services like Key Vault from within a pod.

Example Role Binding:

```
apiVersion: rbac.authorization.k8s.io/v1
kind: RoleBinding
metadata:
name: dev-binding
namespace: default
subjects:
- kind: User
name: "john@company.com"
roleRef:
```

```
kind: Role
name: developer
apiGroup: rbac.authorization.k8s.io
```

CI/CD Integration

- Use **GitHub Actions** or **Azure Pipelines** to automate AKS deployments.
- Leverage tools like **Flux**, **Argo CD**, or **Helm** for GitOps-based workflows.

Example GitHub Action:

```
jobs:
build-and-deploy:
runs-on: ubuntu-latest
steps:
- uses: azure/aks-set-context@v1
with:
creds: ${{ secrets.AZURE_CREDENTIALS }}
cluster-name: myAKSCluster
resource-group: rg-aks
- run: |
kubectl apply -f k8s/
```

Backup and Disaster Recovery

Use **Velero** or **Azure Backup** for:

- Backing up persistent volumes
- Restoring cluster configurations
- Migrating workloads between clusters

Cost Optimization

- Use **spot node pools** for stateless, interruptible workloads.
- Right-size your VM SKU and number of replicas.
- Scale down during off-hours using automation.

Example: Create a spot node pool

az aks nodepool add \

—cluster-name myAKSCluster \

—resource-group rg-aks \

—name spotpool \

—priority Spot \

—eviction-policy Delete \

—spot-max-price -1 \

—node-count 1

Best Practices

- Use **namespaces** to organize workloads and teams.
- Apply **resource requests and limits** to avoid resource contention.
- Use **readiness and liveness probes** for better reliability.
- Regularly rotate **secrets and TLS certificates**.
- Prefer **managed identities** over hardcoded credentials.

Summary

Azure Kubernetes Service (AKS) is a powerful platform for deploying and managing containerized applications at scale. It abstracts away much of the operational burden of Kubernetes while still giving full control over the deployment pipeline, networking, scaling, and security configurations. By integrating with Azure-native services and adhering to Kubernetes best practices, teams can build resilient, scalable, and portable applications suitable for any enterprise environment.

Mastering AKS enables organizations to move beyond traditional VM-based workloads and embrace modern application delivery with microservices, continuous deployment, and self-healing infrastructure. With strong community support and a rapidly evolving ecosystem, AKS continues to be a leading choice for container orchestration in the cloud.

Serverless Architectures in Azure

Serverless computing abstracts away the complexity of infrastructure management, enabling developers to focus solely on code. It offers automatic scaling, pay-per-use billing, and simplified deployment, making it an attractive model for building highly responsive, event-driven applications. In Azure, serverless architecture is primarily supported through services like **Azure Functions**, **Azure Logic Apps**, **Event Grid**, and **Service Bus**, each playing a unique role in composing modern, loosely-coupled systems.

This section explores the landscape of serverless in Azure—from core concepts and service offerings to real-world architectural patterns, implementation practices, cost optimization, and security considerations.

Core Concepts of Serverless

Serverless architecture centers around the following principles:

- **Event-Driven Execution**: Code is triggered by events such as HTTP requests, database updates, queue messages, or timers.
- **Statelessness**: Each function invocation is independent; persistent state must be managed externally.
- **Micro-Billing**: You pay only for execution time and resources consumed during a function's runtime.
- **Auto-Scaling**: Azure handles horizontal scaling based on workload demands, often within milliseconds.

Key Azure Serverless Services

Azure Functions

- Lightweight code execution environment triggered by various events.
- Supports multiple languages (C#, JavaScript, Python, Java, PowerShell, etc.).
- Offers **consumption-based** and **premium** pricing models.
- Ideal for short-lived tasks like data processing, file manipulation, and backend logic.

Azure Logic Apps

- No-code/low-code workflow automation tool.
- Connects to over 300 built-in connectors (Outlook, SharePoint, SQL Server, Twitter, Salesforce, etc.).
- Used for orchestrating business processes, automating workflows, and integrating systems.

Azure Event Grid

- Event routing service that enables event-driven architecture.

- Supports custom events and system events from Azure services.

- Enables pub/sub (publish/subscribe) model at scale.

Azure Service Bus

- Enterprise-grade message broker for reliable communication between distributed systems.

- Offers queues and topics for asynchronous messaging.

- Supports features like dead-lettering, duplicate detection, and sessions.

Building Blocks of a Serverless Solution

A typical serverless application may include:

- **Trigger**: HTTP request, timer, message in queue, blob created

- **Processing Unit**: Azure Function or Logic App

- **State Management**: Azure Cosmos DB, Azure Table Storage, or Durable Functions

- **Event Propagation**: Event Grid or Service Bus

- **Security**: Managed identity, RBAC, and API Management for exposure

---

Real-World Example: Serverless Order Processing

System

Scenario: An eCommerce system processes customer orders using serverless architecture.

Components:

- HTTP-triggered Azure Function for order submission
- Event Grid to route the event
- Azure Function (or Logic App) for processing and updating inventory
- Cosmos DB for storing order data
- Azure Storage for archiving order receipts
- Service Bus for notifying external systems (e.g., logistics)

Azure Functions: Deep Dive

Azure Functions can be configured via:

- **Triggers**: Define what causes the function to run (HTTP, queue, blob, timer, etc.)
- **Bindings**: Connect function inputs/outputs to other services declaratively

Sample HTTP Trigger (JavaScript)

```
module.exports = async function (context, req) {
```

```
context.log('HTTP trigger received request.');
const name = (req.query.name || (req.body && req.body.name));
const responseMessage = name
? `Hello, ${name}.`
: "Please provide a name.";
context.res = {
status: 200,
body: responseMessage
};
}
```

Durable Functions

- Used to build **stateful** workflows in a serverless model
- Patterns include:
  - **Fan-Out/Fan-In**: Parallel tasks with aggregation
  - **Chaining**: Sequential task execution
  - **Human Interaction**: Wait for external input with timeouts

Azure Logic Apps: Deep Dive

Logic Apps provide a GUI for creating workflows using prebuilt connectors.

Example Use Case

- Trigger: New file in OneDrive
- Action: Analyze file with Cognitive Services
- Action: Send summary email via Outlook
- Action: Save analysis results to SQL Database

Features

- Built-in error handling
- Conditionals and loops
- Parallel actions
- Inline code via Azure Functions

Deployment

Logic Apps can be deployed via ARM templates, Azure CLI, or the Portal. Integration with GitHub and Azure DevOps allows CI/CD pipelines.

Event Grid and Serverless Integration

Event Grid is optimized for high-throughput, low-latency event routing.

Example: Connecting Blob Storage to Azure Function

```
az eventgrid event-subscription create \

—name blobTriggerEvent \

—source-resource-id
/subscriptions/<sub-id>/resourceGroups/<rg>/providers/
Microsoft.Storage/storageAccounts/<account> \

—endpoint-type azurefunction \

—endpoint
/subscriptions/<sub-id>/resourceGroups/<rg>/providers/
Microsoft.Web/sites/<functionapp>/functions/<functionname>
```

Service Bus and Serverless

For scenarios requiring ordered, durable, and transactional messaging, Service Bus queues or topics are preferred over Event Grid.

Function Trigger Example (C#)

```
public static class ProcessOrderQueue

{

[FunctionName("ProcessOrderQueue")]

public static void Run(
```

```
[ServiceBusTrigger("orders", Connection = "ServiceBusConnection")] string message,

ILogger log)

{

log.LogInformation($"Order received: {message}");

}

}
```

Serverless Best Practices

Design Principles

- **Small Functions**: Break logic into reusable, single-purpose units.
- **Avoid Stateful Logic**: Use external storage for persistence.
- **Use Durable Functions for Orchestration**: Don't try to manually orchestrate steps with timers or nested functions.
- **Error Handling**: Implement retry policies and dead-lettering.
- **Idempotency**: Ensure functions can safely retry without side effects.
- **Secure Access**: Use Managed Identities and RBAC; avoid hardcoding secrets.

Performance Optimization

- Minimize function cold starts by:
  - Using Premium Plan or Always On
  - Avoiding large dependencies
- Use batching for high-throughput workloads (e.g., Service Bus triggers)

Monitoring Serverless Workloads

Azure provides tools to monitor serverless applications:

- **Application Insights**: Auto-collects telemetry
- **Azure Monitor Logs**: Search, filter, and visualize logs
- **Custom Metrics**: Emit and alert on custom performance indicators

Sample KQL for monitoring function failures:

```
exceptions
| where cloud_RoleName == "my-function-app"
| summarize count() by outerMessage, bin(timestamp, 5m)
```

Cost Considerations

Azure Functions Pricing

- **Consumption Plan**: Pay per execution, with 1 million requests and 400,000 GB-s free monthly.
- **Premium Plan**: Reserved instances, faster cold start performance.
- **Dedicated Plan**: Functions hosted on App Service Plans (rarely used).

Logic Apps Pricing

- **Per-action execution cost**: Each connector and action has its own price.
- **Integration Service Environment (ISE)**: Higher cost, private VNet access, high performance.

Real-World Serverless Patterns

1. **API Backend**
   - Use Azure Functions as a backend for a static frontend (hosted in Azure Static Web Apps)
   - Use API Management to expose, secure, and document APIs
2. **Data Processing Pipeline**

○ Trigger: Blob upload → Event Grid → Azure Function

○ Transform → Store in Data Lake → Notify downstream via Service Bus

3. **Automated Workflow**

○ Trigger: CRM update → Logic App processes record → Sends notification → Archives document

4. **IoT Event Ingestion**

○ Ingest device telemetry using Event Hubs → Azure Functions → Stream Analytics → Dashboard

---

Summary

Serverless architecture in Azure empowers developers to build scalable, cost-efficient, and event-driven applications without the overhead of infrastructure management. Azure Functions, Logic Apps, Event Grid, and Service Bus together form a robust ecosystem that enables powerful workflows and microservices.

With proper architectural patterns, monitoring, and security practices, serverless applications can scale seamlessly, respond to real-time events, and integrate across complex enterprise systems. Embracing serverless not only accelerates development but also reduces operational burden—letting you focus on delivering business value through innovation.

Chapter 4: Networking in Azure

Virtual Networks and Subnets

In any cloud architecture, networking serves as the foundation for building secure, scalable, and high-performing environments. Azure Virtual Network (VNet) is the cornerstone of networking in Azure. It allows you to establish private, isolated, and logically segmented network spaces within the cloud, similar to a traditional on-premises network. These virtual networks enable communication between Azure resources, internet access, secure connectivity with on-premises networks, and the implementation of advanced network security models.

This section will guide you through the core concepts of Azure VNets, subnetting, routing, address management, network isolation, and best practices.

Introduction to Azure Virtual Network (VNet)

An Azure Virtual Network (VNet) is a representation of your own network in the cloud. It enables many types of Azure resources, such as Azure Virtual Machines (VMs), to securely communicate with each other, the internet, and on-premises networks.

Each VNet is isolated from other VNets in Azure unless explicitly peered or connected. This isolation provides security boundaries and supports multi-tenant architecture designs.

Key Properties of VNets

- **Private IP Addressing**: VNets support both IPv4 and IPv6 addresses. You can assign private address ranges to each VNet using CIDR notation, such as 10.0.0.0/16.

- **Subnets**: A VNet is divided into one or more subnets, which helps segment the network based on resource roles or application tiers.

- **Routing**: Azure automatically manages routing between subnets within a VNet and allows custom route tables for advanced control.

- **DNS**: Azure provides default name resolution, but custom DNS servers can be specified.

- **Network Security**: NSGs and route tables offer fine-grained control over traffic flow and access policies.

Creating a Virtual Network

You can create a VNet using the Azure Portal, Azure CLI, PowerShell, ARM templates, or Terraform. Here's an example using Azure CLI:

```
az network vnet create \

—name MyVNet \

—resource-group MyResourceGroup \

—location eastus \

—address-prefix 10.0.0.0/16 \
```

—subnet-name MySubnet \

—subnet-prefix 10.0.1.0/24

This command creates a VNet named MyVNet in the eastus region with a single subnet.

Subnetting in Azure

Subnets divide your VNet address space into smaller segments to organize resources and manage security.

Planning Subnets

Good subnet planning ensures:

- Proper network isolation (e.g., separating web, app, and database tiers)
- Efficient IP utilization
- Simplified routing and security rule implementation

Example Subnet Layout in 10.0.0.0/16:

Subnet Name	CIDR Range	Usage
WebSubnet	10.0.1.0/24	Web frontends
AppSubnet	10.0.2.0/24	App services
DBSubnet	10.0.3.0/24	Database workloads
MgmtSubnet	10.0.4.0/24	Management VMs

Delegation and Service Endpoints

Subnets can be delegated to specific Azure services (e.g., Azure SQL, Container Instances) for tighter integration. You can also enable **Service Endpoints** to extend your subnet's private address space to Azure services like Storage and SQL Database.

az network vnet subnet update \

—name DBSubnet \

—vnet-name MyVNet \

—resource-group MyResourceGroup \

—service-endpoints Microsoft.Sql

IP Address Management

Azure supports both **dynamic** and **static** IP address assignment within subnets. Dynamic IPs are assigned automatically from the subnet range, while static IPs are manually assigned and reserved for resources like load balancers or NAT gateways.

You can reserve IPs with:

az network public-ip create \

—name MyPublicIP \

—resource-group MyResourceGroup \

—allocation-method Static \

—sku Standard

Use the Standard SKU for zone-redundant or production-grade workloads.

VNet Peering

VNet Peering connects two VNets, allowing seamless communication as if they were part of the same network. Peering supports intra-region and global scenarios.

az network vnet peering create \

—name Peer1ToPeer2 \

—resource-group MyResourceGroup \

—vnet-name VNet1 \

—remote-vnet VNet2 \

—allow-vnet-access

Peered VNets must not have overlapping address ranges. Peering is low latency and leverages the Azure backbone, not the public internet.

DNS Integration

By default, Azure assigns its own internal DNS service for name resolution. However, for advanced setups:

- Configure custom DNS in VNet settings.
- Deploy your own DNS server in a subnet.
- Use Azure Private DNS Zones for internal name resolution.

az network vnet update \

—name MyVNet \

—resource-group MyResourceGroup \

—dns-servers 10.0.4.4 10.0.4.5

Private DNS Zones simplify DNS management for resources in a VNet without needing custom DNS servers.

User-Defined Routes (UDRs)

Custom route tables allow you to control traffic flow between subnets or external networks.

For example, to send all internet-bound traffic from a subnet through a network virtual appliance (NVA):

az network route-table create \

—name MyRouteTable \

—resource-group MyResourceGroup

az network route-table route create \

—resource-group MyResourceGroup \

—route-table-name MyRouteTable \

—name InternetRoute \

—address-prefix 0.0.0.0/0 \

—next-hop-type VirtualAppliance \

—next-hop-ip-address 10.0.4.10

az network vnet subnet update \

—vnet-name MyVNet \

```
—name WebSubnet \

—resource-group MyResourceGroup \

—route-table MyRouteTable
```

This ensures all outbound traffic is routed via a specific virtual appliance for inspection or logging.

Network Isolation and Security

To enhance security within a VNet, consider:

- **Network Security Groups (NSGs)**: Control inbound and outbound traffic at the subnet or NIC level.
- **Application Security Groups (ASGs)**: Group similar workloads and apply security rules without IP dependencies.
- **Private Endpoints**: Provide secure, private access to Azure PaaS services using private IPs within your VNet.

Example NSG Rule to Allow HTTP Traffic:

```
az network nsg rule create \

—resource-group MyResourceGroup \

—nsg-name WebNSG \

—name AllowHTTP \

—protocol Tcp \

—direction Inbound \
```

—priority 100 \

—source-address-prefix '*' \

—source-port-range '*' \

—destination-address-prefix '*' \

—destination-port-range 80 \

—access Allow

Integrating with On-Premises Networks

For hybrid environments, VNets can connect to on-premises datacenters using:

- **VPN Gateway** (IPsec tunnels)
- **ExpressRoute** (private, dedicated connectivity)

VPN Gateway Configuration Example:

az network vpn-gateway create \

—name MyVpnGateway \

—public-ip-address MyGatewayIP \

—vnet MyVNet \

—resource-group MyResourceGroup \

—location eastus \

—sku VpnGw2

VPN Gateway works well for dev/test and lower bandwidth needs. ExpressRoute is ideal for production or high-throughput scenarios.

Best Practices

- Plan VNet address space carefully to avoid overlaps, especially with hybrid or peered environments.
- Segment application tiers using subnets and NSGs.
- Use ASGs to reduce IP management overhead.
- Monitor VNet flows using Network Watcher and NSG flow logs.
- Implement UDRs and NVAs for granular control in regulated industries.
- Enable **DDoS Protection Standard** for critical VNets.

Conclusion

Azure Virtual Networks and Subnets are critical components of cloud networking that allow for secure, structured, and scalable infrastructure design. Mastering these concepts lays the foundation for more advanced network configurations and integrations, such as hybrid connectivity, security enforcement, and service mesh architectures.

By combining careful planning, appropriate tooling, and built-in Azure features, organizations can deploy networks that meet performance, availability, and compliance requirements with confidence.

Load Balancers and Application Gateways

As applications scale and require high availability, reliability, and performance, Azure provides advanced load balancing solutions to distribute traffic intelligently. Azure offers several options for traffic distribution, including the **Azure Load Balancer**, **Azure Application Gateway**, and **Azure Traffic Manager**. This section focuses on **Load Balancers** and **Application Gateways**, comparing their capabilities and providing implementation insights for production workloads.

These services ensure that application traffic is distributed across multiple backend resources, such as virtual machines or containers, to avoid bottlenecks, improve fault tolerance, and support seamless updates.

Azure Load Balancer Overview

Azure Load Balancer is a Layer 4 (TCP/UDP) load balancer that enables high availability by distributing incoming network traffic across multiple virtual machines or services within a region. It works at the transport layer of the OSI model and supports inbound and outbound scenarios.

There are two SKUs available:

- **Basic Load Balancer**: Suitable for dev/test environments.
- **Standard Load Balancer**: Offers higher availability, scalability, zone redundancy, and advanced diagnostics for production environments.

Key Features

- Layer 4 load balancing for TCP and UDP traffic.
- Health probes to monitor backend VM instances.
- Supports inbound NAT rules.
- Integration with availability sets and zones.
- Outbound rules for managing SNAT.

Creating a Load Balancer

Using Azure CLI, you can deploy a Load Balancer with a backend pool and health probes.

Step 1: Create Public IP Address

az network public-ip create \

—resource-group MyResourceGroup \

—name MyPublicIP \

—sku Standard \

—allocation-method Static

Step 2: Create Load Balancer

az network lb create \

—resource-group MyResourceGroup \

—name MyLoadBalancer \

—sku Standard \

—public-ip-address MyPublicIP \

—frontend-ip-name LoadBalancerFrontEnd \

—backend-pool-name LoadBalancerBackEnd

Step 3: Configure Health Probes

Health probes help determine the availability of backend instances.

az network lb probe create \

—resource-group MyResourceGroup \

—lb-name MyLoadBalancer \

—name MyHealthProbe \

—protocol Tcp \

—port 80

Step 4: Create Load Balancing Rule

az network lb rule create \

—resource-group MyResourceGroup \

—lb-name MyLoadBalancer \

—name MyLoadBalancingRule \

—protocol Tcp \

—frontend-port 80 \

—backend-port 80 \

—frontend-ip-name LoadBalancerFrontEnd \

—backend-pool-name LoadBalancerBackEnd \

—probe-name MyHealthProbe

Scenarios for Azure Load Balancer

Azure Load Balancer is optimal for:

- Load balancing virtual machines in a scale set.
- Serving internal applications using an **Internal Load Balancer**.
- High-performance scenarios where protocol-level routing is sufficient.
- Simplified deployment where only TCP/UDP is required.

Limitations:

- No SSL termination.
- No cookie-based affinity or path-based routing.
- No Web Application Firewall (WAF) integration.

Azure Application Gateway Overview

Azure Application Gateway operates at Layer 7 (HTTP/HTTPS) and provides advanced web traffic load balancing capabilities. It enables SSL termination, cookie-based session affinity, URL path-based routing, and integrates natively with Web Application Firewall (WAF) to protect web apps from common threats.

Key Features

- HTTP/HTTPS Layer 7 load balancing.
- SSL offloading and end-to-end encryption support.
- URL-based routing and multi-site hosting.
- Autoscaling and zone redundancy.
- Web Application Firewall (WAF) integration.
- Custom error pages and request rewrites.

Application Gateway Architecture

An Application Gateway consists of:

- **Frontend IP Configuration**: Public or private IP.
- **Listeners**: Defines port, protocol, and SSL settings.
- **Rules**: Maps listeners to backend targets.

- **Backend Pools**: Targets like VMs, VMSS, App Services.
- **Probes**: Health checks for backend pool members.
- **WAF**: (Optional) Policy that inspects HTTP requests.

Creating an Application Gateway

Using Azure CLI, here's a basic setup:

Step 1: Create Subnet for App Gateway

```
az network vnet subnet create \
—resource-group MyResourceGroup \
—vnet-name MyVNet \
—name AppGatewaySubnet \
—address-prefix 10.0.5.0/24
```

Step 2: Create Public IP for Gateway

```
az network public-ip create \
—name AppGatewayPublicIP \
—resource-group MyResourceGroup \
—sku Standard \
—allocation-method Static
```

Step 3: Create Application Gateway

az network application-gateway create \

—name MyAppGateway \

—location eastus \

—resource-group MyResourceGroup \

—capacity 2 \

—sku WAF_v2 \

—http-settings-cookie-based-affinity Enabled \

—vnet-name MyVNet \

—subnet AppGatewaySubnet \

—public-ip-address AppGatewayPublicIP

Path-Based Routing and Multi-Site Hosting

Application Gateway can route traffic based on URL path or host headers.

Example: Path-Based Routing

- /api/* routed to backend A
- /images/* routed to backend B

This is configured through **routing rules** and **URL path maps**.

SSL Termination and End-to-End Encryption

SSL termination allows the gateway to decrypt traffic, inspect it, and forward it unencrypted to the backend. Alternatively, you can configure end-to-end encryption for compliance-sensitive workloads.

Uploading a Certificate

az network application-gateway ssl-cert create \

—gateway-name MyAppGateway \

—resource-group MyResourceGroup \

—name MySslCert \

—cert-file /path/to/cert.pfx \

—cert-password MyPassword123

Application Gateway WAF

With the WAF_v2 SKU, you can enable Web Application Firewall to protect against:

- SQL Injection
- Cross-Site Scripting (XSS)
- OWASP Top 10 vulnerabilities

WAF policies are customizable and include logging, IP blocking, and managed rulesets.

az network application-gateway waf-policy create \

—name MyWafPolicy \

—resource-group MyResourceGroup \

—policy-settings-mode Prevention

Attach the policy to your gateway and adjust rules as needed.

Monitoring and Logging

Both Load Balancer and Application Gateway integrate with:

- **Azure Monitor**
- **Log Analytics**
- **Network Watcher**

Enable diagnostics for deep visibility:

az network application-gateway diagnostic-settings create \

—name AppGatewayDiagnostics \

—resource-id $(az network application-gateway show—name MyAppGateway—resource-group MyResourceGroup—query id -o tsv) \

—workspace MyLogAnalyticsWorkspace \

—logs '[{"category": "ApplicationGatewayAccessLog", "enabled": true}]'

Comparing Azure Load Balancer vs. Application Gateway

Feature	Azure Load Balancer	Azure Application Gateway
OSI Layer	Layer 4	Layer 7 (Application Layer)
Protocols Supported	TCP, UDP	HTTP, HTTPS
SSL Termination	No	Yes
Cookie-Based Affinity	No	Yes
Path-Based Routing	No	Yes
Web Application Firewall	No	Yes (WAF_v2)
Autoscaling	VMSS only	Yes (v2 SKU)
Health Probes	Basic TCP/ HTTP	Custom HTTP with headers

Choosing the Right Option

Use Azure Load Balancer when:

- You need ultra-low latency at the TCP/UDP level.
- You're load balancing non-HTTP(S) traffic.
- Backend pool consists of VMs or VMSS.

Use Application Gateway when:

- You need Layer 7 features (path-based routing, host headers).
- Your app uses SSL/TLS and requires WAF.

- You serve multiple web applications via one gateway.

Use both when combining frontend web traffic with backend service balancing.

Conclusion

Azure provides powerful load balancing capabilities for diverse workloads. **Azure Load Balancer** offers performance-focused Layer 4 balancing ideal for VMs and services. **Azure Application Gateway** adds intelligent routing and security features at the application layer, making it essential for web workloads.

Understanding their strengths and configuring them properly ensures high availability, scalability, and security across modern cloud applications. Mastery of these services equips architects and engineers with robust tools to handle complex networking needs and deliver enterprise-grade solutions with confidence.

Azure DNS, Traffic Manager, and Front Door

Azure provides a suite of global traffic distribution and name resolution services to ensure that your applications are discoverable, scalable, and resilient. This section focuses on three core Azure networking services: **Azure DNS**, **Azure Traffic Manager**, and **Azure Front Door**. These services work independently or in combination to route users to the closest and healthiest endpoints, provide reliable name resolution, and accelerate performance.

Understanding and effectively configuring these services is essential for modern cloud applications that span regions, require high availability, or demand ultra-low latency performance.

Azure DNS

Azure DNS is a high-performance, globally distributed domain name system (DNS) service hosted in Azure. It enables you to host your domain names and manage DNS records using Azure's infrastructure, ensuring fast responses and high availability without the need to run your own DNS servers.

Key Features

- Host public DNS zones.
- Manage DNS records using Azure Portal, CLI, or PowerShell.
- Fast propagation times and low latency using Azure's global infrastructure.
- Private DNS zones for name resolution within VNets.

Creating a Public DNS Zone

To use Azure DNS, you must first create a DNS zone and add the appropriate records.

az network dns zone create \

—resource-group MyResourceGroup \

—name mydomain.com

Add an A record pointing to a public IP address:

az network dns record-set a add-record \

—resource-group MyResourceGroup \

—zone-name mydomain.com \

—record-set-name www \

—ipv4-address 52.168.1.1

Common Record Types

Record Type	Description
A	Maps hostname to IPv4 address
AAAA	Maps hostname to IPv6 address
CNAME	Alias to another hostname
MX	Mail exchange records
TXT	Arbitrary text (e.g., SPF records)
NS	Delegates a DNS zone

Azure Private DNS

Azure Private DNS provides name resolution within one or more virtual networks. This is ideal for resolving private IPs of services deployed in VNets without managing a separate DNS infrastructure.

az network private-dns zone create \

—resource-group MyResourceGroup \

—name internal.contoso.com

Link a VNet to the zone:

az network private-dns link vnet create \

—resource-group MyResourceGroup \

—zone-name internal.contoso.com \

—name LinkToMyVNet \

—virtual-network MyVNet \

—registration-enabled false

Azure Traffic Manager

Azure Traffic Manager is a DNS-based global traffic distribution service that directs user requests to the most appropriate endpoint based on routing rules. It does not route the traffic itself but returns the best endpoint to the DNS query.

Key Features

- DNS-based load balancing across regions.
- Multiple routing methods (performance, priority, weighted, geographic).
- Automatic endpoint health checks.
- Supports external and non-Azure endpoints.
- Integration with Azure Monitor for health probes.

Traffic Routing Methods

Method	Description
Performance	Routes to the lowest latency endpoint based on user location
Priority	Routes all traffic to the primary endpoint unless it is unhealthy
Weighted	Distributes traffic based on defined weights
Geographic	Routes users based on the geographic location of their DNS query origin
Multivalue	Returns multiple healthy endpoints in DNS response
Subnet	Routes users based on their IP address range

Creating a Traffic Manager Profile

```
az network traffic-manager profile create \
—name MyTrafficManager \
—resource-group MyResourceGroup \
—routing-method Performance \
—unique-dns-name myappglobal \
—ttl 30 \
—protocol HTTP \
—port 80 \
—path "/"
```

Add endpoints to the profile:

```
az network traffic-manager endpoint create \
—name EastUSApp \
—profile-name MyTrafficManager \
—resource-group MyResourceGroup \
—type azureEndpoints \
—target-resource-id
/subscriptions/.../resourceGroups/.../providers/
Microsoft.Network/publicIPAddresses/EastUSAppIP \
—endpoint-status Enabled
```

You can also add external endpoints by specifying—type externalEndpoints and providing the FQDN.

Health Probes

Traffic Manager uses HTTP, HTTPS, or TCP health probes to determine endpoint status. An unhealthy endpoint is temporarily removed from DNS responses.

Azure Front Door

Azure Front Door is a global, scalable entry point for web applications. It combines application acceleration via split TCP and Anycast, load balancing at Layer 7, SSL offloading, Web Application Firewall (WAF), and instant failover across regions.

It is designed for high-performance, modern web apps with global reach.

Key Features

- Global HTTP/HTTPS load balancing with instant failover.
- Smart health probes and latency-based routing.
- Application acceleration with caching and TCP optimization.
- URL-based routing, SSL termination, and session affinity.
- Web Application Firewall integration for security.
- Custom domain and SSL certificate support.

Front Door vs Traffic Manager

Feature	Azure Traffic Manager	Azure Front Door
Layer	DNS (Layer 7 Routing via DNS)	HTTP/HTTPS proxy (Layer 7)
Failover Speed	DNS TTL-based	Instant (probe-based)
Protocol Support	Any protocol (DNS returns IP)	HTTP/HTTPS only
App Acceleration	No	Yes (split TCP, caching)
Path-Based Routing	Basic via DNS	Advanced and configurable
WAF Support	No	Yes

Creating an Azure Front Door

With Azure CLI:

Step 1: Create Front Door Profile

az network front-door create \

—resource-group MyResourceGroup \

—name MyFrontDoor \

—accepted-protocols Http Https \

—backend-address myapp-eastus.azurewebsites.net \

—frontend-endpoints myfrontend.mydomain.com \

—backend-host-header myapp-eastus.azurewebsites.net

Step 2: Add More Backends

You can add additional regional endpoints and configure routing rules.

az network front-door backend-pool backend add \

—resource-group MyResourceGroup \

—front-door-name MyFrontDoor \

—backend-pool-name DefaultBackendPool \

—address myapp-westus.azurewebsites.net \

—http-port 80 \

—https-port 443 \

```
—weight 50 \
—priority 2
```

Step 3: Configure Routing Rules

Routing rules define how traffic is handled and forwarded.

```
az network front-door routing-rule create \
—resource-group MyResourceGroup \
—front-door-name MyFrontDoor \
—name ForwardToApp \
—frontend-endpoints myfrontend.mydomain.com \
—accepted-protocols Http Https \
—patterns-to-match "/*" \
—route-type Forward \
—backend-pool DefaultBackendPool
```

WAF Integration with Front Door

Azure Front Door integrates with the WAF (Web Application Firewall) for real-time request inspection and protection against common threats.

WAF Policy Example

```
az network front-door waf-policy create \
—resource-group MyResourceGroup \
```

—name MyWafPolicy \

—mode Prevention

Associate the WAF policy with your Front Door instance to enforce global security rules across all frontends.

Best Practices

- Use **Azure DNS** for both public and private zones to centralize name resolution.
- Leverage **Traffic Manager** when global endpoint DNS-based redirection suffices.
- Choose **Front Door** for high-performance, HTTP-based applications requiring WAF, path-based routing, or instant failover.
- Minimize TTL in Traffic Manager for faster failover.
- Secure all DNS zones with Azure RBAC and enable logging.
- For hybrid or secure private DNS scenarios, combine Private DNS zones with conditional forwarding.

Real-World Architecture Example

Scenario: You operate a multi-region web app with frontends in East US and West Europe.

- Use **Azure Front Door** as the primary entry point to globally distribute user traffic based on latency and health.

- Configure **Application Gateway** behind Front Door for SSL offloading, WAF, and path-based routing.

- Manage DNS using **Azure DNS** for www.contoso.com, pointing it to the Front Door frontend.

- Optionally, set up **Traffic Manager** for cross-geo failover between Front Door profiles.

This setup ensures global availability, fast access, and security at every layer.

Conclusion

Azure DNS, Traffic Manager, and Front Door are essential tools in the design and operation of modern, scalable, and resilient cloud applications. Each service plays a unique role:

- **Azure DNS** handles fast, reliable name resolution.

- **Traffic Manager** provides intelligent DNS-level routing for cross-region endpoints.

- **Azure Front Door** delivers HTTP performance acceleration, advanced routing, and deep security features.

By combining these services strategically, architects can meet high demands for uptime, user experience, and global reach. These tools support enterprise-scale cloud-native applications with robust routing, optimized delivery, and secure front-door access.

Network Security Groups and Firewalls

Securing Azure networking infrastructure is critical to ensuring data confidentiality, integrity, and availability. Azure offers several tools to manage traffic flows at various levels, with **Network Security Groups (NSGs)** and **Azure Firewall** serving as two primary mechanisms. NSGs operate at the subnet and NIC level, providing fine-grained access control, while Azure Firewall is a stateful, centralized network security service with advanced threat protection and logging capabilities.

Understanding how to leverage these two tools—independently or together—is essential to building a layered security posture aligned with Zero Trust principles.

Network Security Groups (NSGs)

A **Network Security Group** is a rule-based security boundary that controls inbound and outbound network traffic to and from Azure resources. NSGs can be associated with **subnets** or individual **network interfaces** (NICs) of virtual machines.

Key Features

- Stateless, rule-based filtering for TCP, UDP, and ICMP.
- Rules evaluated based on priority (lower value = higher priority).
- Supports IP address, port, and protocol filtering.

- Can apply to subnets or individual NICs.
- Default rules allow basic communication within Azure and block all inbound traffic by default.

Default NSG Rules

When you create an NSG, it includes the following default rules (in order of priority):

Rule Name	Priority	Direction	Access	Source
AllowVnetInBound	65000	Inbound	Allow	VirtualNe
AllowAzureLoadBalancerInBound	65001	Inbound	Allow	AzureLoa
DenyAllInBound	65500	Inbound	Deny	Any
AllowVnetOutBound	65000	Outbound	Allow	VirtualNe
AllowInternetOutBound	65001	Outbound	Allow	Any
DenyAllOutBound	65500	Outbound	Deny	Any

These can be overridden with custom rules.

Creating and Managing NSGs

Using Azure CLI, you can create and configure NSGs easily.

Create an NSG

```
az network nsg create \

—resource-group MyResourceGroup \

—name MyNSG \

—location eastus
```

Add an Inbound Rule

```
az network nsg rule create \

—resource-group MyResourceGroup \

—nsg-name MyNSG \

—name AllowSSH \

—priority 100 \

—direction Inbound \

—access Allow \

—protocol Tcp \

—source-address-prefix '*' \

—source-port-range '*' \

—destination-address-prefix '*' \
```

—destination-port-range 22

This allows SSH access to a VM. Always use source IP restrictions in production.

Associate NSG with a Subnet

az network vnet subnet update \

—vnet-name MyVNet \

—name MySubnet \

—resource-group MyResourceGroup \

—network-security-group MyNSG

Associate NSG with a NIC

az network nic update \

—name MyNic \

—resource-group MyResourceGroup \

—network-security-group MyNSG

Monitoring NSG Flows

Enable **NSG flow logs** with Network Watcher to analyze traffic flows for diagnostics and auditing.

az network watcher flow-log configure \

—resource-group MyResourceGroup \

—nsg MyNSG \

—enabled true \

—retention 7 \

—storage-account MyStorageAccount

Use **Traffic Analytics** for visualization and deeper insights.

Best Practices for NSGs

- Apply NSGs at both subnet and NIC levels for layered security.
- Use **Application Security Groups (ASGs)** to group VMs logically without relying on IPs.
- Use low-priority numbers (100–399) for custom rules to override defaults.
- Always review effective security rules using the Portal or CLI:

az network nic list-effective-nsg \

—name MyNic \

—resource-group MyResourceGroup

- Deny all by default and explicitly allow known ports and protocols.
- Regularly audit and rotate NSG rules to enforce the principle of least privilege.

Azure Firewall

Azure Firewall is a **stateful** cloud-native network security service that protects Azure Virtual Network resources. It offers **centralized logging, policy enforcement, threat intelligence, and deep packet inspection**. Unlike NSGs, it operates at a more advanced level with full session awareness and inspection.

Key Features

- Fully stateful traffic inspection.
- Built-in high availability and scalability.
- Centralized policy with IP, FQDN, and protocol filtering.
- Application and network rule collections.
- Threat intelligence-based filtering.
- Full logging and monitoring via Azure Monitor.
- Supports both DNAT and SNAT.

Use Cases

- Centralized security enforcement point for hub-and-spoke topology.
- Perimeter control for sensitive workloads.
- Granular filtering with FQDN-based application rules.

- Logging and alerting for audit and compliance requirements.

Deploying Azure Firewall

Azure Firewall requires its own dedicated subnet (AzureFirewallSubnet) in a virtual network.

Step 1: Create VNet and Subnet

```
az network vnet create \

—resource-group MyResourceGroup \

—name MyVNet \

—address-prefix 10.0.0.0/16 \

—subnet-name AzureFirewallSubnet \

—subnet-prefix 10.0.1.0/24
```

Step 2: Create Public IP

```
az network public-ip create \

—resource-group MyResourceGroup \

—name MyFirewallPublicIP \

—sku Standard \

—allocation-method Static
```

Step 3: Create the Firewall

az network firewall create \

—name MyFirewall \

—resource-group MyResourceGroup \

—location eastus

Step 4: Configure IP Configuration

az network firewall ip-config create \

—firewall-name MyFirewall \

—resource-group MyResourceGroup \

—name FWConfig \

—public-ip-address MyFirewallPublicIP \

—vnet-name MyVNet

Application and Network Rules

Azure Firewall supports two rule types:

Application Rules

Used for HTTP/S traffic and FQDN-based filtering.

az network firewall application-rule collection create \

—firewall-name MyFirewall \

—resource-group MyResourceGroup \

—collection-name AppRuleCollection \

—priority 100 \

—action Allow \

—rule-name AllowWeb \

—rule-type ApplicationRule \

—target-fqdns www.microsoft.com \

—protocols Http=80 Https=443 \

—source-addresses 10.0.0.0/24

Network Rules

Used for IP, port, and protocol-based filtering.

az network firewall network-rule collection create \

—firewall-name MyFirewall \

—resource-group MyResourceGroup \

—collection-name NetRuleCollection \

—priority 200 \

—action Allow \

—rule-name AllowDNS \

—rule-type NetworkRule \

—protocols UDP \

—source-addresses 10.0.0.0/24 \

—destination-addresses 8.8.8.8 \

—destination-ports 53

DNAT with Azure Firewall

You can configure **Destination Network Address Translation (DNAT)** to expose internal services.

az network firewall nat-rule collection create \

—firewall-name MyFirewall \

—resource-group MyResourceGroup \

—collection-name DNATCollection \

—priority 300 \

—action Dnat \

—rule-name AllowHTTPInbound \

—rule-type NatRule \

—protocols TCP \

—source-addresses '*' \

—destination-addresses <FirewallPublicIP> \

—destination-ports 80 \

—translated-port 80 \

—translated-address 10.0.2.4

This exposes the internal IP 10.0.2.4 on port 80 through the firewall's public IP.

Monitoring Azure Firewall

All Azure Firewall logs are sent to Azure Monitor. You can enable diagnostics and query logs using Log Analytics:

az monitor diagnostic-settings create \

—resource-id $(az network firewall show—name MyFirewall—resource-group MyResourceGroup—query id -o tsv) \

—workspace MyLogAnalyticsWorkspace \

—name FirewallDiagnostics \

—logs '[{"category": "AzureFirewallNetworkRule", "enabled": true}, {"category": "AzureFirewallApplicationRule", "enabled": true}]'

NSGs vs Azure Firewall

Feature	**NSG**	**Azure Firewall**
Stateful	No	Yes
Layer	Layer 3/4	Layer 3/4/7
Filtering	IP, Port, Protocol	IP, FQDN, Protocol
NAT Support	No	Yes (DNAT/SNAT)
TLS Inspection	No	Planned (Preview in some regions)
Logging	Limited flow logs	Full diagnostics and insights
Application Filtering	No	Yes
Threat Intelligence	No	Yes

Best Practices

- Use NSGs for perimeter and micro-segmentation security within VNets.
- Deploy Azure Firewall as a centralized security policy enforcement point, especially in hub-and-spoke architectures.
- Enable **flow logging** for NSGs and **diagnostic logging** for Firewalls to ensure visibility.
- Combine **Firewall Manager** with policies for enterprise-wide rule management.
- Leverage **Threat Intelligence** in Azure Firewall to block known malicious IPs.
- Regularly audit both NSG and Firewall rule effectiveness and prune unnecessary permissions.

Conclusion

Network Security Groups and Azure Firewall are foundational components of Azure's network security model. NSGs provide lightweight, fast, rule-based filtering at the network and NIC level, while Azure Firewall offers deep packet inspection, centralized security, and intelligent threat protection.

Together, these tools allow Azure architects to build secure, scalable, and manageable network topologies that align with Zero Trust and defense-in-depth strategies. For enterprises, mastering the implementation and optimization of NSGs and Firewalls is essential to ensuring the confidentiality, availability, and integrity of cloud-hosted assets.

VPN Gateway and ExpressRoute

In enterprise and hybrid cloud scenarios, secure and reliable connectivity between on-premises networks and Azure is essential. Azure provides two primary solutions for extending on-premises infrastructure to the cloud: **VPN Gateway** and **ExpressRoute**. Each serves different needs in terms of performance, reliability, security, and cost. This section dives deep into both technologies, exploring their architectures, use cases, configuration steps, and best practices.

Azure VPN Gateway

Azure VPN Gateway provides secure, site-to-site or point-to-site VPN connectivity between your on-premises networks and Azure Virtual Networks using IPsec/IKE protocols. It can also be used for VNet-to-VNet connections within Azure.

Key Features

- Site-to-Site (S2S) and Point-to-Site (P2S) VPN support
- IPsec/IKE-based encryption
- Active-active and zone-redundant gateway configurations
- Integration with Azure Route-Based and Policy-Based VPNs

- High availability and scalability via gateway SKUs
- Supports BGP (Border Gateway Protocol)

VPN Gateway SKUs

SKU	Max Throughput	Max Connections	Zone Redundant	Active-Active
VpnGw1	650 Mbps	250	Yes	Yes
VpnGw2	1 Gbps	1000	Yes	Yes
VpnGw3	1.25 Gbps	2000	Yes	Yes
VpnGw5	10 Gbps	10,000	Yes	Yes

Site-to-Site VPN Architecture

A site-to-site VPN requires:

- A Virtual Network with a dedicated GatewaySubnet
- A public IP for the VPN gateway
- A local network gateway (representing your on-prem router)
- A connection resource linking Azure and on-premises

Step-by-Step VPN Gateway Configuration

Step 1: Create the Virtual Network and Gateway Subnet

az network vnet create \

—name MyVNet \

—resource-group MyResourceGroup \

—address-prefix 10.10.0.0/16 \

—subnet-name GatewaySubnet \

—subnet-prefix 10.10.255.0/27

The GatewaySubnet name is mandatory for VPN Gateway.

Step 2: Create the Public IP for the Gateway

az network public-ip create \

—name MyVpnPublicIP \

—resource-group MyResourceGroup \

—allocation-method Dynamic \

—sku Standard

Step 3: Create the VPN Gateway

az network vnet-gateway create \

—name MyVpnGateway \

—resource-group MyResourceGroup \

—vnet MyVNet \

—public-ip-address MyVpnPublicIP \

—gateway-type Vpn \

—vpn-type RouteBased \

```
—sku VpnGw2 \
—no-wait
```

Step 4: Create the Local Network Gateway

This represents the on-premises VPN device:

```
az network local-gateway create \
—name OnPremGateway \
—resource-group MyResourceGroup \
—gateway-ip-address <ON_PREM_PUBLIC_IP> \
—local-address-prefixes 192.168.0.0/16
```

Step 5: Create the Connection

```
az network vpn-connection create \
—name MyVpnConnection \
—resource-group MyResourceGroup \
—vnet-gateway1 MyVpnGateway \
—local-gateway2 OnPremGateway \
—shared-key "MySharedKey123"
```

Point-to-Site (P2S) VPN

For developers or remote workers, P2S VPN provides a secure connection to an Azure VNet from a single client computer. This is ideal for scenarios where site-to-site is not feasible.

P2S supports:

- Native Azure certificate authentication
- RADIUS server authentication
- Azure Active Directory authentication

To set up P2S, configure:

1. Gateway with a supported SKU (VpnGw1+)
2. Root and client certificates or RADIUS
3. VPN client profiles

az network vnet-gateway update \

—name MyVpnGateway \

—resource-group MyResourceGroup \

—vpn-client-protocols OpenVPN \

—address-prefixes 172.16.201.0/24

Clients can download a configuration package from the Azure Portal and import it into the native OS VPN client.

VPN Gateway Best Practices

- Always use **RouteBased** VPN type for Azure compatibility.
- For high availability, deploy **Active-Active** gateways with multiple on-prem devices.

- Prefer **Standard SKU** IPs and gateways for zone redundancy and security.
- Enable **BGP** for dynamic route propagation across complex networks.
- Monitor VPN health via **Network Watcher** and alerts from Azure Monitor.

Azure ExpressRoute

ExpressRoute provides private, dedicated, high-throughput connections between your on-premises infrastructure and Microsoft's Azure datacenters. Unlike VPN Gateway, which uses the public internet, ExpressRoute uses a private connection established through a connectivity provider.

Key Features

- Layer 3 private connection
- High bandwidth (up to 100 Gbps)
- SLAs on availability and latency
- Dual connections for high availability
- Access to all Microsoft cloud services (Azure, M365, Dynamics 365)
- Supports global reach and peering across regions

Circuit Types

Peering Type	Description
Azure Private	For VNet access (IaaS workloads)
Microsoft	For SaaS access (M365, Dynamics 365)
Azure Public	Deprecated — formerly for public services

ExpressRoute Circuit Creation

An ExpressRoute circuit must be created in Azure and provisioned with a connectivity provider.

```
az network express-route circuit create \
—name MyExpressRoute \
—resource-group MyResourceGroup \
—location eastus \
—bandwidth 200 \
—provider "Equinix" \
—peering-location "Silicon Valley" \
—sku-tier Standard \
—sku-family MeteredData
```

This command provisions the logical circuit. Your provider will give a service key to complete the connection.

ExpressRoute Gateway

To connect an ExpressRoute circuit to a VNet, you need a virtual network gateway of type **ExpressRoute**.

az network vnet-gateway create \

—name MyERGateway \

—resource-group MyResourceGroup \

—vnet MyVNet \

—gateway-type ExpressRoute \

—sku Standard \

—no-wait

Then link the gateway and the ExpressRoute circuit:

az network express-route gateway connection create \

—name MyERConnection \

—resource-group MyResourceGroup \

—gateway-name MyERGateway \

—circuit-name MyExpressRoute \

—peering-type AzurePrivatePeering

ExpressRoute Direct and FastPath

- **ExpressRoute Direct**: Provides dedicated 10Gbps or 100Gbps port pair.

- **FastPath**: Bypasses the virtual network gateway for faster routing.

FastPath is enabled automatically on UltraPerformance gateways.

BGP with ExpressRoute

Border Gateway Protocol (BGP) is used to dynamically exchange routing information between Azure and on-premises networks. BGP is required for:

- Routing between multiple VNets or sites.
- Redundancy and high availability.
- Global Reach (cross-region peering).

Each peering can be configured with a primary and secondary subnet for redundancy.

Security Considerations

- ExpressRoute does not encrypt data by default. Use an IPsec overlay or trusted MPLS provider if required.
- Use **NSGs**, **Azure Firewall**, or **NVA appliances** to control traffic entering the VNet.
- Combine ExpressRoute with **Private Link** for ultra-secure connectivity to PaaS services.

Comparison: VPN Gateway vs ExpressRoute

Feature	VPN Gateway	ExpressRoute
Connection Type	Encrypted over internet	Private connection
Bandwidth	Up to 10 Gbps (VpnGw5)	Up to 100 Gbps
SLA	Limited (99.9%)	Higher SLA (99.95%+)
Security	Encrypted (IPsec/IKE)	Optional encryption
Setup Time	Hours	Days to weeks (provider required)
Use Case	Dev/test, quick deployments	Production, hybrid enterprise
Cost	Lower	Higher (circuit + provider fee)

Hybrid Architecture Example

A large enterprise might deploy:

- **Site-to-Site VPN** for dev/test environments.
- **Point-to-Site VPN** for remote developer access.
- **ExpressRoute** for production workloads with MPLS for high-throughput workloads.
- **VNet Peering** for intra-region traffic.
- **NSGs** and **Firewall** for segmentation and control.
- **Azure Bastion** for secure VM access.

This architecture supports scalability, performance, and regulatory compliance.

Monitoring and Alerts

- Use **Azure Monitor** and **Log Analytics** to track VPN and ExpressRoute metrics.
- Configure alerts on VPN downtime, BGP sessions, or bandwidth thresholds.
- Use **Network Performance Monitor** for hybrid network diagnostics.

Conclusion

Both VPN Gateway and ExpressRoute are vital tools in extending Azure networks to on-premises environments. VPN Gateway offers a cost-effective and flexible option suitable for many scenarios, while ExpressRoute provides high-performance, private connectivity for mission-critical applications.

Understanding their architectures, deployment models, and integration with other Azure services enables network architects to build secure, resilient, and performant hybrid infrastructures. Whether you're building a multi-region enterprise backbone or enabling secure access for remote teams, these connectivity options are the foundation of your hybrid cloud strategy.

Chapter 5: Azure Storage Architecture

Types of Azure Storage: Blob, Queue, Table, File, Disk

Azure offers a comprehensive suite of storage services designed to accommodate a wide range of application requirements, from unstructured data to enterprise-grade virtual machine disks. This section provides an in-depth look at the various types of storage offered in Microsoft Azure: **Blob Storage**, **Queue Storage**, **Table Storage**, **File Storage**, and **Disk Storage**. Understanding these storage types is essential for choosing the right option for your workloads and ensuring performance, scalability, and cost-efficiency.

Azure Blob Storage

Azure Blob Storage is designed to store large volumes of unstructured data, such as images, videos, documents, backups, and big data. It supports three types of blobs:

- **Block blobs**: Optimized for storing text and binary data.
- **Append blobs**: Optimized for append operations, such as logging.
- **Page blobs**: Optimized for random read/write operations, typically used by Azure virtual machine disks.

Storage Tiers

Azure Blob Storage offers multiple access tiers:

Tier	Description	Use Case
Hot	Optimized for frequent access	Real-time analytics, active content
Cool	Optimized for infrequent access	Backup, long-term storage with occasional access
Archive	Optimized for rarely accessed data	Regulatory archives, compliance storage

Creating a Blob Storage Container (Azure CLI)

```
az storage account create \

—name mystorageaccount \

—resource-group MyResourceGroup \

—location eastus \

—sku Standard_LRS \

—kind StorageV2

az storage container create \

—name mycontainer \

—account-name mystorageaccount \

—public-access off
```

Uploading a File to Blob

```
az storage blob upload \
—container-name mycontainer \
—file ./report.pdf \
—name report.pdf \
—account-name mystorageaccount
```

Blob storage also supports lifecycle management policies, redundancy options (LRS, GRS, ZRS), and integration with Azure Data Lake Gen2 for big data analytics.

Azure Queue Storage

Azure Queue Storage provides a simple, reliable, and scalable message queuing service for asynchronous communication between application components.

Each message can be up to 64 KB in size, and a single queue can contain millions of messages. Queues are commonly used in decoupled architectures where background processes need to work through jobs asynchronously.

Common Use Cases

- Decoupling frontend and backend processes
- Distributed task processing
- Order processing systems
- Workflow pipelines

Creating a Queue and Adding a Message (Azure CLI)

```
az storage queue create \
—name myqueue \
—account-name mystorageaccount
az storage message put \
—queue-name myqueue \
—content "New order received" \
—account-name mystorageaccount
```

Retrieving and Deleting Messages

```
az storage message get \
—queue-name myqueue \
—account-name mystorageaccount
az storage message delete \
—queue-name myqueue \
—id <message-id> \
—pop-receipt <receipt>
```

Queue Storage supports message TTL, retry policies, and poison message handling when integrated into enterprise workflows.

Azure Table Storage

Azure Table Storage is a NoSQL key-value datastore for rapid development using structured, non-relational datasets. It's ideal for storing large volumes of data with a flexible schema and provides fast and cost-effective access.

Each table consists of rows with a unique combination of **PartitionKey** and **RowKey**. This design allows for scalable querying and storage across distributed partitions.

Use Cases

- Audit logs and telemetry data
- User profiles
- Configuration data
- Product catalogs

Creating a Table and Inserting Entities (PowerShell Example)

$ctx = New-AzStorageContext -StorageAccountName "mystorageaccount" -StorageAccountKey "yourKey"

New-AzStorageTable -Name "customertable" -Context $ctx

Add-AzTableRow -Table "customertable" -PartitionKey "US" -RowKey "12345" -Property @{"Name"="John Doe"; "Email"="john@example.com"}

Table Querying

Table Storage supports OData-style queries using $filter expressions. For example:

GET https://<account>.table.core.windows.net/customertable()?$filter=PartitionKey eq 'US'

Though Table Storage is cost-effective and scalable, for complex querying and indexing, consider **Cosmos DB Table API**, which provides global distribution and enhanced throughput.

Azure File Storage

Azure File Storage offers fully managed file shares in the cloud, accessible via SMB and NFS protocols. It provides traditional file-sharing capabilities without managing file servers, and is commonly used for lift-and-shift applications, home directories, and shared content across distributed systems.

Key Features

- Standard and Premium tiers
- Active Directory integration
- Snapshot support for backups
- Mountable on Windows, Linux, and macOS
- NFS 4.1 support (preview and GA in select regions)

Creating and Mounting an Azure File Share

```
az storage share create \

—name myshare \

—account-name mystorageaccount \

—quota 100

# Mount on Windows

net use Z: \\mystorageaccount.file.core.windows.net\myshare /u:mystorageaccount <storagekey>
```

File shares can be accessed simultaneously by multiple clients and support fine-grained permissions with Azure AD DS integration.

Snapshot Management

File shares support **incremental snapshots**, allowing fast and efficient backup and restore operations:

```
az storage share snapshot \

—name myshare \

—account-name mystorageaccount
```

Snapshots are read-only and can be used to recover deleted or modified files.

Azure Managed Disks

Azure Managed Disks provide high-performance, durable block storage for Azure Virtual Machines. They come in multiple performance tiers and redundancy options and are fully managed by Azure to handle storage provisioning, availability, and security.

Disk Types

Disk Type	Best For	Max Size	Max IOPS	Max Throughput
Standard HDD	Backup, dev/test workloads	32 TiB	500	60 MB/s
Standard SSD	Web servers, lightly used systems	32 TiB	2,000	500 MB/s
Premium SSD	Production and database workloads	32 TiB	20,000	900 MB/s
Ultra Disk	IO-intensive workloads (SQL, SAP)	64 TiB	160,000	4,000 MB/s

Creating a Managed Disk and Attaching to VM

```
az disk create \

—resource-group MyResourceGroup \

—name MyDataDisk \

—size-gb 128 \

—sku Premium_LRS

az vm disk attach \

—vm-name MyVM \

—resource-group MyResourceGroup \

—name MyDataDisk
```

Azure disks can be encrypted with **Azure Disk Encryption** (ADE) or **customer-managed keys (CMK)** stored in **Azure Key Vault**.

Snapshots and Backup

Azure supports point-in-time backups of managed disks:

az snapshot create \

—resource-group MyResourceGroup \

—source MyDataDisk \

—name MyDataDiskSnapshot

These can be used to create new disks or restore failed VMs.

Choosing the Right Storage Option

Storage Type	Best Use Case	Access Protocol	Optimized For
Blob	Unstructured data (media, logs, backups)	HTTP/ HTTPS	Cost-efficiency, scalability
Queue	Message-based communication	REST	Asynchronous processing
Table	Key-value NoSQL store	REST	High-scale metadata storage
File	Lift-and-shift, shared directories	SMB, NFS	Easy file share integration
Disk	Virtual machines, transactional workloads	iSCSI (via Azure)	High performance, low latency

Security and Compliance

All Azure Storage services support robust security features:

- **Encryption at rest** with Azure-managed or customer-managed keys
- **TLS 1.2** for encryption in transit
- **Shared Access Signatures (SAS)** for fine-grained delegated access
- **Azure AD-based authentication** for File and Blob (preview)
- **Private Endpoints** for isolating traffic within virtual networks

az storage account update \

—name mystorageaccount \

—default-action Deny \

—bypass AzureServices

This restricts public network access and enforces use of **Private Link.**

Monitoring and Diagnostics

Azure Storage integrates with **Azure Monitor, Log Analytics,** and **Storage Metrics:**

- **Transaction metrics:** Number of read/write/delete operations

- **Latency tracking**: Request durations per operation type
- **Capacity metrics**: Utilization, available space
- **Diagnostic logs**: Access, API calls, failures

Enable logging:

```
az storage logging update \
—account-name mystorageaccount \
—log rwd \
—retention 7
```

Conclusion

Microsoft Azure provides a comprehensive set of storage services catering to virtually every workload and use case—from enterprise-scale databases to simple archival storage. Choosing the correct storage service requires a deep understanding of application needs, performance requirements, access patterns, and cost considerations.

By mastering the distinct characteristics of Blob, Queue, Table, File, and Disk Storage—and integrating them effectively into cloud architectures—developers and architects can build secure, resilient, and performant solutions across diverse industries and domains.

Storage Accounts and Performance Tiers

In Azure, all storage services are provisioned within a **Storage Account**, which acts as a container that manages the security, configuration, and billing of your data. The performance, redundancy, and access tier options of the storage account directly affect the behavior and cost-efficiency of the services it hosts. This section explores the structure of storage accounts, the various performance tiers available, redundancy options, and best practices for choosing and managing the right configurations for your workloads.

Understanding Azure Storage Accounts

A **Storage Account** in Azure is a fundamental resource that gives access to Azure Storage services: Blob, Queue, Table, File, and Disk (managed separately). It abstracts the underlying hardware, capacity, and scaling infrastructure, allowing you to focus on data storage, management, and security.

Types of Storage Accounts

Type	Description
General-purpose v2 (GPv2)	Supports all services (Blob, Queue, Table, File) with all features
General-purpose v1 (GPv1)	Legacy account type, lower costs, fewer features (not recommended)
Blob Storage	Specialized for blob-only workloads with tiered pricing
FileStorage	Premium performance tier for Azure File shares
BlockBlobStorage	Premium performance for block blob workloads like video streaming or logs

GPv2 is the recommended account type for nearly all workloads unless a premium workload requires FileStorage or BlockBlobStorage specifically.

Performance Tiers in Azure Storage

Azure provides two main performance tiers for storage accounts: **Standard** and **Premium**. These tiers are further divided based on the type of storage and intended workloads.

Standard Tier

- Backed by HDD or standard SSDs
- Ideal for general-purpose, cost-sensitive applications
- Includes Blob Storage, Queue, Table, and Azure Files
- High durability but moderate performance
- Throughput and IOPS suitable for small to medium applications

Premium Tier

- Backed by high-performance SSDs
- Optimized for low-latency, high-throughput workloads
- Required for scenarios like:
  - Enterprise databases

- ○ High-speed analytics
- ○ Real-time media serving
- Includes **Premium Page Blobs**, **Premium Azure Files**, and **Premium Block Blob**

Example: Creating a Premium Block Blob Account

```
az storage account create \
—name mystoragepremium \
—resource-group MyResourceGroup \
—sku Premium_LRS \
—kind BlockBlobStorage \
—location eastus
```

Azure Blob Storage Access Tiers

In addition to performance tiers, Azure Blob Storage offers **Access Tiers** to manage cost based on how frequently data is accessed:

Tier	Access Frequency	Retrieval Cost	Storage Cost	Best For
Hot	Frequent	Low	High	Active content, real-time access
Cool	Infrequent (<30 days)	Medium	Lower	Backup, older files
Archive	Rare (months/ years)	High (rehydration required)	Very Low	Compliance data, archives

You can set access tiers at both the blob level and account level.

Changing Blob Tier with Azure CLI

```
az storage blob set-tier \
—account-name mystorageaccount \
—container-name mycontainer \
—name bigdata.csv \
—tier Cool
```

Lifecycle Management

You can automate tier transitions using **Lifecycle Management Policies**, which optimize storage costs by moving data between tiers.

```
{
"rules": [
{
"enabled": true,
"name": "archive-old-data",
"type": "Lifecycle",
"definition": {
"filters": {
"blobTypes": [ "blockBlob" ],
```

```
"prefixMatch": [ "logs/" ]
},
"actions": {
"baseBlob": {
"tierToCool": { "daysAfterModificationGreaterThan": 30 },
"tierToArchive": { "daysAfterModificationGreaterThan": 90 },
"delete": { "daysAfterModificationGreaterThan": 365 }
}
}
}
}
]
}
```

You can apply this policy using ARM templates or the Azure Portal.

Redundancy Options in Storage Accounts

Redundancy ensures data durability and availability, especially during hardware failures or regional outages. Azure provides several **Replication** options:

Replication Type	Description	Use Case
LRS (Locally-redundant storage)	Replicates data 3 times within a single datacenter	Cost-effective, not fault-tolerant
ZRS (Zone-redundant storage)	Replicates data across availability zones in the same region	High availability, regional durability
GRS (Geo-redundant storage)	LRS + replication to paired region (read-only)	Disaster recovery, high durability
RA-GRS (Read-access GRS)	GRS + read access to secondary	Geo-read scenarios
GZRS (Geo-zone-redundant)	ZRS + geo-replication to secondary region	Best of ZRS and GRS
RA-GZRS	GZRS with read access to secondary	Highly available and readable backup

Configuring Redundancy in Storage Account Creation

```
az storage account create \
—name mysecurestore \
—resource-group MyResourceGroup \
—sku Standard_GZRS \
—kind StorageV2 \
—location eastus
```

You can upgrade some replication types later (e.g., LRS → GRS), but not all transitions are supported in reverse.

Storage Account Security

Azure Storage accounts offer multiple layers of security:

- **Encryption at rest** with Microsoft-managed or customer-managed keys (CMKs)
- **Transport Layer Security (TLS 1.2)** for data in transit
- **Shared Access Signatures (SAS)** for delegated access
- **Azure AD-based identity management** for Blob and Queue
- **Firewalls and virtual network integration** for network isolation
- **Private Endpoints** for secure access over Azure Backbone

Enabling Storage Firewall

```
az storage account update \
—name mystorageaccount \
—default-action Deny \
—bypass AzureServices
```

Creating a Private Endpoint

az network private-endpoint create \

—name myPrivateEndpoint \

—resource-group MyResourceGroup \

—vnet-name MyVNet \

—subnet mySubnet \

—private-connection-resource-id /subscriptions/xxx/resourceGroups/xxx/providers/Microsoft.Storage/storageAccounts/mystorageaccount \

—group-id blob

Storage Account Monitoring and Diagnostics

Azure provides built-in tools to monitor performance, availability, capacity, and security:

- **Metrics**: Transactions, latency, availability
- **Logs**: Read, write, delete operations
- **Alerts**: Threshold breaches
- **Workbooks**: Custom dashboards
- **Log Analytics**: Deep log analysis

Enabling Diagnostic Logging

az monitor diagnostic-settings create \

—name StorageDiag \

—resource-id /subscriptions/<id>/resourceGroups/<rg>/providers/Microsoft.Storage/storageAccounts/mystorageaccount \

—workspace MyLogAnalyticsWorkspace \

—logs '[{"category": "StorageRead", "enabled": true}, {"category": "StorageWrite", "enabled": true}]'

Quotas and Limits

Storage accounts have defined limits to ensure operational performance:

Resource	Limit
Max storage accounts per region	250 (standard), 100 (premium)
Max capacity per standard account	Up to 5 PiB (pay-as-you-go)
Max IOPS per account	20,000 (standard), 80,000+ (premium)
Max blob size (block blob)	Up to 200 GiB (PutBlob), 4.75 TiB (Block List)

Use **Premium BlockBlobStorage** for higher throughput needs and **Data Lake Gen2** for hierarchical namespace support.

Best Practices

- Use **StorageV2** accounts for modern features and flexibility.
- Leverage **lifecycle policies** to control storage costs.

- Apply **encryption with CMKs** for regulatory compliance.
- Use **ZRS or GZRS** for high availability requirements.
- Avoid **public network access** by using **Private Endpoints**.
- Enable **soft delete** for blobs, file shares, and containers to recover from accidental deletions.
- Set **resource locks** and **tags** for operational governance.

Conclusion

Choosing the right storage account configuration—performance tier, redundancy, and access tier—has a significant impact on application performance, availability, and cost. By understanding how to structure and manage Azure Storage Accounts effectively, you can optimize your architecture for any workload, from cost-efficient archival to low-latency, high-throughput enterprise applications.

Azure's flexibility, combined with policy-based automation and deep monitoring tools, ensures that storage remains reliable, scalable, and secure across a wide range of scenarios. Whether you're handling terabytes of logs or provisioning disk storage for mission-critical applications, mastering storage accounts and their performance characteristics is essential for building cloud-native systems with confidence.

Securing and Managing Data Access

Securing and managing data access in Azure Storage is a critical responsibility for ensuring the confidentiality, integrity, and availability of data across diverse workloads. Azure provides a comprehensive security model that includes encryption, access control, identity integration, networking restrictions, and auditing. Proper configuration of these features helps organizations meet regulatory compliance requirements and protect against internal and external threats.

This section explores identity-based access, shared access signatures (SAS), encryption mechanisms, private networking, logging, and access governance best practices for all Azure Storage types—Blob, File, Table, Queue, and Disk.

Azure Identity Integration

Azure Storage supports two primary authentication and authorization models:

- **Azure Active Directory (Azure AD) integration**
- **Shared Key and Shared Access Signature (SAS)**

Azure AD Authentication

Azure AD provides **identity-based access control** to Azure Storage services. With Azure AD, users, groups, and managed identities can be assigned roles to access resources without managing shared credentials or keys.

Steps to Enable Azure AD Authentication for Blob and Queue

1. Ensure the storage account has the **Azure role-based access control (RBAC)** model enabled.
2. Assign a role (e.g., **Storage Blob Data Reader**, **Storage Blob Data Contributor**) to the identity.
3. Use Azure AD token to authenticate from applications or CLI.

Assigning RBAC Role with Azure CLI

```
az role assignment create \

—assignee <user-or-app-id> \

—role "Storage Blob Data Contributor" \

—scope
/subscriptions/<sub-id>/resourceGroups/<rg>/providers/
Microsoft.Storage/storageAccounts/<account-name>
```

Azure AD authentication is the preferred model for security-sensitive and enterprise workloads.

Shared Access Signatures (SAS)

SAS tokens provide time-bound, permission-limited access to storage resources. They are ideal for sharing files securely with limited scope and duration.

Types of SAS

SAS Type	Description
Account SAS	Grants access to all services in the account
Service SAS	Grants access to a specific service and resource (e.g., blob)
User Delegation SAS	Created using Azure AD credentials, offering higher security

Example: Create a Service SAS for a Blob

```
az storage blob generate-sas \

—account-name mystorageaccount \

—container-name mycontainer \

—name myfile.txt \

—permissions r \

—expiry 2025-12-31T23:59Z \

—https-only \

—output tsv
```

To access the blob with the SAS token:

https://mystorageaccount.blob.core.windows.net/mycontainer/myfile.txt?<SAS_TOKEN>

Best Practices for SAS

- Always use **HTTPS-only** connections.

- Set short expiration times.
- Avoid account-level SAS unless necessary.
- Prefer **user delegation SAS** for secure, identity-based token generation.
- Use **Azure Key Vault** to store SAS tokens securely.

Azure Role-Based Access Control (RBAC)

RBAC allows for granular access management across Azure Storage. It uses built-in roles or custom-defined roles that can be scoped to:

- Entire subscription
- Resource group
- Storage account
- Individual containers or shares (for data actions)

Built-In Roles for Storage

Role	Scope	Permissions
Storage Account Contributor	Management	Full control of storage account settings
Storage Blob Data Reader	Data	Read access to blob content
Storage Blob Data Contributor	Data	Read/write access to blob content
Storage File Data SMB Share Contributor	Data	Create, read, write, delete in file share (SMB)

RBAC is preferable to access keys or SAS for enterprise workloads due to centralized control and auditing.

Access Keys and Key Rotation

Every storage account includes two **access keys** that can be used for authentication in legacy scenarios. These keys provide full administrative access to the account and should be used cautiously.

Retrieving and Rotating Keys

az storage account keys list \

—account-name mystorageaccount \

—resource-group MyResourceGroup

To regenerate a key:

az storage account keys renew \

—account-name mystorageaccount \

—resource-group MyResourceGroup \

—key primary

Automated key rotation can be implemented using Azure Automation or Azure Key Vault integration.

Encryption for Data Security

Azure Storage encrypts data **at rest** and **in transit** by default.

Encryption at Rest

- Uses **Storage Service Encryption (SSE)** with Microsoft-managed keys.
- Optionally, use **Customer-Managed Keys (CMK)** stored in Azure Key Vault.

Enabling Customer-Managed Key

az storage account update \

—name mystorageaccount \

—resource-group MyResourceGroup \

—encryption-key-source Microsoft.Keyvault \

—encryption-key-vault /subscriptions/.../resourceGroups/.../providers/ Microsoft.KeyVault/vaults/myKeyVault \

—encryption-key-name myKey \

—encryption-key-version <version>

Encryption in Transit

- Enforced via **HTTPS-only** setting on the storage account.
- TLS 1.2 is used for all client connections.

az storage account update \

—name mystorageaccount \

—https-only true

Network Security for Storage

Azure Storage supports multiple options for network security:

Firewall Rules

Restrict access to specific IP ranges:

az storage account network-rule add \

—resource-group MyResourceGroup \

—account-name mystorageaccount \

—ip-address 192.168.1.0/24

Virtual Network Integration

Enable access only from specific VNets:

az storage account network-rule add \

—resource-group MyResourceGroup \

—account-name mystorageaccount \

—vnet-name MyVNet \

—subnet MySubnet

Private Endpoints

Provision a private IP address within your VNet to securely access the storage account via Azure Backbone network.

az network private-endpoint create \

—name myPrivateEndpoint \

—resource-group MyResourceGroup \

—vnet-name MyVNet \

—subnet MySubnet \

—private-connection-resource-id <storage-account-resource-id> \

—group-id blob

Private endpoints eliminate public exposure, enhance compliance, and reduce attack surface.

Auditing and Logging

Auditing is essential for tracking access and changes to data.

Enable Diagnostics

az monitor diagnostic-settings create \

—resource-id /subscriptions/<id>/resourceGroups/<rg>/providers/Microsoft.Storage/storageAccounts/mystorageaccount \

—workspace MyLogAnalyticsWorkspace \

—name "storage-logs" \

—logs '[{"category": "StorageRead", "enabled": true}, {"category": "StorageWrite", "enabled": true}, {"category": "StorageDelete", "enabled": true}]'

Common Audit Scenarios

- Who accessed a blob and when?
- Was a file share deleted or overwritten?
- Are SAS tokens being misused or expired?
- What IPs are accessing the storage account?

Logs can be analyzed using **Azure Log Analytics**, **Microsoft Sentinel**, or custom **workbooks.**

Access Governance

To maintain control over access and permissions, implement:

- **Privileged Identity Management (PIM)** for role elevation
- **Azure Policy** for enforcing encryption, HTTPS, private link usage

- **Blueprints** to ensure storage standards across environments
- **Soft Delete** to recover from accidental deletions

az storage blob service-properties update \

—account-name mystorageaccount \

—enable-delete-retention true \

—delete-retention-days 30

Best Practices

- Prefer **Azure AD and RBAC** over access keys and SAS.
- Use **user delegation SAS** when temporary scoped access is required.
- Store all secrets and tokens in **Azure Key Vault**.
- Enforce **HTTPS-only** and **firewall rules**.
- Enable **logging and diagnostics** across all services.
- Use **customer-managed keys** for regulatory compliance.
- Isolate traffic using **Private Endpoints**.
- Regularly audit role assignments and token usage.

Conclusion

Securing and managing data access in Azure Storage is a multidimensional task that encompasses identity, encryption, network isolation, and governance. Azure provides powerful tools to enforce least privilege, monitor usage, and align with compliance frameworks such as ISO, HIPAA, and GDPR.

By integrating identity-based access controls, enforcing encrypted communications, and adopting Zero Trust principles across storage services, organizations can safeguard their critical data while enabling secure collaboration and operational agility. Whether handling personal customer data or high-volume telemetry, mastering access control in Azure Storage ensures long-term resilience and trustworthiness in any cloud-native application.

Backup, Replication, and Disaster Recovery

Ensuring the durability, availability, and recoverability of data is one of the most critical responsibilities in cloud architecture. Azure Storage services are designed with resilience in mind, offering a combination of **replication**, **backup**, and **disaster recovery** mechanisms. These capabilities help protect against accidental deletions, hardware failures, corruption, and large-scale regional disasters.

This section explores Azure's native data protection features, from storage-level redundancy and backup solutions to geo-replication and failover strategies. Properly implementing these practices ensures that enterprise data remains safe, recoverable, and compliant.

Storage-Level Replication

At the foundation of Azure's data protection model is **replication**, which ensures your data is duplicated across multiple physical locations, either within a region or across regions.

Replication Types

Replication Type	Scope	Durability	Availability	Use Case
LRS (Locally Redundant Storage)	Same data center	11 9s	Low	Development, low-cost environments
ZRS (Zone-Redundant Storage)	Across availability zones in region	12 9s	High	Production workloads needing high availability
GRS (Geo-Redundant Storage)	Primary + secondary region	16 9s	High	Regulatory backup, large-scale DR
RA-GRS (Read-Access GRS)	GRS + read access	16 9s	Very High	Read-only access during outages
GZRS (Geo-Zone-Redundant Storage)	ZRS + GRS	16 9s	Very High	Critical workloads, HA + DR
RA-GZRS	GZRS + read access	16 9s	Very High	Premium availability + regional access

Choosing the Right Redundancy

- Use **ZRS** for workloads requiring high uptime within a region.
- Use **GRS** or **GZRS** if disaster recovery across regions is mandatory.
- Use **RA-GRS** or **RA-GZRS** when read-access is required during DR events.

Enabling Replication (During Account Creation)

```
az storage account create \
—name myreplicatedstore \
—resource-group MyResourceGroup \
—sku Standard_GRS \
—location eastus \
—kind StorageV2
```

You can upgrade from LRS to GRS or GZRS, but not the other way around.

Azure Backup Integration

Azure Backup provides built-in, secure, scalable backup services for Azure resources and on-premises data. For Azure Storage, backup capabilities are primarily focused on **Azure Files** and **Azure Blob Storage**.

Backing Up Azure File Shares

Azure Backup natively supports file share protection through Recovery Services Vaults.

Step 1: Create Recovery Services Vault

```
az backup vault create \
—name MyRecoveryVault \
—resource-group MyResourceGroup \
—location eastus
```

Step 2: Register the Storage Account

```
az backup protection enable-for-azurefileshare \
—vault-name MyRecoveryVault \
—resource-group MyResourceGroup \
—storage-account mystorageaccount \
—azure-file-share myshare \
—policy-name DefaultPolicy
```

Azure Backup automatically handles snapshots, retention policies, and recovery workflows.

Blob Storage Backup

While Blob Storage does not use Azure Backup natively, it provides several built-in features for backup-like functionality:

- **Soft Delete for Blobs and Containers**
- **Blob Versioning**
- **Point-in-Time Restore**
- **Immutable Blob Storage (WORM)**

Enabling Soft Delete

```
az storage blob service-properties update \
—account-name mystorageaccount \
—enable-delete-retention true \
—delete-retention-days 30
```

Enabling Blob Versioning

```
az storage blob service-properties update \
—account-name mystorageaccount \
—enable-versioning true
```

These capabilities enable restoring accidentally deleted or modified blobs with minimal configuration.

Point-in-Time Restore (PITR)

PITR allows you to restore an entire container to a previous state based on a timestamp. This is crucial for mitigating widespread data loss or corruption incidents.

Requirements

- Versioning and soft delete must be enabled.
- Applies to **General Purpose v2** accounts with **Blob Storage**.

az storage blob restore \

—account-name mystorageaccount \

—time-to-restore "2025-01-10T00:00:00Z"

PITR can restore to a precise time, effectively "rewinding" the container state.

Immutable Blob Storage

Immutable Blob Storage allows data to be written once and read many times (WORM). This is important for compliance with financial, legal, and medical records retention policies.

Creating a Legal Hold or Time-Based Retention Policy

az storage container immutability-policy create \

—account-name mystorageaccount \

—container-name securecontainer \

```
—period 365

az storage container legal-hold set \

—account-name mystorageaccount \

—container-name securecontainer \

—tags "audit" "legal"
```

These protections prevent deletion or modification of blobs until the retention period expires.

Snapshots and Incremental Backups

Blob and File Storage support **snapshots**, which are read-only versions of a blob or file share at a specific point in time.

Creating a Blob Snapshot

```
az storage blob snapshot \

—account-name mystorageaccount \

—container-name mycontainer \

—name myblob.txt
```

Snapshots can be used for rollback, duplication, or recovery.

Copying From Snapshot

```
az storage blob copy start \

—source-uri <snapshot-url> \

—destination-blob myblob-restored.txt \
```

—destination-container mycontainer \

—account-name mystorageaccount

Azure charges only for the differences between the base blob and its snapshots (incremental).

Cross-Region Replication and Failover

In GRS and GZRS accounts, Microsoft replicates data asynchronously to a paired region. While the secondary region is not directly accessible, **read-access geo-redundant accounts (RA-GRS / RA-GZRS)** allow read operations from the replica.

Initiating Manual Failover (GRS Accounts)

If the primary region is unavailable, you can manually fail over to the secondary.

az storage account failover \

—name mystorageaccount \

—resource-group MyResourceGroup

After failover, the secondary becomes primary, and the previous primary becomes inaccessible. This process is irreversible.

Disaster Recovery Planning

An effective disaster recovery (DR) strategy requires:

- **Redundancy and replication** setup
- **Geo-redundant storage** with read-access

- **Backup scheduling and retention** via Recovery Services Vaults
- **Snapshot and versioning strategies**
- **SAS and RBAC controls** to prevent unauthorized deletions
- **Audit logs and alerting** for suspicious access or deletions
- **Private Link and NSGs** to secure recovery paths

Use **Azure Site Recovery** for VMs, and **Azure Backup** and **storage-native features** for files and blobs.

Monitoring and Alerting

To ensure your data protection systems are working correctly:

- Set up **Log Analytics** queries for backup job status.
- Use **Azure Monitor Alerts** for snapshot success/failure.
- Configure **Storage diagnostic logs** to track deletions and access.

Example: Alert for Blob Deletion

```
az monitor metrics alert create \
—name BlobDeleteAlert \
—resource-group MyResourceGroup \
```

```
—scopes /subscriptions/<sub>/resourceGroups/<rg>/providers/Microsoft.Storage/storageAccounts/mystorageaccount \

—condition "total Transactions > 0 where OperationName == 'DeleteBlob'" \

—window-size 5m \

—evaluation-frequency 1m \

—action-group myAlertGroup
```

Best Practices

- **Always enable soft delete and versioning** for Blob Storage.
- Use **ZRS or GZRS** for production workloads requiring high durability.
- Implement **Azure Backup** for File Shares and critical workloads.
- Use **Snapshots** for quick recovery and rollback.
- Configure **immutable storage** where regulatory compliance requires.
- **Test failovers** and **restore procedures** regularly.
- Implement **automated lifecycle policies** to manage older data.
- Use **Tagging** to classify data for backup and recovery priorities.

- **Use Azure Policy** to enforce DR configurations across the organization.

Conclusion

Azure provides a powerful, layered set of capabilities to ensure that your data is protected from loss, corruption, or disasters. By combining replication strategies with native backup tools, point-in-time recovery, and automated monitoring, organizations can implement robust and cost-effective disaster recovery architectures.

Whether you're protecting mission-critical applications, archival records, or development environments, mastering Azure's backup, replication, and DR tooling ensures long-term data resilience, reduced risk, and compliance with modern regulatory standards.

Chapter 6: Identity and Access Management

Azure Active Directory (AAD) Deep Dive

Azure Active Directory (AAD) is Microsoft's cloud-based identity and access management service that provides secure access to resources, both internal and external, for users, groups, and applications. It plays a crucial role in securing cloud infrastructure, enabling single sign-on (SSO), multi-factor authentication (MFA), conditional access, and seamless integration with on-premises environments.

AAD is foundational in the Azure ecosystem. It's not just a directory service—it's an identity platform that integrates identity, security, and compliance, enabling organizations to manage and protect access to apps and data at cloud scale.

Core Concepts of Azure Active Directory

Azure AD provides identity services for both Microsoft cloud services (like Microsoft 365, Azure, and Dynamics 365) and third-party services.

- **Tenants**: A dedicated instance of AAD that an organization receives when signing up for Azure or Microsoft 365.

- **Users and Groups**: Individuals who can be granted access to resources. Groups allow easier role and policy management.

- **Applications**: Both first-party and third-party apps registered in AAD for authentication and authorization purposes.

- **Service Principals**: Security identities used by apps or services to access specific Azure resources.

- **Managed Identities**: Special types of service principals automatically managed by Azure, used for secure resource access.

Azure AD Editions

There are several tiers of Azure AD, each with progressively more features:

1. **Free** – Basic user and group management, SSO for a few apps.
2. **Office 365 Apps** – Includes features for Microsoft 365 apps.
3. **Premium P1** – Adds Conditional Access, hybrid identity, and more.
4. **Premium P2** – Adds Identity Protection and Privileged Identity Management (PIM).

Understanding what features are available at each level is crucial for compliance, governance, and security planning.

Identity Models in Azure

Azure supports three identity models:

- **Cloud-only identity**: All user identities exist only in Azure AD.

- **Synchronized identity**: Identities are synchronized from on-premises Active Directory using Azure AD Connect.

- **Federated identity**: Authentication is handled via federation with an on-premises identity provider like ADFS.

Azure AD Connect

Azure AD Connect is the tool that synchronizes on-premises directories with Azure AD. Key capabilities:

- **Password Hash Sync (PHS)** – Default method; syncs password hashes.

- **Pass-through Authentication (PTA)** – Authenticates users directly against on-prem AD.

- **Federation with ADFS** – Allows full SSO with customized policies.

Admins can configure Azure AD Connect to control which attributes are synced, manage write-back features, and handle hybrid identity scenarios.

User and Group Management

AAD allows fine-grained control over identity lifecycle through:

- **Dynamic groups**: Automatically assign users to groups based on attributes.

- **Nested groups**: Simplifies access control by inheriting permissions.

- **Access reviews**: Periodic access audits to ensure appropriate access.
- **Self-service features**: Enable password reset, group join requests, etc.

Here's an example of creating a dynamic group with a rule:

```
New-AzureADMSGroup -DisplayName "Marketing Team" `
-MailEnabled $false `
-MailNickname "MarketingTeam" `
-SecurityEnabled $true `
-GroupTypes "DynamicMembership" `
-MembershipRule "(user.department -eq 'Marketing')" `
-MembershipRuleProcessingState "On"
```

Application and API Access Management

AAD manages access to both internal and external applications. When registering an app, AAD issues an Application ID and allows configuration of:

- Redirect URIs
- Client secrets or certificates
- API permissions (Microsoft Graph, custom APIs)
- Role-based access and scopes

Example: Registering an app via Azure CLI

```
az ad app create \
—display-name "MyApp" \
—identifier-uris "https://myapp.contoso.com" \
—reply-urls "https://myapp.contoso.com/auth"
```

Once registered, service principals are used to assign roles or permissions:

```
az ad sp create—id <app-id>
az role assignment create—assignee <sp-id>—role Contributor—scope /subscriptions/<sub-id>/resourceGroups/<rg>
```

Conditional Access Policies

Conditional Access allows policy-based decision-making based on conditions like:

- User/group membership
- Application
- Sign-in risk
- Device platform or compliance state
- Location or IP address

Policy example:

```
New-AzureADMSConditionalAccessPolicy -DisplayName "Block Legacy Auth" `
```

-State "Enabled" `

-Conditions @{ClientAppTypes=@("Other")} `

-GrantControls @{Operator="OR"; BuiltInControls=@("Block")}

�This policy blocks legacy applications that don't support modern authentication.

Multi-Factor Authentication (MFA)

AAD MFA is a vital security control that requires a second form of authentication. It can be enforced in various ways:

- Per-user basis
- Conditional Access
- Security defaults (for small organizations)

Options for second factors:

- Microsoft Authenticator app
- Phone call or SMS
- FIDO2 hardware keys
- Windows Hello for Business

Admins can enforce registration during first sign-in and monitor usage with reports.

Identity Protection

AAD Identity Protection uses risk-based detection to proactively secure identities.

It classifies:

- **User risk** – likelihood a user's credentials are compromised.
- **Sign-in risk** – probability that a sign-in attempt isn't legitimate.

Admins can configure automatic responses such as:

- Requiring MFA
- Forcing password change
- Blocking access

Policies can be set through the Azure Portal or via CLI:

�az identity-protection policy update—user-risk-policy 'RequireMfa'—sign-in-risk-policy 'BlockAccess'

�Privileged Identity Management (PIM)

AAD PIM enables just-in-time access to privileged roles. Benefits include:

- Time-bound role activation
- Approval workflow
- Access reviews

- Auditing and alerting

Admins can configure eligible assignments (users must activate the role) versus permanent active assignments.

Example: Assign a user as eligible for the Owner role

�New-AzureADMSPrivilegedRoleAssignmentRequest -ResourceId <resource-id> `

-RoleDefinitionId <role-id> `

-SubjectId <user-id> `

-AssignmentState "Eligible"

�Integration with Other Identity Providers

AAD supports integration with:

- **External Identities** – B2B/B2C collaboration
- **Social Identities** – Facebook, Google, etc.
- **SAML/OIDC providers** – For federated login
- **LDAP and on-premises directories** – Through Azure AD Domain Services (AAD DS)

AAD B2B collaboration allows adding external users with their own credentials. Admins can invite external users and set up restrictions on what resources they can access.

Best Practices for Azure AD Implementation

1. **Use Conditional Access with MFA** – Enforce MFA

using conditions.

2. **Enable Identity Protection** – Detect risky sign-ins early.
3. **Separate admin accounts** – Don't use personal accounts for privileged access.
4. **Limit global admins** – Follow least privilege principle.
5. **Audit and rotate secrets regularly** – Use certificates where possible.
6. **Implement access reviews and lifecycle policies** – Ensure stale accounts are removed.
7. **Enable logging and monitoring** – Integrate with Azure Monitor, Log Analytics, and Sentinel.

Summary

Azure Active Directory is the backbone of identity in Azure. Understanding its architecture, capabilities, and security mechanisms is essential for any cloud administrator or architect. From SSO and MFA to risk-based policies and integration with on-premises systems, AAD enables secure, manageable, and scalable identity infrastructure in the cloud.

The next sections in this chapter will build upon this foundation, diving into governance, conditional access, and hybrid integration strategies.

Identity Protection and Governance

In modern cloud environments, managing access to resources is not enough—organizations must also proactively protect identities and enforce governance to ensure secure and compliant operations. Azure Active Directory (AAD) offers a comprehensive set of tools for identity protection and governance, focusing on minimizing risk, enhancing visibility, and controlling access through structured policies and automation.

Understanding Identity Protection

Azure AD Identity Protection is a feature in the Azure AD Premium P2 tier that uses adaptive machine learning algorithms and heuristics to detect potential vulnerabilities affecting an organization's identities, configure automated responses, and investigate incidents.

Identity Protection provides three key capabilities:

- **Risk Detection** – Flags risky sign-ins and users based on suspicious activity.
- **Automated Risk Response** – Automatically respond to risky activity via Conditional Access policies.
- **Security Reports** – Detailed information on identity risks and resolution recommendations.

Types of Risk Detections

1. **User Risk**: Measures the probability that an identity has been compromised.

   ○ Examples: Leaked credentials, high sign-in failure rate.

2. **Sign-In Risk**: Evaluates the risk of a specific sign-in attempt.

○ Examples: Sign-ins from anonymous IP addresses, unusual locations.

3. **Risk Events**: Individual risk detections that feed into aggregated risk scores.

These risks are surfaced in the Azure Portal under *Azure Active Directory > Security > Identity Protection.*

Risk-Based Policies

Administrators can create policies to automatically handle high-risk scenarios. For example:

- Require password change for high-risk users.
- Block access or enforce MFA for high-risk sign-ins.

Example using Azure CLI to update a sign-in risk policy:

az identity-protection policy update \

—policy-name "signInRiskPolicy" \

—user-group "AllUsers" \

—actions "blockAccess" \

—risk-level "high"

These policies ensure threats are addressed swiftly without requiring constant administrative oversight.

Governance: The Need for Control

Governance ensures that access is granted according to policy, only for as long as needed, and with appropriate oversight. Azure AD Governance tools allow organizations to manage:

- **Privileged Access**
- **Guest Access (B2B collaboration)**
- **Group Membership**
- **Access Lifecycle**
- **Policy Enforcement and Auditing**

Azure offers three primary governance tools:

1. **Entitlement Management**
2. **Access Reviews**
3. **Privileged Identity Management (PIM)**

Let's break down each of these tools.

Entitlement Management

Entitlement management in Azure AD is a part of **Identity Governance** that allows organizations to manage identity and access lifecycle at scale.

Access Packages are at the core of entitlement management. These packages bundle:

- Groups and Teams
- Applications

- SharePoint sites
- Role assignments

Users can request access to packages based on policies, which can include:

- Expiration rules
- Approval workflows
- Justification requirements

Creating an Access Package

Steps:

1. Navigate to *Azure AD* > *Identity Governance* > *Entitlement Management*.
2. Define a **catalog**.
3. Create an **access package** under the catalog.
4. Assign **resources**.
5. Configure **request policies** and **lifecycle settings**.

Access packages are ideal for managing onboarding and project-based access.

Access Reviews

Access reviews help ensure users have only the access they need. Regular reviews are crucial for compliance and reducing insider threats.

You can review:

- Group memberships
- App access
- Role assignments (especially privileged roles)

Features:

- Scheduled recurrence
- Delegation of reviewers
- Auto-apply of decisions (e.g., remove if not reviewed)

PowerShell Example: Starting a Review

```
Start-AzureADMSAccessReview -ReviewId <review-id>
```

Admins can monitor results and export decisions for auditing purposes.

Guest User Governance (B2B)

Azure AD B2B collaboration allows external users to access internal resources. However, without proper governance, this can create security and compliance risks.

Best practices for managing guest users:

- Require redemption of invitations through secure mechanisms.
- Enforce terms of use upon first sign-in.
- Configure Conditional Access for guests (e.g., block access from risky IPs).

- Set expiration for guest access.
- Periodically review and remove inactive or unnecessary guests.

AAD offers automatic expiration policies using the **Access Lifecycle** feature. This can be done via the portal or programmatically using Graph API.

```
az ad user update—id <guest-id>—account-enabled false
```

Or with lifecycle policy configuration:

```
az ad policy create—definition '{
"ExpirationDays": 30,
"Action": "disable",
"Target": "GuestUsers"
}'
```

Privileged Identity Management (PIM)

We touched on PIM in the previous section, but from a governance perspective, its auditability and control mechanisms are critical.

PIM supports:

- **Just-in-time (JIT) access** to Azure AD and Azure resource roles
- **Approval-based workflows** for elevated permissions
- **Access justification**

- **Time-bound access assignments**
- **Access reviews and auditing**

Using PIM reduces the standing privilege problem and ensures that elevated access is always deliberate, approved, and limited in duration.

Role-Based Access Control (RBAC)

While RBAC is a broader Azure concept, it's tightly linked with identity governance. Azure RBAC allows you to assign fine-grained access permissions to resources, based on:

- **Built-in roles** (e.g., Reader, Contributor)
- **Custom roles** (defined per need)
- **Scope** (management group, subscription, resource group, or individual resource)

Governance best practices include:

- Avoid using Owner role unnecessarily.
- Always apply **least privilege**.
- Use **resource-specific roles** when possible.
- Regularly **review role assignments**.

Example: Assign a Reader role at the resource group level

```
az role assignment create \
—assignee <user-id> \
```

```
—role Reader \
—scope /subscriptions/<sub-id>/resourceGroups/<rg-name>
```

Combine RBAC with PIM for full governance over who has what level of access and when.

Logging and Auditing

Visibility into identity events is essential for both operational and compliance purposes.

AAD provides several logs:

- **Sign-in logs** – Successful and failed attempts
- **Audit logs** – Directory changes
- **Risky sign-in/user reports**
- **Access review decisions**

You can export these logs to:

- **Azure Monitor / Log Analytics**
- **Azure Sentinel**
- **SIEM tools via Event Hubs**

Example of querying sign-in logs in Log Analytics:

```
SigninLogs
| where ResultType != 0
| summarize count() by UserPrincipalName, ResultDescription
```

This allows admins to detect patterns like failed sign-ins, brute force attempts, or unauthorized access.

Governance Automation

For organizations managing large numbers of users, automation is key. Azure AD supports:

- **Graph API** – Programmatic management of users, groups, roles.
- **Azure Automation / Logic Apps** – Workflow automation for access approvals, terminations, etc.
- **Microsoft Entra Workflows (preview)** – Built-in low-code workflows for identity lifecycle events.

Example: Automatically remove users after end date using Graph API:

```
PATCH https://graph.microsoft.com/v1.0/users/{id}

Content-type: application/json

{

"accountEnabled": false

}
```

Recommendations and Best Practices

- **Implement MFA and Conditional Access for all users.**
- **Use PIM for privileged roles.**

- **Enforce expiration and reviews for guest users.**
- **Automate access decisions and lifecycle events.**
- **Monitor and act on identity risks.**
- **Regularly review and remove excessive permissions.**
- **Centralize logging and auditing for all identity activities.**
- **Educate users on phishing, social engineering, and secure password usage.**

Summary

Identity protection and governance in Azure AD go far beyond simple authentication. With advanced tools like Identity Protection, Entitlement Management, Access Reviews, and PIM, administrators can automate security, maintain compliance, and manage access intelligently. These features work together to form a resilient and secure identity framework that scales with organizational needs while adapting to evolving security threats.

As threats grow more sophisticated and compliance requirements more stringent, leveraging Azure's governance and identity protection capabilities becomes not just advisable—but essential.

Conditional Access and Multi-Factor Authentication

Conditional Access and Multi-Factor Authentication (MFA) are two cornerstone features in Azure Active Directory (Azure AD) that enhance identity security without compromising usability. Together, they enable adaptive access control strategies that protect against evolving threats while aligning with modern productivity requirements.

Conditional Access acts as a gatekeeper, evaluating sign-in attempts based on context (such as user identity, location, device, and risk) and enforcing policies that can block access, require MFA, or grant access with restrictions. MFA ensures that even if a password is compromised, unauthorized access is prevented by requiring a second form of verification.

The Evolution of Access Control

Traditional perimeter-based security models are no longer sufficient in a world where users work remotely, access resources from personal devices, and use a mix of cloud and on-premises apps. Conditional Access offers a more granular, identity-driven approach to access control.

It evaluates real-time signals to make decisions, such as:

- Who the user is
- Where they are signing in from
- What device they're using
- What application they're accessing
- The risk level of the sign-in or user

Conditional Access Policies

Conditional Access (CA) policies are if-then statements:

- **If** a user signs in under certain conditions (e.g., from an untrusted device),
- **Then** apply certain controls (e.g., require MFA).

Components of a CA Policy

1. **Assignments**:

   ○ **Users and Groups**: Specify who the policy applies to.

   ○ **Cloud Apps or Actions**: Define what the policy is protecting.

   ○ **Conditions**: Additional filters (e.g., location, device platform, sign-in risk).

2. **Access Controls**:

   ○ **Grant**: Require MFA, device compliance, or specific authentication strength.

   ○ **Session**: Limit session lifetime or sign-in frequency.

   ○ **Block**: Deny access completely under certain conditions.

3. **Enable Policy**: Set to *Report-only*, *On*, or *Off*.

Example CA Policy: Require MFA for Admins

To enforce MFA for all users in the "Global Admins" group accessing the Azure portal:

```
New-AzureADMSConditionalAccessPolicy -DisplayName "Admin MFA" `

-State "Enabled" `

-Conditions @{

Users = @{

IncludeGroups = @("<global-admin-group-id>")

}

Applications = @{

IncludeApplications = @("797f4846-ba00-4fd7-ba43-dac1f8f63013") # Azure portal app ID

}

} `

-GrantControls @{

Operator = "OR"

BuiltInControls = @("Mfa")

}
```

Common Conditional Access Scenarios

1. **Block access from risky locations or anonymous IPs**
2. **Require compliant devices for high-value apps like SharePoint or Exchange**
3. **Enforce sign-in frequency (e.g., every 12 hours)**
4. **Require MFA when user or sign-in is marked as high risk**

5. **Restrict access to approved apps only (via App Enforced Restrictions)**

These scenarios provide flexibility and strong security posture for both employees and external users.

Multi-Factor Authentication (MFA)

MFA requires users to verify their identity using at least two of the following:

- **Something you know** (password)
- **Something you have** (phone, hardware token)
- **Something you are** (biometrics)

Azure AD supports several MFA methods:

- Microsoft Authenticator app (push notifications, OTP)
- Phone call
- Text message
- FIDO2 security keys
- Windows Hello for Business
- Temporary access pass (TAP)

Enforcing MFA

There are three primary ways to enable MFA in Azure AD:

1. **Security Defaults**: Basic policies for small organizations.
2. **Per-user MFA**: Legacy method, simple toggle per user.
3. **Conditional Access MFA**: Recommended approach for enterprise environments.

Enabling MFA via Conditional Access

1. Go to *Azure AD* > *Security* > *Conditional Access*
2. Create a new policy targeting specific users/groups
3. Select the apps or actions the policy will apply to
4. Under *Grant*, select *Require multi-factor authentication*
5. Enable and save the policy

MFA Registration Policy

To enforce MFA registration during sign-in:

- Go to *Azure AD* > *Security* > *Authentication Methods* > *Registration*
- Set *Require users to register when signing in* to *Yes*
- Choose target groups (e.g., All users)

Authentication Strengths

Azure AD allows admins to define **authentication strengths**, which specify what combination of methods are required for a policy.

For example, a policy might enforce the use of **phishing-resistant MFA** like FIDO2 keys or Windows Hello for Business, avoiding weaker methods like SMS.

```
New-AzureADMSAuthenticationStrengthPolicy -DisplayName "PhishingResistant" `
-Requirements @{
AllowedCombinations = @("fido2", "windowsHelloForBusiness")
}
```

Attach the policy to a CA rule to enforce advanced MFA.

Report-Only Mode

Before enforcing a policy, admins can test it in **report-only mode** to monitor its impact without blocking users. This allows fine-tuning of conditions and controls.

Monitor results in *Azure AD > Sign-in Logs*, where report-only decisions are displayed alongside actual outcomes.

Monitoring and Auditing

Azure AD provides rich auditing and logging capabilities:

- **Sign-in Logs**: Show MFA requirement, whether satisfied, and sign-in success/failure.
- **Audit Logs**: Track changes to Conditional Access and MFA settings.
- **Insights and Reporting**: Dedicated dashboards for Conditional Access coverage and effectiveness.

You can also query logs with Kusto Query Language (KQL) in Log Analytics:

```
SigninLogs
```

```
| where ConditionalAccessStatus == "failure"

| project UserPrincipalName, ConditionalAccessPolicies, FailureReason
```

Use alerts and workbooks to surface anomalous patterns and response trends.

Integrating Conditional Access with Other Services

Conditional Access integrates tightly with:

- **Microsoft Defender for Cloud Apps**: Apply real-time controls such as session restrictions and monitoring.
- **Microsoft Entra Verified ID**: Use verified credentials as part of CA conditions.
- **Intune Compliance**: Only allow access from compliant, managed devices.

Admins can enforce policies like "Only allow access from Intune-compliant devices" by combining CA with device compliance settings.

```
az ad conditional-access policy create \

—name "Require Compliant Device" \

—conditions "{ 'users': { 'includeGroups': ['<group-id>'] }, 'clientAppTypes': ['all'] }" \

—grant-controls "{ 'operator': 'OR', 'builtInControls': ['compliantDevice'] }"
```

Best Practices for Conditional Access and MFA

1. **Start with security defaults**, especially for small orgs.
2. **Move to Conditional Access for enterprise flexibility and scale.**
3. **Use report-only mode** before enforcing new policies.
4. **Target high-value apps and privileged roles first.**
5. **Avoid blanket "allow all" exclusions**, especially for MFA.
6. **Leverage sign-in risk and device compliance** to improve user experience.
7. **Enforce strong authentication methods** like FIDO2.
8. **Monitor policy impact and iterate regularly.**

Common Pitfalls

- **Too many exclusions**: Excluding service accounts or execs can open gaps.

- **Overcomplicating policies**: Avoid conflicting or redundant CA rules.

- **Ignoring guest user security**: Apply policies to external identities.

- **Not educating users**: Ensure they understand MFA registration and usage.

Real-World Implementation Strategy

1. **Assessment**: Identify which apps, users, and roles need protection.

2. **MFA Rollout**: Begin with per-user MFA or Security Defaults.

3. **Conditional Access Design**:

○ Start with report-only mode.

○ Define tiered policies (e.g., baseline, privileged, high-risk).

○ Add session controls for SaaS apps.

4. **Pilot and Review**:

○ Test in staging environment.

○ Review logs for false positives or failures.

5. **Full Enforcement**:

○ Roll out to production.

○ Monitor continuously.

6. **Maintenance**:

○ Update policies with changing business needs.

○ Rotate authentication methods and secrets.

Summary

Conditional Access and Multi-Factor Authentication are fundamental to a secure identity posture in Azure AD. They allow organizations to adaptively respond to threats while preserving usability. Through strategic policy design, reporting, automation, and strong authentication enforcement, enterprises can minimize risk, support remote work, and meet compliance requirements efficiently. As threat landscapes evolve, Conditional Access and MFA remain two of the most impactful tools in an administrator's arsenal for enforcing secure, context-aware access to critical resources.

Integration with On-Premises Identity Systems

Many organizations operate in a hybrid identity model, where existing on-premises infrastructure must integrate seamlessly with cloud services such as Azure Active Directory (Azure AD). This integration is crucial to ensure a consistent and secure user experience across environments, streamline identity management, and maintain compliance with organizational policies.

Azure AD provides a variety of tools and methodologies to bridge the gap between traditional on-premises identity systems—primarily Windows Server Active Directory—and the modern cloud identity platform. This section explores these tools, best practices, and implementation strategies for integrating on-premises identity with Azure AD.

Why Hybrid Identity?

A hybrid identity enables organizations to:

- Maintain a single identity per user across on-premises and cloud services
- Reuse existing investments in on-premises infrastructure (e.g., Group Policy, security groups)

- Support legacy applications that depend on Windows Integrated Authentication

- Implement centralized access governance and security controls

- Simplify the transition to the cloud over time, reducing user disruption

Microsoft supports three main hybrid identity authentication models:

1. **Password Hash Synchronization (PHS)**
2. **Pass-through Authentication (PTA)**
3. **Federation with Active Directory Federation Services (AD FS)**

Each model has its use cases and considerations.

Azure AD Connect: The Integration Bridge

Azure AD Connect is a free Microsoft tool used to synchronize on-premises directories with Azure AD. It is the cornerstone of hybrid identity implementation.

Core capabilities include:

- Synchronizing user, group, and contact objects

- Password hash sync or pass-through authentication

- Device write-back and group write-back

- Hybrid Azure AD join for Windows devices

- Filtering by OU, group, or attribute

Installing Azure AD Connect

Installation is typically performed on a Windows Server joined to the domain. The server should be dedicated, up-to-date, and meet hardware and network requirements.

```
# Prerequisite installation example

Install-WindowsFeature -Name RSAT-ADDS
```

Once installed, launch the **Azure AD Connect Wizard**, select the appropriate sign-in method (PHS, PTA, or Federation), and configure synchronization settings.

Sync Configuration Example

- Synchronize only specific Organizational Units (OUs)
- Filter objects by attribute (e.g., only users with extensionAttribute10 = 'sync')
- Enable password writeback for self-service password reset
- Schedule synchronization (default every 30 minutes)

You can verify sync status using:

```
Get-ADSyncScheduler
```

To trigger a manual sync:

Start-ADSyncSyncCycle -PolicyType Delta

For initial troubleshooting, use:

Get-ADSyncConnectorRunStatus

Password Hash Synchronization (PHS)

With PHS, the password hashes from the on-premises AD are synchronized with Azure AD in a secure and non-reversible format. Users can use the same password for both environments, simplifying the user experience.

Pros:

- Simple to configure and maintain
- Supports SSO with seamless sign-in
- No need for additional infrastructure
- Compatible with cloud-only environments after decommissioning on-prem

Cons:

- Delayed revocation (up to 30 min)
- Passwords exist in the cloud (though encrypted)

PHS is ideal for most small to medium-sized organizations or enterprises starting their cloud journey.

Pass-through Authentication (PTA)

PTA allows users to authenticate directly against the on-premises Active Directory without syncing password hashes to the cloud.

How it works:

- Authentication request is encrypted and securely passed from Azure AD to an on-premises authentication agent
- Agent validates credentials against AD and returns the result

Pros:

- No password stored in the cloud
- Near real-time credential validation and revocation
- Simpler than federation

Cons:

- Requires high availability (minimum 2 agents)
- Depends on on-prem connectivity

Install additional PTA agents using:

Install-AzureADPTHAgent

Register agents with your Azure tenant during setup to ensure redundancy.

Federation with Active Directory Federation

Services (AD FS)

Federation provides full control over authentication, including custom policies, multi-factor authentication (MFA), and third-party integrations.

Architecture:

- Users are redirected to on-premises AD FS servers for authentication
- AD FS uses token-based authentication (SAML, WS-Federation)
- Azure AD trusts the token issued by AD FS

Pros:

- Centralized authentication control
- Support for legacy, non-modern auth apps
- Customizable login experience

Cons:

- Complex to deploy and maintain
- Requires highly available federation infrastructure
- Latency and failure risks if not designed correctly

Federation is typically reserved for complex, highly regulated environments.

To configure Azure AD for federation:

Connect-MsolService

Set-MsolDomainAuthentication -DomainName yourdomain.com -Authentication Federated `

-IssuerUri "https://youradfs.yourdomain.com/adfs/services/trust"

Hybrid Azure AD Join

Hybrid Azure AD Join allows domain-joined Windows 10/11 devices to automatically register with Azure AD while still being managed by on-prem AD. This enables:

- Seamless SSO to cloud resources
- Conditional Access enforcement
- Device compliance reporting

To configure hybrid join:

1. Ensure devices are domain-joined and connected to the internet
2. Use Group Policy to enable auto-registration
3. Sync computer accounts via Azure AD Connect
4. Verify with dsregcmd /status on the device

Seamless Single Sign-On (SSO)

Azure AD supports **Seamless SSO** for users on domain-joined devices. When enabled, users are automatically signed in to Azure AD without entering passwords if they're on the corporate network.

Configure via Azure AD Connect setup or:

Enable-AzureADSSO -Domain yourdomain.com

Users' browser or Office clients pick up their Windows sign-in credentials and authenticate transparently.

Device and Application Integration

Hybrid environments often require that devices and applications are identity-aware across clouds and data centers. Key integrations include:

- **Intune + GPO coexistence**: Support for both MDM and GPO-managed settings.
- **Azure AD Application Proxy**: Securely expose on-prem apps to external users without a VPN.
- **SCCM with Co-Management**: Combine ConfigMgr and Intune for device lifecycle management.
- **Line-of-business apps**: Configure legacy apps to use Azure AD or AD FS for auth.

Monitoring and Troubleshooting

Key tools include:

- **Azure AD Connect Health**: Monitors sync and authentication health.
- **Sign-in logs**: Indicate auth source (e.g., PHS, PTA, AD FS).
- **Event Viewer**: Use Directory Synchronization and AD FS logs for root cause analysis.

- **dsregcmd**: Check device registration status.

```
dsregcmd /status
```

Azure AD Connect Health alerts administrators to sync failures, high latency, or outdated agents, ensuring proactive resolution.

Migration and Transition Considerations

Organizations may start with federation and later move to PHS or PTA for simplification. Microsoft supports these transitions.

Steps to move from AD FS to PHS:

1. Ensure PHS is enabled in Azure AD Connect
2. Validate password sync and user access
3. Update domain authentication to "Managed"

```
Set-MsolDomainAuthentication -DomainName yourdomain.com -Authentication Managed
```

1. Decommission federation infrastructure after validation

Migrating from federation reduces complexity and improves availability, especially in remote work scenarios.

Best Practices for Hybrid Identity

- **Use PHS unless specific requirements dictate otherwise**
- **Ensure high availability for PTA or AD FS**
- **Sync only required users and groups**

- **Enable SSO for optimal user experience**
- **Secure Azure AD Connect with least privilege and tiered admin model**
- **Monitor sync health and authentication metrics**
- **Regularly review hybrid identity logs and reports**
- **Implement conditional access policies on hybrid-joined devices**

Summary

Integrating on-premises identity systems with Azure AD provides a flexible, secure, and user-friendly identity experience across hybrid environments. Whether using PHS, PTA, or federation, organizations can maintain continuity with existing investments while adopting modern identity solutions. Through Azure AD Connect, hybrid join, and seamless SSO, administrators gain the tools needed to build a resilient, scalable identity platform that bridges legacy systems and the future of cloud-based identity.

Chapter 7: Security, Compliance, and Governance

Azure Security Center and Defender

As organizations migrate workloads to the cloud, ensuring robust security is essential to protect data, maintain compliance, and defend against evolving cyber threats. Azure provides a comprehensive suite of security services under the umbrella of **Microsoft Defender for Cloud** (formerly Azure Security Center and Azure Defender). This platform enables organizations to assess, secure, and monitor their Azure, hybrid, and multi-cloud environments.

Microsoft Defender for Cloud delivers unified security management, threat protection, and security posture management for both cloud-native and hybrid workloads.

Microsoft Defender for Cloud: An Overview

Defender for Cloud offers two primary capabilities:

1. **Cloud Security Posture Management (CSPM)** – Assesses current configurations, identifies vulnerabilities, and provides recommendations to improve security.
2. **Cloud Workload Protection Platform (CWPP)** – Delivers advanced, threat protection for workloads such as VMs, containers, databases, and more.

These features are delivered through three core pillars:

- **Secure Score** and security recommendations

- **Threat Protection** for workloads
- **Regulatory Compliance** monitoring and reporting

Security Posture Management

Secure Score is a quantifiable metric (out of 100) that represents your current security posture. It is based on recommendations and their respective weights. A higher score indicates stronger security practices.

Secure Score is calculated from:

- Resource configuration assessments
- Remediation status
- Severity and potential impact of issues

Administrators can view Secure Score from:

Microsoft Defender for Cloud > Secure Score

Example Recommendation:

- *"Enable Just-In-Time (JIT) VM access"*
- *"Apply system updates to virtual machines"*
- *"Restrict access to management ports"*

Admins can remediate directly from the portal or export reports for further action.

Threat Protection for Workloads

Defender for Cloud offers **native protection** for a wide range of Azure resources:

- **Virtual Machines (VMs)**: Monitors for malware, suspicious activity, and missing OS patches.
- **App Services**: Detects web app vulnerabilities.
- **Containers (AKS)**: Scans container images and runtime behavior.
- **SQL Databases**: Protects against SQL injection and other database threats.
- **Storage Accounts**: Monitors access patterns and flags anomalous behavior.

You can enable protection per resource or subscription level. Each workload type has its own agent or integration:

- Azure Monitor Agent (AMA) or Log Analytics agent for VMs
- Defender extension for Kubernetes clusters
- Defender for SQL integration with advanced threat protection

Example: Enabling Defender for Servers via Azure CLI

az security pricing create—name VirtualMachines—tier 'Standard'

To confirm configuration:

az security pricing show—name VirtualMachines

This provides access to endpoint detection and response (EDR), file integrity monitoring, and adaptive network hardening.

Just-In-Time VM Access (JIT)

JIT allows administrators to reduce exposure by enabling access to management ports (e.g., SSH, RDP) only when needed. This limits brute-force attacks on always-open ports.

How it works:

- Admin requests access for a specific time window and IP address
- JIT opens ports temporarily
- Access is logged and monitored

Configuring JIT in PowerShell:

```
Set-AzJitNetworkAccessPolicy -ResourceGroupName "rg1" `

-Location "eastus" `

-Name "vm1" `

-VirtualMachine "vm1" `

-Port 22 -Protocol TCP -AllowedSourceAddress "192.168.1.10" -MaxRequestAccessDuration "PT1H"
```

Access is removed automatically after the defined period.

Adaptive Application Controls

Defender for Cloud provides **adaptive application controls**, a form of whitelisting that defines which applications are allowed to run on a VM. Any unauthorized execution triggers an alert.

Benefits:

- Protect against malware or unauthorized software
- Reduce attack surface
- Enhance compliance with organizational policies

Admins can configure policies through Defender for Cloud recommendations and monitor compliance through alerts.

File Integrity Monitoring

File Integrity Monitoring (FIM) detects changes to critical files and registry settings. This feature is especially important for compliance-driven environments (e.g., PCI-DSS).

Examples of monitored changes:

- System file modifications
- Registry key alterations
- Unauthorized configuration changes

Admins can define FIM rules and monitor logs via Log Analytics or Sentinel.

Security Alerts and Incidents

Microsoft Defender for Cloud generates **security alerts** based on threat intelligence and anomaly detection. Alerts include:

- Suspicious authentication attempts
- Network intrusions
- Malware detection
- Lateral movement in VMs or containers

Each alert includes:

- Severity level
- Affected resources
- Recommended remediation steps

Alerts can be routed to **Azure Sentinel**, SIEM tools, Logic Apps, or email notifications.

Example alert scenario:

- *"Crypto mining malware detected on VM X from IP 198.51.100.2"*

Integration with Microsoft Defender for Endpoint

For endpoint protection, Defender for Cloud integrates with **Microsoft Defender for Endpoint** (MDE). This combination enhances threat detection on Windows and Linux servers and provides:

- Behavioral analysis
- Threat intelligence correlation
- Automated investigation and response

Integration can be enabled from Defender for Cloud and requires enabling MDE for the target machines.

az security setting update—name 'MCAS'—enabled true

Regulatory Compliance Management

Defender for Cloud maps your environment against **industry-specific compliance standards**:

- ISO 27001
- NIST SP 800-53
- CIS Microsoft Benchmarks
- PCI-DSS
- HIPAA

The **Compliance Dashboard** provides:

- Compliance score
- Control-by-control pass/fail results
- Remediation guidance

Admins can generate reports, track remediation efforts, and demonstrate compliance during audits.

Custom compliance standards can also be created using **Azure Policy initiatives.**

```
{
"properties": {
"displayName": "Custom HIPAA Initiative",
"policyDefinitions": [
{
"policyDefinitionId": "/providers/Microsoft.Authorization/policyDefinitions/audit-vm-agent",
"parameters": {}
}
]
}
}
```

This enables alignment with internal or regulatory frameworks.

Secure Score Optimization

Organizations should routinely monitor and improve their **Secure Score** using these strategies:

- Prioritize high-severity recommendations
- Automate remediation via Azure Policy
- Set score improvement targets across teams

- Assign security roles for accountability

- Track trend over time and share results with stakeholders

Role-Based Access for Security Management

Defender for Cloud is tightly integrated with Azure Role-Based Access Control (RBAC). Assign least-privilege roles such as:

- **Security Reader** – View security recommendations and alerts

- **Security Admin** – Configure policies, manage alerts, take action

- **Resource Owner** – Remediate issues in their scope

Use built-in roles or define custom roles:

```
{
"Name": "CustomSecurityOperator",
"Actions": [
"Microsoft.Security/*/read",
"Microsoft.Security/securityContacts/write"
]
}
```

Assign these roles using:

az role assignment create—assignee <user-id>—role "CustomSecurityOperator"—scope /subscriptions/<sub-id>

Best Practices for Defender for Cloud

- **Enable Defender for Cloud on all subscriptions** (including non-Azure via multi-cloud support)
- **Integrate with Azure Policy for compliance automation**
- **Use JIT and NSG rules to limit port exposure**
- **Enable vulnerability assessment for SQL and VM workloads**
- **Continuously monitor Secure Score and compliance dashboard**
- **Connect to Sentinel or SIEM for advanced investigation**
- **Regularly review and respond to alerts**
- **Apply adaptive controls like app whitelisting and file monitoring**

Summary

Microsoft Defender for Cloud (formerly Azure Security Center) provides a powerful and centralized solution to monitor, assess, and secure cloud and hybrid environments. With tools like Secure Score, threat protection, JIT access, and compliance tracking, organizations can achieve a higher level of security maturity, reduce attack surface, and maintain regulatory alignment. Whether protecting VMs, containers, or databases, Defender for Cloud is a critical component of an enterprise cloud security strategy.

Managing Compliance Frameworks in Azure

Compliance is a critical component of cloud governance and enterprise security. Organizations across various industries must adhere to regulatory standards such as ISO 27001, HIPAA, PCI-DSS, SOC 2, and NIST. Microsoft Azure offers an extensive suite of compliance and risk management tools that empower organizations to manage compliance requirements at scale, enforce controls automatically, and maintain audit readiness across services.

Azure's compliance offerings extend beyond documentation and certifications. Through **Azure Policy**, **Microsoft Defender for Cloud**, **Compliance Manager**, and **Azure Blueprints**, enterprises can design, implement, monitor, and enforce policies that align with industry frameworks.

Understanding Compliance Frameworks

A compliance framework is a structured set of guidelines, controls, and requirements an organization must meet to demonstrate that it operates securely and responsibly. Azure supports compliance for numerous international, regional, and industry-specific standards, including:

- **General frameworks**: ISO/IEC 27001, SOC 1/2/3, NIST SP 800-53, CSA STAR
- **Industry-specific**: HIPAA (healthcare), PCI-DSS (payment), FERPA (education), CJIS (law enforcement)

- **Regional**: GDPR (EU), CCPA (California), IRAP (Australia), ENS (Spain)

Microsoft maintains over 100 compliance certifications, and customers can access documentation through the **Microsoft Trust Center** and **Compliance Documentation Center** in the Azure portal.

Microsoft Compliance Manager

Microsoft Compliance Manager is a centralized dashboard that helps organizations manage data protection, compliance posture, and risk assessments.

Key features:

- Provides **compliance score** based on your controls' implementation status
- Maps Azure and Microsoft 365 settings to common frameworks
- Tracks improvement actions and assigns ownership
- Generates reports for audits

You can find it at *Microsoft Purview* > *Compliance Manager.*

Example: Setting up HIPAA assessment

1. Navigate to *Compliance Manager*
2. Click + **Add Assessment**
3. Choose HIPAA or custom template
4. Assign improvement actions to responsible team

members

5. Track implementation status and overall compliance score

Each action includes details, testing guidance, and mapping to the corresponding control requirement.

Azure Policy and Compliance

Azure Policy allows you to define and enforce organizational standards. It evaluates resources for compliance and can automatically remediate non-compliant configurations.

Azure Policy is crucial in ensuring compliance frameworks are implemented at the resource level.

Common policy types:

- Enforce tag and naming conventions
- Restrict location of resource deployment
- Require encryption at rest and in transit
- Prevent public IP assignment
- Enforce secure configurations (e.g., TLS, HTTPS, disk encryption)

Example: Enforce resource location to UK regions

```
{
"properties": {
"displayName": "Allowed Locations",
```

```
"policyType": "BuiltIn",
"mode": "All",
"parameters": {
"listOfAllowedLocations": {
"value": ["UK South", "UK West"]
}
},
"policyRule": {
"if": {
"not": {
"field": "location",
"in": "[parameters('listOfAllowedLocations')]"
}
},
"then": {
"effect": "deny"
}
}
}
}
```

This policy ensures no resources are deployed outside of specified compliant regions.

Policies can be grouped into **initiatives** that map to specific compliance standards.

Compliance Initiatives

Policy initiatives are collections of related policies representing a broader goal, such as GDPR or NIST compliance.

Azure provides many **built-in initiatives**, including:

- NIST SP 800-53 Rev. 5
- ISO 27001:2013
- UK NHS
- CMMC Level 3
- Azure CIS 1.3.0

These initiatives can be assigned to subscriptions, management groups, or resource groups and monitored for compliance through the **Policy Compliance Dashboard**.

Assigning an initiative via CLI:

```
az policy assignment create \
—name "ISO27001" \
—display-name "ISO 27001 Compliance" \
—policy-set-definition "ISO27001" \
```

—scope "/subscriptions/<sub-id>"

Once assigned, Azure evaluates existing resources and future deployments against the initiative's requirements.

Microsoft Defender for Cloud Compliance Reports

Microsoft Defender for Cloud provides built-in **regulatory compliance standards** that map recommendations to specific controls.

The **Regulatory Compliance Dashboard** includes:

- Compliance standards summary
- Control-level evaluation
- Remediation recommendations
- Integration with Azure Policy

Example: Enabling PCI-DSS compliance tracking

1. Navigate to *Defender for Cloud > Environment Settings*
2. Select the target subscription
3. Under *Regulatory Compliance*, enable *PCI-DSS 3.2.1*
4. View progress and address failed assessments

Defender for Cloud continuously scans resources and updates compliance status in real time.

Azure Blueprints

Azure Blueprints offer a repeatable way to define, deploy, and manage a compliant environment. A blueprint combines:

- Role assignments
- Policy assignments
- Resource templates (ARM templates)
- Resource groups

Use blueprints to ensure consistent deployment of environments that conform to required compliance standards.

Example Blueprint for NIST 800-53

A NIST-aligned blueprint may include:

- Policies for logging, encryption, and auditing
- Assignment of Security Admin role
- Deployment of Log Analytics workspace
- Deny public access to storage accounts

Blueprints are especially valuable for DevOps and infrastructure-as-code workflows.

```
az blueprint create \
—name "nist-blueprint" \
—description "NIST 800-53 Baseline Blueprint" \
—subscription <sub-id>
```

After publishing a blueprint, you can assign it to an environment and enforce consistent compliance.

Logging, Auditing, and Evidence Gathering

Azure Monitor, **Log Analytics**, **Azure Activity Logs**, and **Microsoft Purview** (formerly Compliance Center) provide visibility and traceability.

- Use **Log Analytics** for querying resource compliance over time.
- Store logs in immutable storage for long-term evidence retention.
- Enable **Azure Resource Graph** to query compliance status at scale.

Example: Query non-compliant resources

```
PolicyResources

| where ComplianceState == "NonCompliant"

| summarize count() by ResourceType, ResourceGroup
```

Enable diagnostic logs:

```
az monitor diagnostic-settings create \

—name "send-to-log-analytics" \

—resource <resource-id> \

—workspace <workspace-id> \

—logs '[{"category": "AuditLogs", "enabled": true}]'
```

This ensures that all activity, especially changes to policy or resource configuration, is auditable.

Third-Party Compliance Integrations

Azure supports integration with third-party tools like:

- **ServiceNow** for compliance ticketing
- **Splunk / QRadar** for SIEM use cases
- **AWS / GCP connectors** for multi-cloud compliance via Defender for Cloud
- **Power BI** for custom compliance reporting dashboards

Organizational Strategy for Cloud Compliance

1. **Map regulations to technical controls**: Understand how HIPAA or PCI translates to Azure policies.
2. **Assign control ownership**: Define who is responsible for remediation and evidence gathering.
3. **Automate policy enforcement**: Use Azure Policy and Blueprints to reduce human error.
4. **Continuously assess and improve**: Monitor compliance posture regularly, not just before audits.
5. **Use built-in standards**: Start with Microsoft's built-in initiatives and customize as needed.
6. **Educate teams**: Ensure DevOps and IT understand their role in maintaining compliance.

Summary

Managing compliance in Azure is a multi-faceted, continuous process that requires alignment between technical controls, organizational policies, and regulatory requirements. With tools like Azure Policy, Compliance Manager, Microsoft Defender for Cloud, and Azure Blueprints, organizations can automate enforcement, reduce manual overhead, and maintain audit readiness across environments. As regulatory landscapes evolve, Azure's dynamic compliance ecosystem empowers enterprises to adapt quickly while maintaining trust, transparency, and control.

Policy Enforcement and Cost Management

In the dynamic landscape of cloud computing, policy enforcement and cost management are critical pillars of operational governance. While the cloud offers scalability and flexibility, it also introduces risks of resource sprawl, non-compliance, and budget overruns. Azure provides robust, integrated tools to define and enforce policies, control spending, optimize resource usage, and ensure accountability.

Organizations that effectively manage policies and costs can reduce waste, meet regulatory requirements, and maintain a secure and predictable cloud environment. This section explores how to implement these strategies using native Azure features such as **Azure Policy**, **Azure Cost Management + Billing**, **Azure Budgets**, **Azure Reservations**, and **Resource Tagging**.

Azure Policy: Defining and Enforcing Organizational Standards

Azure Policy is the primary mechanism for ensuring that resources across subscriptions adhere to predefined rules. It evaluates resource configurations for compliance and can deny, audit, or remediate non-compliant resources.

Policy Modes

Azure Policy supports several modes:

- **All** – Works for all resource types
- **Indexed** – Used for resource properties only available at request time
- **Microsoft.Kubernetes.Data** – For policies that evaluate Kubernetes clusters
- **Microsoft.ContainerService.Data** – AKS-specific policy definitions

Common Policy Scenarios

- Enforce tagging for cost tracking
- Restrict allowed SKUs for VMs or databases
- Enforce use of managed disks
- Deny use of deprecated regions
- Require encryption for storage accounts

Example: Enforce Resource Tagging

This policy ensures that all resources include a CostCenter tag.

```
{
"properties": {
"displayName": "Require CostCenter Tag",
"policyRule": {
"if": {
"field": "[concat('tags[', parameters('tagName'), ']')]",
"exists": "false"
},
"then": {
"effect": "deny"
}
},
"parameters": {
"tagName": {
"type": "String",
"defaultValue": "CostCenter"
}
}
}
}
```

Assign the policy using CLI or portal to subscriptions or management groups.

az policy assignment create \

—name "require-costcenter-tag" \

—policy "CostCenterTagPolicy" \

—scope "/subscriptions/<sub-id>"

Initiative Definitions

Group related policies into **initiatives** to enforce broader organizational requirements. For instance, a cost control initiative might include policies to:

- Limit VM SKUs
- Require tagging
- Deny unapproved regions
- Enforce shutdown schedules

Azure Policy Effects

Azure Policy supports multiple enforcement types:

- **Deny** – Block resource creation if non-compliant
- **Audit** – Allow but log non-compliance
- **DeployIfNotExists** – Automatically deploy a resource or setting if absent

- **Modify** – Alter incoming requests to make them compliant
- **Append** – Add required configuration values

Use **Audit** and **DeployIfNotExists** to roll out compliance in stages without immediate disruption.

Azure Blueprints and Governance at Scale

For standardized deployments, **Azure Blueprints** combine policy definitions, RBAC assignments, ARM templates, and resource groups into a repeatable package.

Use blueprints to:

- Establish environment baselines
- Enforce naming and tagging conventions
- Deploy security controls
- Assign cost management roles

Blueprints help operationalize governance at the management group level, ensuring new subscriptions adhere to corporate policies from day one.

Azure Cost Management and Billing

Azure provides a comprehensive **Cost Management + Billing** suite to help you track, analyze, and optimize spending across resources, subscriptions, and departments.

Key capabilities:

- **Cost analysis** and forecasting
- **Budget creation and enforcement**
- **Cost alerts**
- **Tag-based cost breakdowns**
- **Reservation and savings plan tracking**

Access the dashboard via *Azure Portal > Cost Management + Billing*.

Cost Analysis

Use **Cost Analysis** to:

- Visualize spend by service, region, or resource group
- Identify spending trends
- Filter costs by tag (e.g., CostCenter, Environment)
- Export reports for stakeholders

Example: Show Daily Cost by Resource Group

In the portal:

- Navigate to *Cost Management > Cost Analysis*
- Group by *Resource Group*
- Set granularity to *Daily*

- Export as Excel or CSV

This helps pinpoint unexpected spikes or inefficient deployments.

Azure Budgets

Azure Budgets allow you to set spending thresholds for resources, resource groups, or subscriptions. You can trigger alerts or automate actions when usage approaches or exceeds these thresholds.

Creating a Budget via CLI

```
az consumption budget create \
—amount 1000 \
—time-grain monthly \
—name "MonthlyDevBudget" \
—resource-group "DevRG" \
—start-date 2024-01-01 \
—end-date 2024-12-31 \
—category cost \
—notifications
'{"Actual_GreaterThan_80":{"enabled":true,"operator":"GreaterThan","thre
```

Automating Responses

Integrate budgets with **Azure Action Groups** or **Logic Apps** to:

- Scale down VMs
- Deallocate underused services
- Notify finance or DevOps teams

Reservations and Savings Plans

Azure Reservations and **Savings Plans** offer discounted pricing for committing to consistent resource usage over 1- or 3-year terms.

Use for:

- Virtual Machines (VMs)
- SQL Database Compute
- App Services
- Cosmos DB

Example: Estimate Reservation Savings

1. Navigate to *Cost Management > Reservations*
2. Use the **Azure Pricing Calculator** to estimate savings
3. Purchase and assign reservations to specific subscriptions or shared scope

Use **Advisor Recommendations** to identify eligible resources for reservations.

Tagging Strategy for Cost Management

Tags are essential for cost visibility and accountability. Design a consistent tagging strategy with required keys such as:

- CostCenter
- Environment (dev, test, prod)
- Project
- Owner
- Department

Automate tagging through:

- **Azure Policy**
- **ARM templates**
- **Terraform**
- **Tag inheritance scripts**

Example: Add Tags to a VM

```
az resource tag \

—tags CostCenter=1234 Environment=Dev Owner=team@company.com \

—resource-id "/subscriptions/<sub-id>/resourceGroups/DevRG/providers/Microsoft.Compute/virtualMachines/myVM"
```

Use **Tag Governance** policies to enforce required tags at provisioning.

Cost Allocation and Chargeback

Azure supports **cost allocation** to internal teams or business units. You can:

- Use tags or resource groups to define ownership
- Export billing data to **Azure Storage**
- Process costs in **Power BI** or **Excel**
- Build dashboards using **Log Analytics**

Example: Enable Cost Data Export

```
az consumption export create \
—name "DailyExport" \
—timeframe "MonthToDate" \
—recurrence "Daily" \
—recurrence-period start=2024-01-01T00:00:00Z end=2024-12-31T00:00:00Z \
—destination "https://yourstorage.blob.core.windows.net/exports"
```

This allows integration with internal reporting systems and custom analysis.

FinOps and Governance

FinOps (Financial Operations) is a growing discipline that brings together IT, finance, and business to manage cloud spend collaboratively.

Key principles:

- **Visibility**: Provide real-time, tag-based views of cost
- **Optimization**: Continuously analyze and right-size workloads
- **Accountability**: Assign ownership and budgets
- **Automation**: Enforce limits and optimize resource usage

Azure-native tools align closely with FinOps best practices, enabling a data-driven approach to governance.

Best Practices for Policy and Cost Governance

- **Start with audit policies**, then move to enforce/deny
- Use **initiatives** to group and apply policies consistently
- **Implement tagging from day one**
- **Set and monitor budgets for every environment**
- **Use reservations for steady workloads**
- **Automate unused resource cleanup**

- **Create chargeback reports** for transparency
- **Review Azure Advisor and Cost Management monthly**

Summary

Effective policy enforcement and cost management are essential to maintaining control in the cloud. Azure equips organizations with powerful tools like Azure Policy, Cost Management, Budgets, Reservations, and Tags to drive compliance and financial accountability. By automating governance, enforcing standards, and optimizing spend, teams can achieve a secure, cost-efficient, and scalable cloud environment tailored to business goals.

Secure DevOps and Infrastructure as Code

Secure DevOps, also known as **DevSecOps**, is the practice of integrating security throughout the DevOps lifecycle. In Azure, this involves embedding security controls, policies, and monitoring mechanisms directly into the planning, development, deployment, and operational stages of application and infrastructure delivery. When combined with **Infrastructure as Code (IaC)**, Secure DevOps ensures that environments are not only automated but also compliant, repeatable, and secure by default.

Modern DevOps workflows embrace automation, CI/CD, and microservice architectures—but without integrated security, these practices can introduce risks. Secure DevOps with Azure helps mitigate these risks through continuous policy enforcement, threat modeling, secrets management, and infrastructure verification.

Core Pillars of Secure DevOps in Azure

1. **Infrastructure as Code (IaC)**
2. **Automated Security Testing**
3. **Secrets and Credential Management**
4. **Role-Based Access and Least Privilege**
5. **Policy-as-Code Enforcement**
6. **Continuous Monitoring and Threat Detection**

These pillars combine to deliver robust, automated security postures for both application code and the infrastructure it runs on.

Infrastructure as Code (IaC)

IaC allows infrastructure provisioning through code instead of manual processes. Azure supports multiple IaC tools:

- **ARM Templates**: Native Azure declarative JSON templates.

- **Bicep**: A domain-specific language that simplifies ARM templates.

- **Terraform**: Popular open-source tool for multi-cloud IaC.

- **Pulumi**: Code-based IaC using familiar programming languages.

IaC promotes consistency, repeatability, and versioning of infrastructure configurations, reducing human error.

Example: Bicep Template for Secure Storage Account

```
resource storage 'Microsoft.Storage/storageAccounts@2022-09-01' = {

name: 'securestorage${uniqueString(resourceGroup().id)}'

location: resourceGroup().location

sku: {

name: 'Standard_GRS'

}

kind: 'StorageV2'

properties: {

minimumTlsVersion: 'TLS1_2'

allowBlobPublicAccess: false

supportsHttpsTrafficOnly: true

}

}
```

This ensures TLS 1.2, disables public access, and enforces HTTPS—all embedded directly in the code.

Integrating Security into CI/CD Pipelines

Azure DevOps and GitHub Actions provide the framework for automating builds, testing, and deployments. Security should be integrated as early and often as possible.

Key integrations include:

- **Static Application Security Testing (SAST)**: Analyze code for vulnerabilities during build.
- **Dynamic Application Security Testing (DAST)**: Simulate attacks on live apps in staging.
- **Dependency Scanning**: Identify known vulnerabilities in third-party packages.
- **Infrastructure Drift Detection**: Compare deployed infrastructure with IaC definitions.

Example: Azure DevOps Pipeline with SAST and IaC Linting

```
trigger:
- main
pool:
vmImage: 'ubuntu-latest'
jobs:
- job: SecurePipeline
steps:
- task: UseDotNet@2
inputs:
packageType: 'sdk'
version: '7.x'
```

```
- script: dotnet build—no-restore
displayName: 'Build Project'
- script: dotnet sonarscanner begin /k:"MyApp" /d:sonar.login="$(sonarToken)"
displayName: 'Start SonarQube Scan'
- script: dotnet test
displayName: 'Run Tests'
- script: dotnet sonarscanner end /d:sonar.login="$(sonarToken)"
displayName: 'End SonarQube Scan'
- task: AzureCLI@2
inputs:
azureSubscription: '<subscription>'
scriptType: 'bash'
scriptLocation: 'inlineScript'
inlineScript: |
az bicep build—file ./main.bicep
```

Secrets and Credential Management

Secrets should never be stored in source control or IaC files. Instead, use **Azure Key Vault** for secure storage and access.

Key Vault allows you to manage:

- API keys

- Connection strings
- Certificates
- Passwords
- Encryption keys

Integrate Key Vault with CI/CD by referencing secrets at runtime rather than embedding them.

Example: Accessing Key Vault Secret in Azure CLI

az keyvault secret show—vault-name MyVault—name DbPassword—query value -o tsv

In Azure Pipelines, link secrets using service connections and variable groups.

Best practices:

- Use **managed identities** for automated pipelines
- Implement **access policies** with least privilege
- Enable **logging and alerting** on key access

Policy as Code and Governance Integration

Security policies should be codified and enforced through automation. Azure Policy enables **policy-as-code**, which is essential for Secure DevOps.

Use **Terraform** or **Bicep** to assign Azure Policies during infrastructure deployment. Combine with **Azure Blueprints** for full environment configuration.

Terraform Example: Enforcing Tagging Policy

```
resource "azurerm_policy_definition" "require_tags" {
name = "require-tags"
policy_type = "Custom"
mode = "All"
display_name = "Require Tags"
policy_rule = <<POLICY
{
"if": {
"not": {
"field": "tags['Environment']",
"exists": "true"
}
},
"then": {
"effect": "deny"
}
```

```
}

POLICY

}
```

Integrate policy checks into CI/CD pipelines using tools like **Checkov**, **TFLint**, or **PSRule for Azure**.

Role-Based Access Control (RBAC) and Privilege Management

A key part of Secure DevOps is limiting who can access what. Azure's **Role-Based Access Control (RBAC)** enables granular permissions assignment to users, groups, and service principals.

RBAC principles:

- Use **built-in roles** such as Reader, Contributor, or Owner
- Create **custom roles** if specific permissions are needed
- Assign at the **lowest appropriate scope** (resource, group, subscription)

Example: Assign Reader Role with Azure CLI

```
az role assignment create \

—assignee "<user-object-id>" \

—role "Reader" \

—scope "/subscriptions/<sub-id>/resourceGroups/<rg-name>"
```

Use **Privileged Identity Management (PIM)** for time-bound access to sensitive roles, reducing the risk of standing privilege.

Security Baseline Templates

Microsoft provides **Security Baseline Blueprints** for standardizing secure configurations. These blueprints include:

- Audit policies
- Logging setup
- RBAC assignments
- Network restrictions
- Key Vault and diagnostic settings

Adopt these as a base for new projects and modify to suit business requirements.

Blueprints can be enforced using Azure CLI or ARM templates, making secure deployment consistent and repeatable.

Continuous Monitoring and Threat Detection

Security doesn't stop after deployment. Use continuous monitoring to detect vulnerabilities, misconfigurations, and threats.

Recommended tools:

- **Microsoft Defender for Cloud**: Threat detection and Secure Score for posture management
- **Azure Monitor and Log Analytics**: Custom queries and alerts

- **Azure Sentinel**: SIEM and SOAR capabilities
- **Security Center integrations**: Container scanning, OS patching

Configure alerts for:

- Unusual resource access
- Failed login attempts
- Changes to critical configurations
- Suspicious lateral movement

Example: Azure Monitor Alert for Failed Logins

```
SigninLogs
| where ResultType != 0
| summarize count() by UserPrincipalName
```

Automate responses using **Logic Apps** or **Azure Automation.**

Secure DevOps Kit for Azure (AzSK)

Microsoft's **Secure DevOps Kit for Azure** (AzSK) is a set of PowerShell-based tools to check security configurations and generate compliance reports.

Modules include:

- ARM Template Analyzer
- Subscription Security Scans

- DevOps Pipeline Integration
- Continuous Assurance Scanning

Install via PowerShell:

```
Install-Module AzSK -Scope CurrentUser
```

Run a scan:

```
Get-AzSKSubscriptionSecurityStatus -SubscriptionId "<sub-id>"
```

Best Practices for Secure DevOps and IaC

- **Shift security left**: Identify and fix issues during development
- **Integrate scanning tools** into every stage of the pipeline
- **Use managed identities** instead of hardcoded credentials
- **Enforce policies automatically** during deployment
- **Review RBAC regularly** and remove unused assignments
- **Encrypt all data at rest and in transit**
- **Use tag enforcement** for tracking and compliance
- **Monitor continuously** and act on alerts
- **Version-control infrastructure code** and perform code reviews

Summary

Secure DevOps and Infrastructure as Code together redefine how security is applied in the cloud. By embedding security practices into automated workflows, using policy-as-code, managing secrets securely, and monitoring systems proactively, organizations can build resilient, scalable, and compliant systems. In Azure, tools like Azure Policy, Key Vault, Defender for Cloud, and Azure DevOps pipelines allow developers and operations teams to embrace security as a shared responsibility—without slowing down innovation.

Chapter 8: Monitoring, Diagnostics, and Performance Tuning

Azure Monitor and Log Analytics

Effective monitoring is a cornerstone of reliable, scalable, and secure cloud applications. In the Azure ecosystem, **Azure Monitor** and **Log Analytics** form the foundation for observability. Together, they allow organizations to collect, analyze, and act on telemetry data from applications and infrastructure deployed in Azure—and beyond.

What is Azure Monitor?

Azure Monitor is a comprehensive monitoring solution that provides full-stack observability across applications, infrastructure, and networks. Its capabilities include:

- **Metrics**: Numerical values describing aspects of a system at a particular time.
- **Logs**: Structured data generated by resources or applications.
- **Alerts**: Notifications based on metrics or logs.
- **Dashboards**: Visual representations of data trends.
- **Insights**: Built-in monitoring solutions for specific services (VMs, Containers, etc.).

Azure Monitor provides telemetry from a variety of sources:

- **Application telemetry** via Application Insights

- **Infrastructure telemetry** from Azure resources
- **Guest OS telemetry** via diagnostics extensions
- **Custom telemetry** from APIs or SDKs

Understanding Log Analytics

Log Analytics is a tool within Azure Monitor that collects and analyzes log data using the **Kusto Query Language (KQL)**. It's part of the broader Azure Monitor Logs capability and enables users to:

- Run complex queries across logs
- Correlate logs from different resources
- Visualize trends
- Power alerts and automation

To use Log Analytics effectively, you must first connect resources to a **Log Analytics workspace**.

Key Concepts

- **Workspace**: The central repository where logs are collected and analyzed.
- **Tables**: Logs are stored in schema-defined tables (e.g., Heartbeat, Perf, Event).
- **Retention**: Data can be retained from days to years, depending on configuration.

- **Data Sources**: Azure services, custom apps, on-premises machines, and other clouds.

Configuring Azure Monitor

Enable Diagnostics Settings: You can configure most Azure services to send telemetry to Azure Monitor. This is done via Diagnostic Settings.

```
az monitor diagnostic-settings create \

—name 'send-logs' \

—resource
/subscriptions/<sub-id>/resourceGroups/<rg>/providers/
Microsoft.Compute/virtualMachines/<vm-name> \

—workspace <log-analytics-workspace-id> \

—logs '[{"category": "AuditLogs", "enabled": true}]'
```

1.

Install Agent: To collect OS-level logs, install the **Azure Monitor Agent** (AMA).

```
Install-AzMonitorAgent -ResourceId "/subscriptions/xxx/
resourceGroups/xxx/providers/Microsoft.Compute/
virtualMachines/xxx"
```

2.

3. **Connect to Workspace**: For virtual machines:

○ Use Azure Portal or CLI to link the VM to the Log Analytics workspace.

◦ Ensure network rules permit outbound access to the ingestion endpoints.

Querying with Kusto Query Language (KQL)

KQL is the powerful query language used in Azure Monitor and Log Analytics. A simple example:

```
Heartbeat

| where TimeGenerated > ago(1h)

| summarize Count = count() by Computer
```

This returns the number of heartbeat signals from each monitored computer over the past hour.

Common operators in KQL include:

- where: Filters data
- summarize: Aggregates results
- join: Merges data from multiple tables
- project: Selects specific columns
- extend: Adds new calculated fields

Advanced Example:

```
Perf

| where CounterName == "% Processor Time"

| summarize AvgCPU=avg(CounterValue) by bin(TimeGenerated, 5m), Computer
```

```
| order by TimeGenerated desc
```

This aggregates CPU usage per computer in 5-minute bins.

Setting Up Alerts

Alerts enable real-time response to potential issues. In Azure Monitor, you can configure:

- **Metric Alerts**: For example, when CPU exceeds 80%.
- **Log Alerts**: Based on KQL queries.
- **Activity Log Alerts**: When specific administrative operations occur.

Example of creating a metric alert using Azure CLI:

```
az monitor metrics alert create \

—name "HighCPUAlert" \

—resource-group "myResourceGroup" \

—scopes "/subscriptions/<sub-id>/resourceGroups/myResourceGroup/providers/Microsoft.Compute/virtualMachines/myVM" \

—condition "avg Percentage CPU > 80" \

—description "CPU usage exceeded 80%"
```

For log alerts, you define a KQL query and evaluation frequency.

Dashboards and Visualization

Azure dashboards provide a flexible way to visualize telemetry data.

- Native integration with Azure Monitor.
- Support for pinned queries, metrics, and charts.
- Shared or private dashboards.

To create a dashboard:

1. Navigate to **Azure Monitor > Dashboards**
2. Click **New Dashboard**
3. Use widgets to add:
   - Metric charts
   - Log Analytics queries
   - Alerts summary

Example KQL query pinned to a dashboard:

```
AzureActivity
| where ActivityStatus == "Failed"
| summarize Failures = count() by bin(TimeGenerated, 1h), Resource
```

This tracks failed operations by resource.

Application Insights

Application Insights is tailored for developers to monitor live applications. It provides:

- Application performance telemetry

- Distributed tracing
- Smart detection and usage analytics

It can be integrated via SDKs for .NET, Java, JavaScript, and others.

Sample telemetry:

appInsights.trackEvent({ name: "UserSignup", properties: { plan: "Pro" } });

Application Insights also supports:

- Custom events and metrics
- Automatic dependency tracking (e.g., HTTP calls)
- Performance counters and exceptions

Best Practices

1. **Centralize Logs**: Use a single Log Analytics workspace across environments for easier management.

2. **Structure Tags**: Apply consistent tags across resources (e.g., Environment, Owner) to enable scoped queries.

3. **Retention Management**: Adjust data retention based on compliance requirements.

4. **Automation**: Use **Azure Monitor Action Groups** to trigger:

   - Email

- Webhook
- Logic Apps
- Azure Functions

5. **Cost Control**:

- Enable sampling in Application Insights
- Retain only necessary logs
- Use filters in Diagnostic Settings

6. **Monitor Hybrid Resources**: Install Azure Monitor Agent on-premises or use **Azure Arc** to onboard non-Azure machines.

Integration with Other Tools

Azure Monitor integrates with:

- **Grafana**: Visualize data using native Azure Monitor plugin.
- **SIEM tools**: Forward logs to Splunk, Sentinel, or third-party platforms.
- **DevOps**: Link alerts to Azure DevOps work items or GitHub issues.

Example: Forward logs to Sentinel via Data Connector.

Common Troubleshooting Tips

- **No data in workspace:**

  - Check if agent is installed and connected.
  - Validate permissions to workspace.
- **High ingestion costs**:
  - Use filters in diagnostic settings.
  - Set up data caps and alerts on ingestion volume.
- **Slow queries**:
  - Use indexing (summarize, project) to reduce output.
  - Bin time-based queries (bin(TimeGenerated, 1h)).

Summary

Azure Monitor and Log Analytics enable full observability across your environment, from virtual machines and Kubernetes clusters to serverless apps and on-premises servers. By leveraging metrics, logs, alerts, dashboards, and advanced querying with KQL, organizations can gain proactive insights, diagnose issues faster, and ensure optimal performance. Proper configuration and adherence to best practices ensure you maintain a secure, scalable, and cost-effective monitoring solution.

Application Insights and Workbooks

Monitoring applications effectively goes beyond just tracking infrastructure. **Application Insights** provides deep visibility into application performance, failures, and user behavior. It is part of Azure Monitor and supports proactive diagnostics, usage analytics, and live metrics for applications running in the cloud or on-premises.

Azure Workbooks, on the other hand, offer a powerful and flexible way to visualize data, create interactive reports, and build rich dashboards by combining metrics, logs, and external data sources. Together, Application Insights and Workbooks enable full-stack observability and advanced analytics for any application.

Introduction to Application Insights

Application Insights is an **application performance monitoring (APM)** service for developers and DevOps professionals. It automatically detects performance anomalies, logs telemetry data from your app, and helps you diagnose issues and understand user interactions.

Key capabilities include:

- Live application monitoring
- Telemetry collection (requests, dependencies, exceptions, traces, events)
- Distributed tracing
- Analytics powered by KQL (Kusto Query Language)
- Usage and performance insights
- Smart alerts and anomaly detection

You can instrument your app with Application Insights via SDKs or by enabling **Auto-Instrumentation** (for services like Azure App Service and AKS).

Instrumenting Your Application

Application Insights supports most major platforms and languages:

- **.NET / .NET Core**
- **Java / Java EE**
- **Node.js**
- **Python**
- **JavaScript / SPA frameworks**

Here's a simple example for a Node.js app:

```
npm install applicationinsights
```

```
const appInsights = require("applicationinsights");

appInsights.setup("<YOUR_INSTRUMENTATION_KEY>").start();
```

For a .NET Core application:

```
dotnet add package Microsoft.ApplicationInsights.AspNetCore
```

In Startup.cs:

```
services.AddApplicationInsightsTelemetry("<YOUR_INSTRUMENTAT
```

Once configured, Application Insights collects telemetry such as:

- **Request Telemetry**: Incoming HTTP requests
- **Dependency Telemetry**: Outbound calls (e.g., SQL, HTTP)

- **Exception Telemetry**: Unhandled exceptions
- **Event Telemetry**: Custom events
- **Trace Telemetry**: Logging data

Live Metrics and Performance

Live Metrics Stream enables real-time monitoring of key performance indicators. It includes:

- Request rates
- Failure rates
- Response time
- Dependency call status
- Custom metrics

Live metrics are especially useful during incident response or after deployment to observe real-time behavior without full ingestion latency.

To enable Live Metrics in the Azure portal:

1. Navigate to your Application Insights resource.
2. Click **Live Metrics Stream.**
3. Authorize access via a **Live Metrics Access Control**.

Distributed Tracing

Modern applications are often composed of many microservices. Application Insights supports **distributed tracing**, which lets you track requests across services and components.

Each request gets a **correlation ID**, and telemetry such as requests, dependencies, and exceptions are linked.

You can visualize traces using:

- **End-to-end transaction views**
- **Timeline explorers**
- **Dependency maps**

These tools help you isolate bottlenecks and pinpoint failures across services.

Custom Events and Metrics

You can send custom telemetry using the SDK to track user behavior or specific business logic.

Example: Logging a user action in JavaScript:

appInsights.trackEvent({ name: "ClickedSubscribe", properties: { plan: "Pro" } });

Example: Logging a custom metric:

appInsights.trackMetric({ name: "SignupDuration", value: 3.42 });

Custom telemetry can be visualized, queried via KQL, and used in alerts and workbooks.

Application Map and Smart Detection

Application Map provides a visual representation of all components and how they interact. You can see:

- Topology of services
- Health and failure trends
- Call latency between services

Smart Detection uses machine learning to identify anomalies such as:

- Sudden increase in failure rate
- Performance degradation
- Dependency latency spikes

Smart Detection alerts are generated automatically without manual thresholds.

KQL Queries with Application Insights Data

Once telemetry is in Application Insights, you can query it using **Kusto Query Language (KQL)**.

Example: Top 10 slowest requests:

```
requests
| order by duration desc
| take 10
```

Example: Exceptions by type over the last 7 days:

```
exceptions
| where timestamp > ago(7d)
| summarize count() by type
```

Example: Average response time by URL:

```
requests
| summarize avg(duration) by name
| order by avg_duration desc
```

These queries can power dashboards, alerts, and visualizations.

Introduction to Azure Workbooks

Azure Workbooks is a visualization and reporting tool that allows you to create dynamic, interactive reports and dashboards using metrics, logs, and data from Application Insights and other sources.

Key features:

- Support for both time-series and tabular data
- Query integration with KQL
- Parameterized controls (dropdowns, checkboxes)
- Cross-resource queries
- Markdown, metrics, text boxes, and grids

You can use Workbooks to:

- Build dashboards for performance and SLA metrics

- Create custom health reports for your apps
- Track incidents and triage history
- Combine multiple data sources (metrics, logs, usage)

Creating a Workbook

To create a workbook:

1. Navigate to your Application Insights or Azure Monitor resource.
2. Go to **Workbooks.**
3. Click **+ New.**
4. Choose the visualization format (e.g., query, chart, markdown).
5. Add a **Log Analytics query** or a metric.
6. Save and optionally share the workbook.

Example query block (average response time over time):

```
requests
| summarize avg(duration) by bin(timestamp, 1h)
| render timechart
```

You can mix multiple query blocks, charts, and markdown explanations in a single workbook.

Parameters and Interactivity

Workbooks allow user interaction through parameter controls like:

- Time pickers
- Resource selectors
- Drop-down lists
- Boolean toggles

Example: Filter requests by selected operation name.

```
requests
| where name == "{OperationName}"
| summarize count() by bin(timestamp, 1h)
| render timechart
```

This makes workbooks highly customizable and useful for teams and stakeholders.

Sharing and Governance

Workbooks can be:

- **Shared across teams** using Azure role-based access control (RBAC)
- **Exported and imported** as JSON
- **Embedded in dashboards** or external apps

You can manage workbook permissions using built-in Azure roles or assign custom roles for granular control.

Best Practices

1. **Use Tags for Context**: Apply consistent tagging (like environment, owner) to resources and query filters.
2. **Sample Data Intelligently**: To reduce ingestion costs, implement **adaptive sampling** in SDKs.
3. **Create Shared Workbooks**: For common health, SLA, and incident dashboards.
4. **Organize Telemetry**: Use naming conventions for events, operations, and metrics.
5. **Combine Metrics and Logs**: Mix both types of data for holistic views in Workbooks.
6. **Limit Query Scope**: Use filters (where) and time bins to improve performance.

Integration with DevOps and Automation

Application Insights and Workbooks integrate seamlessly with DevOps pipelines and automation tools:

- **Export telemetry to Azure DevOps** work items via alerts
- **Integrate Workbooks into release gates**
- **Use API/ARM templates to deploy Workbooks**
- **Incorporate Application Insights telemetry into CI/CD decisions**

Example: Create a deployment gate that checks for failure spikes post-release using a KQL query.

Summary

Application Insights and Azure Workbooks form a powerful duo for monitoring, troubleshooting, and optimizing applications. Application Insights provides rich telemetry, distributed tracing, smart detection, and real-time insights. Workbooks offer a customizable, interactive canvas to visualize and share these insights across teams.

By leveraging KQL, SDK integrations, custom telemetry, and powerful dashboards, teams can go beyond basic monitoring to create a proactive, intelligent observability strategy that supports rapid development, quick incident response, and continuous performance improvement.

Alerts, Dashboards, and Action Groups

Monitoring is only effective when it leads to timely and meaningful action. In Azure, the trio of **Alerts**, **Dashboards**, and **Action Groups** empowers teams to detect issues, visualize system health, and respond proactively. This ecosystem allows you to automate responses, coordinate incident management, and ensure that telemetry drives value.

This section dives into how these features work, how to configure them, and how to apply best practices to create reliable, maintainable, and proactive monitoring strategies.

Alerts: An Overview

Azure Alerts notify you when conditions defined in monitoring data are met. These alerts can be configured on:

- **Metrics** (numeric data points like CPU usage)

- **Logs** (custom queries on diagnostic and telemetry data)
- **Activity Logs** (management operations in Azure)
- **Resource Health** (service-level or availability issues)
- **Platform Events** (e.g., scaling operations)

Alerts are useful for a variety of scenarios:

- Detecting performance degradation
- Identifying failed deployments
- Notifying stakeholders of security incidents
- Triggering automated remediation workflows

Types of Alerts

1. **Metric Alerts**
   - Operate on performance metrics.
   - Ideal for threshold-based conditions (e.g., CPU > 80%).
2. **Log Alerts**
   - Use **KQL queries** on log data.
   - Support complex logic and cross-resource analysis.
3. **Activity Log Alerts**

○ Triggered when specific administrative operations are performed.

4. **Prometheus Alerts**

○ Used with Azure Monitor for containers when Prometheus metrics are collected.

5. **Dynamic Threshold Alerts**

○ Automatically calculate thresholds using machine learning.

Creating a Metric Alert

Example: Alert when CPU usage exceeds 80% for 5 minutes.

Via Azure CLI:

az monitor metrics alert create \

—name "HighCPUAlert" \

—resource-group "MyResourceGroup" \

—scopes "/subscriptions/<sub-id>/resourceGroups/MyResourceGroup/providers/Microsoft.Compute/virtualMachines/MyVM" \

—condition "avg Percentage CPU > 80" \

—description "Alert when CPU > 80%" \

—window-size 5m \

—evaluation-frequency 1m \

—action-group "/subscriptions/<sub-id>/resourceGroups/MyResourceGroup/providers/microsoft.insights/actionGroups/MyActionGroup"

Via Portal:

1. Go to Azure Monitor > Alerts.
2. Click + **New Alert Rule**.
3. Select the resource, condition (e.g., CPU), and threshold.
4. Attach an action group and review settings.

Creating a Log Alert

You can also base alerts on Log Analytics queries using KQL.

Example KQL: High number of failed requests

requests

| where resultCode startswith "5"

| summarize count() by bin(timestamp, 5m)

Configure alert logic:

- Trigger if result count > threshold (e.g., > 100 in 5 mins)
- Set severity and frequency

Best Practices for Alerts

- **Granularity**: Use specific, actionable conditions.

- **Severity Levels**: Define levels (Sev0–Sev4) to prioritize incidents.
- **Suppression**: Prevent alert fatigue using **alert rules suppression.**
- **Aggregation**: Group alerts per incident when possible.
- **Use Smart Detection**: Leverage machine-learning-based dynamic thresholds to minimize noise.

Action Groups

Action Groups define how Azure responds to alerts. They decouple alert logic from response logic and are reusable across multiple alerts.

Components:

- Email/SMS/Push Notifications
- Webhook URLs
- Azure Function
- Logic App
- Automation Runbook
- ITSM (ServiceNow, Cherwell, etc.)
- Secure webhook (HMAC signature)

Creating an Action Group (CLI):

```
az monitor action-group create \
—name MyActionGroup \
—resource-group MyResourceGroup \
—action email MyAdmin myadmin@example.com \
—short-name AGCPU
```

Action groups support **user-defined fields**, which allow dynamic data to be passed into webhook payloads or automation scripts.

Common Use Cases for Action Groups

- **Email escalation to engineering teams**
- **Triggering auto-remediation scripts via Logic Apps**
- **Opening tickets in incident management systems**
- **Invoking a webhook for CI/CD integration**
- **Publishing to Microsoft Teams or Slack channels**

Azure Dashboards

Azure Dashboards provide a **customizable canvas** for visualizing metrics, logs, and alerts. Dashboards enable teams to track system health at a glance and are especially useful for operations, NOC, or development teams.

Types:

- **Private Dashboards**: Visible only to the creator.
- **Shared Dashboards**: Visible to users with access permissions.

Dashboard Elements:

- Metrics charts
- Log query visualizations
- Markdown text blocks
- Alerts summary
- Workbooks and pinned content

Creating a Dashboard

From Azure Portal:

1. Navigate to **Dashboard > + New Dashboard**.
2. Use **Tiles** to add:
    - Metric charts (e.g., CPU, Memory)
    - KQL visualizations from Log Analytics
    - Markdown sections (descriptions, instructions)
3. Pin tiles from other Azure resources (e.g., Application Insights charts).
4. Save and share the dashboard with team members.

Programmatic Creation (ARM template):

Dashboards can be exported/imported using ARM templates or deployed using Bicep/Terraform.

Example:

```
{
"type": "Microsoft.Portal/dashboards",
"apiVersion": "2020-09-01-preview",
"name": "MyDashboard",
"properties": {
"lenses": { ... },
"metadata": { ... }
},
"location": "eastus"
}
```

Interactive Dashboards with Workbooks

You can also **embed Workbooks** into Dashboards for interactive controls such as drop-downs, filters, and dynamic charts. This enables rich drill-down capability directly from a static dashboard environment.

Use this for:

- Daily health summaries

- Interactive SLA tracking
- On-call runbooks

Alert Management and Remediation

Azure offers several built-in features for managing alert lifecycles:

- **Alert State Management**: New, Acknowledged, Closed
- **Action Rule Suppression**: Prevent action groups from firing during planned maintenance
- **Alert Processing Rules (APRs)**: Modify alert payloads or suppress them based on conditions

Example use case: Suppress alerts from Dev environment between 10 PM and 6 AM using an action rule.

```
az monitor action-rule create \

—name SuppressNightDevAlerts \

—resource-group MyResourceGroup \

—scope "/subscriptions/<sub-id>/resourceGroups/dev" \

—condition description "Suppress after hours" \

—action-type Suppress \

—schedule "22:00" "06:00"
```

Alerts Analytics

For deeper insights into alert trends, you can use **Log Analytics queries** or Workbooks. Azure provides data on:

- Most frequent alerts
- Average time to acknowledge or resolve
- False positives
- Distribution by severity or resource type

Example Query:

```
AlertEvidence
| summarize Count = count() by AlertName, SeverityLevel
| order by Count desc
```

Use this data to tune thresholds, adjust routing logic, and improve your monitoring posture.

Integration with External Systems

Azure alerts and dashboards are not siloed. You can extend them to integrate with:

- **DevOps Tools**: GitHub Actions, Azure DevOps Pipelines
- **ITSM**: ServiceNow, PagerDuty, OpsGenie
- **Messaging Platforms**: Slack, Microsoft Teams
- **Custom APIs**: Via Webhooks and Logic Apps

Example: Trigger a GitHub workflow from an alert:

```
{
"url": "https://api.github.com/repos/org/repo/actions/workflows/alert-response.yml/dispatches",
"headers": { "Authorization": "Bearer <token>" },
"body": { "ref": "main" }
}
```

Summary

Azure's alerting system, coupled with dashboards and action groups, forms a complete feedback and response loop for modern cloud infrastructure. By combining real-time alerts with automated and manual response actions, users can create robust observability pipelines that support high availability and operational excellence.

The key is not just to monitor, but to **visualize, alert, and act**—with minimal delay and maximum precision. When implemented correctly, this trio becomes a critical part of DevOps, SRE, and ITSM strategies, enabling data-driven decision-making and resilient cloud-native systems.

Performance Optimization Strategies

Optimizing performance in Azure is not a one-time task but an ongoing discipline that spans across compute, networking, storage, databases, and application architecture. Azure provides a rich set of services and tools to monitor, analyze, and improve the responsiveness, scalability, and efficiency of cloud-based solutions.

In this section, we will explore core strategies and best practices for performance optimization within the Azure ecosystem.

Core Principles of Performance Optimization

Before diving into service-specific techniques, it's essential to align with several core principles:

- **Measure First**: Always base optimizations on metrics, not assumptions. Use data from Azure Monitor, Application Insights, and Log Analytics.
- **Minimize Latency**: Identify bottlenecks and reduce hops between services.
- **Scale Intelligently**: Use auto-scaling and elasticity principles to adapt to demand.
- **Right-Size Resources**: Avoid overprovisioning by evaluating actual usage patterns.
- **Cache Aggressively**: Use in-memory caching where applicable to reduce I/O.
- **Asynchronous Design**: Avoid blocking operations, especially in web and mobile apps.

Optimizing Virtual Machines

1. Right-Sizing VMs

- Regularly analyze CPU, memory, and disk utilization.

- Use **Azure Advisor** and **Metrics** to identify underused or overused VMs.
- Switch to burstable B-series VMs for spiky workloads.

Example – Resize a VM using Azure CLI:

```
az vm resize \
—resource-group MyResourceGroup \
—name MyVM \
—size Standard_DS2_v2
```

2. Use Managed Disks and Premium Storage

- Premium SSDs reduce latency and increase IOPS for high-performance apps.
- Use **Ultra Disks** for databases requiring low latency.

3. Enable Accelerated Networking

- Reduces latency, jitter, and CPU utilization for VM-to-VM communication.
- Available for supported VM sizes and OS configurations.

```
az network nic update \
—name myNic \
—resource-group myResourceGroup \
—accelerated-networking true
```

Application Performance

1. Application Insights Profiler

- Use the Profiler in Application Insights to capture method-level performance data.
- Identify code bottlenecks like N+1 queries or expensive method calls.

2. Asynchronous Programming

- In .NET, use async/await patterns to avoid blocking threads.
- In Node.js, ensure long operations use promises or callbacks.

3. Reduce Cold Start in Azure Functions

- Choose Premium Plans or use **pre-warmed instances.**
- Keep dependencies minimal to reduce startup time.

```
{
"functionTimeout": "00:05:00",
"preWarmedInstanceCount": 2
}
```

Database Optimization

1. Azure SQL Database

- **Query Performance Insight**: Identify high-resource-consuming queries.
- **Index Advisor**: Automatically recommends indexes based on usage patterns.
- **Elastic Pools**: Optimize cost and performance for multiple databases with variable usage.

Sample Query: Top 5 Longest-Running Queries

```
SELECT TOP 5 query_hash, total_dop, avg_cpu_time, avg_duration

FROM sys.query_store_query

ORDER BY avg_duration DESC;
```

2. Cosmos DB

- Use **Partitioning** effectively to distribute load.
- Enable **Automatic Indexing** only when necessary.
- Monitor **RU/s consumption** to avoid throttling.

```
{
"partitionKey": {
"paths": ["/region"],
"kind": "Hash"
}
}
```

3. Azure Database for PostgreSQL/MySQL

- Enable **query logging** to identify slow queries.
- Adjust parameters like work_mem or innodb_buffer_pool_size for better performance.
- Use **read replicas** for scaling read-heavy workloads.

API and Gateway Optimization

1. Azure API Management (APIM)

- Use **caching policies** to reduce backend load.
- Apply **rate-limiting** to protect against abuse.
- Use **compression** to minimize payload size.

```
<cache-lookup vary-by-developer="false" vary-by-developer-groups="false" />
```

2. Azure Front Door

- Use global edge nodes to accelerate app delivery.
- Enable **HTTP/2**, **compression**, and **TLS session resumption**.
- Apply **Web Application Firewall (WAF)** for security and performance.

Caching Strategies

1. Azure Cache for Redis

- Use Redis to store session data, shopping carts, or frequently accessed results.
- Choose appropriate cache eviction policies (LRU, volatile-lru, allkeys-lru).
- Use Pub/Sub to broadcast changes to subscribers in real time.

Sample Redis usage in .NET:

```
IDatabase cache = Connection.GetDatabase();

cache.StringSet("user:123", "John Doe", TimeSpan.FromMinutes(30));
```

2. CDN Caching

- Leverage Azure CDN to cache static assets like images, stylesheets, and JavaScript files.
- Use **cache-control** headers to manage cache behavior.
- Integrate with Azure Blob Storage for seamless content delivery.

```
Cache-Control: public, max-age=86400
```

Auto-Scaling and Load Balancing

1. Auto-Scaling

- Configure rules to scale out based on metrics (CPU, queue length, etc.).
- Azure App Service and Azure Virtual Machine Scale Sets support custom autoscale rules.

```
az monitor autoscale rule create \
—resource-group MyResourceGroup \
—autoscale-name MyScaleSetting \
—condition "Percentage CPU > 75 avg 5m" \
—scale out 1
```

2. Load Balancing

- Use **Azure Load Balancer** for L4 traffic (TCP/UDP).
- Use **Application Gateway** for L7 traffic (HTTP/HTTPS) with WAF.
- Use **Traffic Manager** for DNS-based global load balancing.

Networking Performance

1. Reduce DNS Lookup Time

- Use **Azure DNS** with low TTL values for dynamic environments.

- Co-locate services within the same virtual network or region to minimize latency.

2. Use ExpressRoute for Hybrid Connections

- Provides private, dedicated connectivity between on-prem and Azure.
- Offers predictable latency and higher throughput compared to VPNs.

3. Optimize Network Security

- Use **NSGs and ASGs** for fine-grained control.
- Avoid overly broad rules that may route traffic inefficiently.

Monitoring for Performance

1. Azure Monitor Alerts

Set alerts for:

- High CPU or memory
- Throttled requests
- Query duration thresholds
- Under-utilized resources (to right-size)

2. Azure Workbooks

Create dynamic dashboards to visualize:

- App latency trends
- Dependency maps
- Load distribution

Sample KQL Query:

```
requests
| summarize avg(duration) by bin(timestamp, 5m)
```

Visualize this in a workbook to track performance trends.

Cost and Performance Tradeoffs

Often, performance improvements increase cost. Optimize based on application profile:

- **Mission-Critical**: Use Premium SKUs, pre-warmed instances, geo-redundancy.
- **Dev/Test**: Use lower-cost SKUs, shared instances, or spot VMs.
- **Burst Workloads**: Use serverless or autoscaling patterns.

Use **Azure Cost Management + Advisor** to align performance with budget.

Continuous Optimization Cycle

Performance tuning is not a one-time effort. Implement the following feedback loop:

1. **Measure**: Collect metrics using Application Insights and Azure Monitor.
2. **Analyze**: Use KQL, Workbooks, and Dashboards.
3. **Act**: Apply architectural changes, resource scaling, or code optimization.
4. **Review**: Validate impact via post-deployment performance tracking.

This cycle should be integrated into CI/CD pipelines with pre- and post-deployment metrics.

Summary

Performance optimization in Azure spans every layer of your architecture—from the smallest function to the largest distributed system. By leveraging metrics, alerts, scaling mechanisms, and caching strategies, you can ensure your applications remain fast, resilient, and cost-effective. Tools like Application Insights, Azure Monitor, and Workbooks provide visibility, while services like Redis, Front Door, and SQL Elastic Pools help deliver concrete improvements.

Optimization should be both proactive and reactive, driven by real-time data, historical trends, and the evolving needs of users. With these strategies in place, you're equipped to build and maintain cloud-native applications that meet demanding performance SLAs at scale.

Chapter 9: High Availability, Scaling, and Resiliency

Designing for Redundancy and Disaster Recovery

Ensuring high availability and implementing effective disaster recovery strategies are foundational principles in designing resilient cloud solutions. In Azure, this involves architecting systems to tolerate failures, minimizing downtime, and recovering quickly when disruptions occur. Whether you're deploying enterprise applications, mission-critical services, or customer-facing APIs, designing for redundancy and disaster recovery is a non-negotiable aspect of achieving operational excellence.

This section will explore the essential concepts, tools, architectural patterns, and best practices involved in building highly available and resilient systems on Microsoft Azure.

Understanding High Availability and Disaster Recovery

High Availability (HA) refers to the design of systems that aim to remain accessible and operational during failures of components or services. The goal is to minimize downtime and avoid single points of failure.

Disaster Recovery (DR) is the process of restoring application functionality and data after a major incident, such as a regional outage, data corruption, or cyberattack.

Key terms:

- **RPO (Recovery Point Objective)**: Maximum tolerable period of data loss.
- **RTO (Recovery Time Objective)**: Maximum acceptable time to restore service.

These two metrics help define the level of redundancy and recovery needed for each application component.

Azure Infrastructure Building Blocks for HA and DR

Azure provides various services and configurations that support HA and DR out-of-the-box:

- **Availability Zones**
- **Availability Sets**
- **Geo-redundant Storage (GRS)**
- **Azure Site Recovery**
- **Traffic Manager**
- **Azure Backup**
- **Load Balancers and Gateways**

Each of these plays a role in enabling fault tolerance, automatic recovery, and data durability.

Redundancy with Availability Zones

Azure **Availability Zones** are physically separate datacenters within a region, each with independent power, cooling, and networking. Deploying across zones ensures resiliency against localized failures.

Use cases:

- Mission-critical workloads
- Stateful applications like databases
- Applications requiring high SLA guarantees (up to 99.99%)

Example: Deploying a VM scale set across zones (CLI)

```
az vmss create \
—resource-group MyRG \
—name MyScaleSet \
—image UbuntuLTS \
—zones 1 2 3 \
—upgrade-policy-mode automatic
```

This command provisions the VM scale set in all three availability zones, providing zone redundancy.

Availability Sets

Availability Sets offer a cost-effective way to improve availability for Virtual Machines by distributing them across **fault domains** and **update domains**.

- **Fault domains** simulate physical server racks.
- **Update domains** allow rolling OS or app updates.

SLA: VMs in an availability set can achieve a 99.95% SLA.

Example: Create an Availability Set

```
az vm availability-set create \
—name MyAvailabilitySet \
—resource-group MyRG \
—platform-fault-domain-count 2 \
—platform-update-domain-count 5
```

Use availability sets when deploying legacy applications that aren't zone-aware but still need some level of resiliency.

Redundancy in Data Storage

Azure Storage offers several replication options:

- **LRS (Locally Redundant Storage)**: Data is replicated within a single datacenter.
- **ZRS (Zone-Redundant Storage)**: Replication across availability zones.

- **GRS (Geo-Redundant Storage)**: Data is asynchronously copied to a paired region.
- **GZRS (Geo-Zone Redundant Storage)**: Combines zone redundancy with geo-replication.

Choosing the right replication:

Replication	Scope	Use Case
LRS	Single datacenter	Low-cost, low-risk apps
ZRS	Multiple zones	High availability in a region
GRS	Secondary region	Disaster recovery
GZRS	ZRS + GRS	Critical apps requiring both HA and DR

Azure Site Recovery (ASR)

Azure Site Recovery enables replication, failover, and recovery of workloads across regions or from on-premises to Azure.

Features:

- Application-consistent snapshots
- Orchestration of failover and failback
- Support for VMs, physical servers, and databases
- Automated DR drills

Steps to configure ASR:

1. Enable replication for target VMs.

2. Define a recovery plan with steps for failover.
3. Test failover periodically without affecting production.
4. Monitor health using Azure Monitor integration.

Example: Enable replication for a VM

```
az backup protection enable-for-vm \

—resource-group MyRG \

—vault-name MyRecoveryVault \

—vm MyVM \

—policy-name DefaultPolicy
```

Designing Geo-Redundant Architectures

Active-Active Configuration

- Both primary and secondary regions are active and handle live traffic.
- Use **Traffic Manager** or **Front Door** for global load balancing.
- Challenges: Data synchronization, session affinity, higher complexity.

Active-Passive Configuration

- Primary region serves all traffic.
- Secondary region remains on standby.
- Lower cost and simpler to manage.

Traffic Manager Example:

az network traffic-manager profile create \

—name MyTrafficProfile \

—resource-group MyRG \

—routing-method Priority \

—unique-dns-name myapp \

—ttl 30 \

—monitor-path "/" \

—monitor-port 80 \

—monitor-protocol HTTP

Then add endpoints with primary (priority 1) and secondary (priority 2) regions.

Database Resiliency Patterns

1. Azure SQL Database

- **Geo-Replication**: Configure active secondary in a paired region.
- **Failover Groups**: Automatic redirection of traffic in case of failure.

az sql failover-group create \

—name MyFailoverGroup \

—partner-server MySecondarySQL \

—resource-group MyRG \

—server MyPrimarySQL \

—failover-policy Automatic \

—grace-period 1

2. Cosmos DB

- Multi-region writes and reads.
- Manual or automatic failover.

3. PostgreSQL/MySQL Flexible Server

- High availability enabled during creation.
- Use backup and geo-restore for DR.

Application Architecture Considerations

Stateless Applications

- Easier to scale and recover.
- Store session in Redis or external state store.

Stateful Applications

- Require replication and consistency strategies.
- Use availability sets/zones and backup solutions.

Decoupled Services

- Use messaging queues (Service Bus, Event Grid) to isolate failures.
- Asynchronous processing improves resilience.

Example architecture:

- Frontend behind Application Gateway
- Backend services deployed in VMSS across zones
- Redis Cache for session
- SQL Database with Geo-Replication
- Azure Storage using GZRS
- Traffic Manager with failover policy

Testing and Validating Resiliency

Chaos Engineering and **Disaster Recovery Drills** should be a regular part of your process.

- Schedule test failovers.
- Use Azure Chaos Studio to simulate outages.
- Validate RTO/RPO objectives.

Example Chaos Studio Test Plan:

1. Target a VM or AKS node.
2. Introduce latency or CPU pressure.
3. Monitor failover response and app behavior.

Cost Optimization and Trade-Offs

Balancing availability with cost is critical:

Component	Basic Option	High Availability Option	Trade-Off
VMs	LRS disk, single VM	VMSS across zones, Premium SSD	Higher cost
Databases	Single region	Geo-replication, auto-failover	Extra compute/ storage
Storage	LRS	GZRS	Higher storage cost
App Hosting	Basic App Service	App Service Environment, Traffic Manager	Complexity, licensing

Use **Azure Advisor** to identify underused HA features or cost-saving opportunities.

Summary

Designing for redundancy and disaster recovery in Azure ensures that your systems are prepared for both expected and unexpected disruptions. With the help of built-in features like Availability Zones, Azure Site Recovery, Traffic Manager, and replication options, you can architect robust systems that meet your business continuity goals.

By considering recovery objectives, choosing the right tools for each layer, and regularly testing your plans, you can dramatically reduce downtime and data loss. Whether you're building a new cloud-native system or migrating legacy applications, high availability and disaster recovery should be embedded into every architectural decision.

Auto-Scaling and Load Testing

Modern cloud applications must be able to dynamically adapt to changes in demand without manual intervention. Azure provides robust support for **auto-scaling** to maintain performance and cost efficiency, as well as **load testing tools** to simulate traffic and validate system scalability before real users encounter issues.

This section explores the strategies, tools, and best practices for implementing auto-scaling and conducting effective load testing in Azure-based architectures.

Why Auto-Scaling Matters

Traditional scaling requires manual provisioning of resources, leading to inefficiencies:

- **Under-provisioning** causes performance degradation during high traffic.
- **Over-provisioning** wastes resources and inflates costs during low traffic.

Auto-scaling enables applications to grow or shrink resources based on real-time metrics or schedules. Benefits include:

- Improved application availability
- Reduced manual effort and response time
- Optimized cost management

- Better end-user experience under fluctuating load

Types of Scaling in Azure

Azure supports several types of scaling mechanisms:

- **Vertical Scaling (Scale Up/Down):** Increase or decrease the size (SKU) of a resource.
- **Horizontal Scaling (Scale Out/In):** Add or remove instances of a resource (e.g., VMs, pods).
- **Manual Scaling:** User-triggered scaling via CLI/ Portal.
- **Automatic Scaling:** Based on metrics or time-based schedules.

Azure Services That Support Auto-Scaling

Service	Supports Auto-Scaling	Notes
Azure Virtual Machine Scale Sets	⍰	Works with custom images and autoscale rules
Azure App Service	⍰	Built-in rules for HTTP queue length, CPU, etc.
Azure Kubernetes Service (AKS)	⍰	Horizontal Pod Autoscaler + Cluster Autoscaler
Azure Functions	⍰	Consumption plan scales automatically
Azure Logic Apps	⍰	Scales based on trigger rates
Azure SQL Database	⍰	Elastic Pools and serverless plans

Configuring Auto-Scaling

1. Virtual Machine Scale Sets

VMSS lets you deploy and manage a set of identical VMs. Auto-scaling can be configured based on CPU, memory, or custom metrics.

Example – Create a scale rule based on CPU usage:

```
az monitor autoscale create \

—resource-group MyRG \

—resource MyScaleSet \

—resource-type Microsoft.Compute/virtualMachineScaleSets \
```

```
—name MyScaleRule \
—min-count 2 \
—max-count 10 \
—count 2
az monitor autoscale rule create \
—resource-group MyRG \
—autoscale-name MyScaleRule \
—condition "Percentage CPU > 70 avg 5m" \
—scale out 1
az monitor autoscale rule create \
—resource-group MyRG \
—autoscale-name MyScaleRule \
—condition "Percentage CPU < 30 avg 5m" \
—scale in 1
```

2. Azure App Service

App Service Plans provide auto-scaling capabilities out-of-the-box. Rules can be based on CPU, memory, HTTP queue length, and custom metrics via Application Insights.

Steps in Azure Portal:

1. Navigate to your App Service.
2. Select **Scale out (App Service Plan)**.

3. Choose **Custom auto-scale.**
4. Add scale conditions (e.g., CPU > 80%).

3. Azure Kubernetes Service (AKS)

AKS supports both pod-level and node-level auto-scaling.

Horizontal Pod Autoscaler:

Automatically adjusts the number of pods in a deployment.

kubectl autoscale deployment webapp \

—cpu-percent=50 \

—min=2 \

—max=10

Cluster Autoscaler:

Manages the number of VM nodes in your AKS cluster. Enabled via node pool configuration in ARM/Bicep or through the Azure Portal.

Best Practices for Auto-Scaling

- **Baseline Metrics:** Establish a baseline of typical performance (CPU, memory, queue length).
- **Cooldown Periods:** Prevent rapid scaling in/out by setting cooldown intervals.
- **Predictive Scaling:** Use historical data to anticipate spikes.

- **Avoid Flapping**: Set thresholds with a buffer to prevent frequent scaling.
- **Combine Rules**: Use compound conditions (CPU + queue length) for smarter decisions.
- **Minimum/Maximum Boundaries**: Always define min/max instance counts.

Load Testing: An Essential Practice

Auto-scaling is only effective if the infrastructure is tested under simulated load conditions. Load testing validates your scaling strategy and uncovers performance bottlenecks.

Azure Load Testing is a fully managed service designed to simulate high user traffic on applications.

Key Goals of Load Testing:

- Identify bottlenecks
- Validate auto-scaling triggers
- Determine resource limits
- Assess user experience under stress
- Ensure disaster recovery failover works under load

Azure Load Testing Service

Features:

- Apache JMeter test support
- Azure resource monitoring integration
- CI/CD pipeline integration
- Test from multiple regions

Creating a Load Test:

1. Prepare a JMeter test plan (.jmx).
2. Upload to Azure Load Testing.
3. Configure test parameters (users, duration, ramp-up).
4. Monitor in real-time.

Example – Azure CLI (preview):

az load test create \

—resource-group MyRG \

—name MyLoadTest \

—test-plan path/to/test.jmx \

—engine-instances 3 \

—display-name "WebApp Load Test"

Metrics to Observe:

- Response time (P50, P90, P99)
- Throughput (requests per second)
- Error rate

- CPU/memory metrics of backend services

Integrating Load Testing with CI/CD

Incorporate load tests into deployment pipelines using GitHub Actions or Azure DevOps.

Example – GitHub Workflow Snippet:

- name: Run Load Test

uses: azure/load-testing@v1

with:

loadTestConfigFile: load-test.yaml

Add test gates to stop rollouts if performance thresholds are exceeded.

Real-World Scenario: E-Commerce Application

Architecture:

- Azure App Service (frontend)
- Azure Function (checkout processing)
- Cosmos DB (inventory)
- Azure Redis (session)
- Traffic Manager (global routing)

Auto-Scaling Configuration:

- App Service: Scales out when CPU > 75%
- Azure Functions: Consumption plan handles burst
- Cosmos DB: Autoscale RU/s enabled
- Redis: Clustered for scale
- Load Test: Simulates Black Friday traffic spike

Results:

- App Service scaled from 3 to 10 instances
- Cosmos DB autoscaled from 4000 to 12000 RU/s
- 99.9% of requests under 500ms

Monitoring Auto-Scaling Performance

Use **Azure Monitor**, **Workbooks**, and **Application Insights** to observe scaling behavior.

Example KQL to visualize instance count over time:

Perf

| where ObjectName == "Processor" and CounterName == "% Processor Time"

| summarize avg(CounterValue) by bin(TimeGenerated, 5m), Computer

Create dashboards to correlate load test timing with scale events.

Summary

Auto-scaling and load testing are foundational elements in ensuring that cloud applications remain resilient, responsive, and cost-effective under varying demand. Azure provides powerful built-in support across services to automate scaling decisions based on real-time telemetry, while load testing services ensure these systems behave predictably under pressure.

A successful strategy balances intelligent scaling policies, proactive testing, and continuous monitoring. With the right configurations, your applications can seamlessly handle traffic surges, avoid outages, and deliver exceptional user experiences—at scale.

Azure Availability Zones and Sets

Designing fault-tolerant systems is a cornerstone of any cloud architecture. Azure provides two foundational constructs to achieve high availability: **Availability Zones** and **Availability Sets.** Both are designed to protect workloads from different types of failures—ranging from local hardware issues to full datacenter outages.

This section explores the differences between these two constructs, their use cases, how to configure them, and how to integrate them into enterprise-grade Azure deployments.

Understanding Fault Domains and Update Domains

Before diving into Availability Sets and Zones, it's important to understand two fundamental concepts that Azure uses to manage resiliency:

- **Fault Domain (FD)**: A group of hardware that shares a common power source and network switch. If a rack or power unit fails, all VMs in that fault domain may be affected.

- **Update Domain (UD)**: A logical group of VMs that can undergo maintenance (e.g., OS patching) together. Azure cycles through update domains one at a time to reduce downtime.

Availability Sets utilize both FDs and UDs, while **Availability Zones** offer much stronger isolation by spanning entire physical datacenters.

Availability Sets

An **Availability Set** is a logical grouping of VMs that are deployed across multiple fault and update domains. This protects against localized hardware or software failures within a single datacenter.

Characteristics:

- Deployed within a **single Azure region** and **single datacenter**.

- VMs are spread across at least **2 fault domains** and **5 update domains** by default.

- Designed to ensure that no single point of failure can affect all instances.

Service-Level Agreement (SLA):

- 99.95% uptime when using two or more VMs in an availability set.

When to Use:

- Legacy workloads that can't easily be redeployed across zones.
- Stateful services like custom databases or middleware stacks.
- Applications that run on infrastructure-as-a-service (IaaS) VMs only.

Create an Availability Set with Azure CLI:

```
az vm availability-set create \
—name MyAvailabilitySet \
—resource-group MyResourceGroup \
—platform-fault-domain-count 2 \
—platform-update-domain-count 5
```

Then create VMs within the set:

```
az vm create \
—name WebServer01 \
—availability-set MyAvailabilitySet \
—resource-group MyResourceGroup \
—image UbuntuLTS \
—admin-username azureuser \
—generate-ssh-keys
```

This ensures that the VM is automatically placed in a fault and update domain distinct from others in the same set.

Availability Zones

Availability Zones (AZs) are unique physical datacenters within an Azure region. Each zone is independent in terms of power, networking, and cooling, ensuring high resiliency against data center-level failures.

Key Features:

- Each Azure region with AZ support has **at least three separate zones.**
- Workloads can be deployed across zones for **zone-redundancy**.
- Resources like Virtual Machines, Managed Disks, Load Balancers, and Kubernetes clusters can be **zonal** or **zone-redundant.**

Service-Level Agreement (SLA):

- 99.99% uptime for VMs deployed across Availability Zones.

When to Use:

- Mission-critical applications requiring maximum uptime.
- Cloud-native applications designed for distributed deployment.

- Systems where tolerance to full datacenter failures is mandatory.

Create a Zonal VM:

az vm create \

—name WebServerZone1 \

—resource-group MyResourceGroup \

—zone 1 \

—image UbuntuLTS \

—admin-username azureuser \

—generate-ssh-keys

To deploy multiple VMs across zones, repeat with different—zone values (1, 2, 3).

Comparing Availability Sets vs Availability Zones

Feature	Availability Set	Availability Zones
Isolation Scope	Fault/Update Domain (same DC)	Separate Physical Datacenters
SLA	99.95%	99.99%
Zone Resiliency	◈	◈
Cost	Standard	Slightly Higher (due to replication)
Ideal Use Case	Legacy VMs, Stateful Apps	High Availability, Mission-Critical Apps
Regional Limitation	Available in all regions	Only in Zone-enabled Azure regions

Example Use Case:

- Use **Availability Sets** for a legacy SQL Server cluster.
- Use **Availability Zones** for microservices running on Azure Kubernetes Service.

Zone-Redundant Services

Azure natively supports zone-redundancy for many PaaS and IaaS services. This ensures that even if an entire zone becomes unavailable, the service continues uninterrupted.

Examples of Zone-Redundant Services:

- Azure Load Balancer (Standard SKU)
- Azure Public IP (Standard)

- Azure VPN Gateway (with Zonal Gateway SKU)
- Azure SQL Database (Zone Redundant Configuration)
- Azure Kubernetes Service (Zonal control plane + node pools)
- Azure Application Gateway (Zonal deployment)

Enable Zone Redundancy for SQL DB:

```
az sql db create \
—name mydb \
—server myserver \
—resource-group MyResourceGroup \
—zone-redundant true \
—edition GeneralPurpose \
—compute-model Serverless
```

Load Balancing Across Zones

For applications deployed across multiple zones, it is essential to have proper traffic distribution.

- **Azure Load Balancer (Standard)**: Distributes traffic to VMs in multiple zones.
- **Application Gateway**: Can be deployed in a zonal or zone-redundant mode.

- **Azure Front Door**: Offers global load balancing and failover across regions and zones.

Zone-aware Backend Pool for Azure Load Balancer:

```
az network lb address-pool address add \

—lb-name MyLoadBalancer \

—resource-group MyRG \

—pool-name MyBackendPool \

—vnet MyVnet \

—ip-address 10.0.0.4 \

—zone 1
```

Repeat the process for zones 2 and 3 to ensure full coverage.

Designing a Multi-Zone Architecture

Let's break down a practical, zone-resilient architecture:

1. **Frontend Web App**:

   ○ Deployed on App Service Plan with Zone Redundant setting.

   ○ Connected to Azure Front Door for global entry point.

2. **Application Layer**:

   ○ Hosted on Virtual Machine Scale Sets deployed across 3 AZs.

○ Autoscale rules based on CPU and memory metrics.

3. **Database Layer**:

○ Azure SQL Database with zone redundancy enabled.

○ Automatic failover groups to secondary region for DR.

4. **State Management**:

○ Azure Redis Cache (Premium tier with zone support).

○ Session data replicated for low-latency access.

5. **Monitoring and Resilience**:

○ Azure Monitor for alerting and metrics.

○ Application Insights with multi-region telemetry ingestion.

High Availability Pitfalls to Avoid

1. **Single-Zone Deployment**: Don't assume redundancy unless explicitly configured.
2. **No Load Balancer**: VMs across zones still need a load balancer to distribute traffic.
3. **Shared Resources**: Avoid shared disks or state between zonal VMs unless replicated.
4. **Improper Scaling Policies**: Ensure scaling and failover policies align with your zone deployment.
5. **Lack of DR Planning**: Zone redundancy helps with

availability but not necessarily disaster recovery.

Monitoring Zone Distribution and Health

Use **Azure Resource Graph** or **Azure Monitor** to confirm and track resource zone distribution.

Sample Query in Azure Resource Graph Explorer:

```
resources

| where type =~ "microsoft.compute/virtualmachines"

| project name, location, zones
```

Azure Monitor Alert Example:

Trigger an alert if all VMs in a zone become unresponsive:

```
Heartbeat

| where TimeGenerated > ago(5m)

| summarize Count = count() by Computer, _ResourceId, Location

| where Count == 0
```

Summary

Azure Availability Zones and Sets offer complementary approaches to achieving high availability. Availability Sets provide a cost-effective way to mitigate single datacenter failures, while Availability Zones deliver full datacenter isolation and SLA-backed uptime guarantees.

By thoughtfully architecting your applications using these constructs, combined with intelligent load balancing, autoscaling, and monitoring, you can ensure that your systems remain resilient, performant, and always available. The key is to match your availability strategy to the criticality of each workload component, leveraging Azure's zone and set-based capabilities to their fullest.

Business Continuity Planning

Business Continuity Planning (BCP) in Azure focuses on ensuring that critical business operations can continue during and after disruptions. These disruptions can include infrastructure failures, regional outages, cyberattacks, software bugs, or even natural disasters. While high availability and disaster recovery are core components of BCP, the full scope also includes processes, people, and policies—ensuring organizational resilience beyond just technical configurations.

This section provides a deep dive into the architecture, planning, testing, and management of business continuity in Azure, covering everything from data resilience to automated failover strategies and compliance considerations.

Core Concepts of Business Continuity

Business Continuity (BC) is the capability of an organization to maintain essential functions during a disruption.

Disaster Recovery (DR) is a subset of BC that deals with restoring IT services after a disruption.

Key metrics used in BCP:

- **RTO (Recovery Time Objective)**: How quickly a service must be restored.
- **RPO (Recovery Point Objective)**: How much data loss is acceptable.

A solid BCP ensures:

- Critical operations are defined and protected.
- Stakeholders know their roles during a disruption.
- Systems are recoverable with minimal loss.
- Compliance requirements (e.g., ISO, HIPAA, SOC) are met.

Business Continuity Architecture in Azure

Azure offers a wide set of tools and patterns to support business continuity across infrastructure, platform, and software layers.

1. Data Resiliency

- Use **Geo-Redundant Storage** (GRS) or **Geo-Zone-Redundant Storage** (GZRS) to replicate storage across regions.
- Database solutions like **Azure SQL Database**, **Cosmos DB**, and **PostgreSQL Flexible Server** offer built-in geo-replication.

2. Compute Continuity

- Use **Virtual Machine Scale Sets (VMSS)** with health probes.
- Deploy workloads across **Availability Zones**.
- For extreme cases, deploy active-active workloads across regions using **Traffic Manager** or **Azure Front Door**.

3. Networking Continuity

- Configure redundant VPN gateways.
- Use **Azure Load Balancer** and **Application Gateway** with zone redundancy.
- Use **Private Link** and **ExpressRoute Global Reach** to ensure continuity of private connections.

Designing a Resilient Business Continuity Strategy

Step 1: Identify Critical Services

Start by categorizing services based on criticality:

Service Name	Criticality	RTO	RPO
Customer Web App	High	1 hour	5 mins
Internal API	Medium	4 hours	30 mins
Admin Dashboard	Low	1 day	1 hour

This will guide the level of redundancy and recovery investment required for each service.

Step 2: Implement Cross-Region Redundancy

Use **paired regions** or custom region pairings to replicate services.

Example: SQL Database Failover Group

az sql failover-group create \

—name sqlfg \

—partner-server myserver-secondary \

—resource-group myRG \

—server myserver-primary \

—failover-policy Automatic \

—grace-period 1

This configuration automatically redirects traffic to the secondary region during outages.

Step 3: Build and Test Runbooks

Document recovery procedures for each service. Use **Azure Automation** or **Logic Apps** to codify these procedures.

Example Use Case: VM Recovery

- Triggered by Azure Monitor alert
- Executes Azure Automation Runbook
- Restores VM from snapshot or deploys replacement from image

Step 4: Use Traffic Routing Services

Azure provides several tools for global traffic management:

- **Traffic Manager**: DNS-based routing across endpoints in different regions.
- **Front Door**: Global HTTP load balancer with health probes and failover.
- **Application Gateway**: Web traffic routing within a region, with zone redundancy.

Example Traffic Manager setup:

```
az network traffic-manager profile create \
—name MyTrafficManager \
—resource-group MyRG \
—routing-method Priority \
—unique-dns-name mybcpapp \
—ttl 30 \
—monitor-path "/" \
—monitor-port 443 \
—monitor-protocol HTTPS
```

Add primary and secondary endpoints with priority levels to enable failover.

Automating Business Continuity

Automation ensures swift, consistent execution during a disruption:

1. Azure Site Recovery

- Automate failover and failback of VMs.
- Supports DR for on-premises and Azure workloads.

2. Azure Backup

- Protects VMs, SQL databases, file shares, and more.
- Retention policies can be tailored per compliance requirements.

Example – Enable Backup for a VM

```
az backup protection enable-for-vm \
—vm MyVM \
—vault-name MyRecoveryVault \
—resource-group MyRG \
—policy-name DefaultPolicy
```

3. Azure Resource Manager Templates / Bicep

- Infrastructure as Code (IaC) allows redeployment of resources quickly.
- Store DR configurations and test scripts in source control.

4. GitHub Actions or Azure DevOps Pipelines

- Create "One-click DR" pipelines to initiate resource deployment and re-routing in emergencies.

Simulating Failures and DR Drills

Regular testing of business continuity strategies is critical to ensuring real-world readiness.

Chaos Testing Tools:

- **Azure Chaos Studio**: Simulate failures such as VM crashes, latency spikes, CPU pressure.
- **Custom scripts**: Restart services, simulate region-level failover using CLI or REST APIs.

Example Chaos Studio test (VM shutdown):

```
az chaos experiment create \
—name test-shutdown \
—resource-group MyRG \
—targets vm-1 \
—actions shutdown \
—duration PT5M
```

Disaster Recovery Drills:

- Test every 3–6 months.

- Include stakeholders (technical and non-technical).
- Use runbooks, confirm RTO/RPO, and document findings.

Business Continuity Compliance and Documentation

Many industries require formal business continuity documentation for compliance:

- **Financial Services**: FCA, PCI-DSS
- **Healthcare**: HIPAA
- **Public Sector**: FedRAMP, CJIS

Key components of BCP documentation:

- Service Impact Analysis
- Recovery Objectives
- Communication Plan
- Data Retention and Archival Policies
- Audit and Test Logs

Use **Azure Policy** to enforce compliance-related configurations:

Example: Ensure Geo-Redundant Storage is enabled

```
{
"if": {
```

```
"allOf": [
{
"field": "type",
"equals": "Microsoft.Storage/storageAccounts"
},
{
"field": "Microsoft.Storage/storageAccounts/sku.name",
"notEquals": "Standard_GRS"
}
]
},
"then": {
"effect": "deny"
}
}
```

Integrating with Organizational BCP

Business continuity is not only about infrastructure—it must include people, processes, and communications.

BCP Checklist:

- ◈ Documented recovery plans for each service

- ◈ Stakeholder contacts and escalation paths
- ◈ Communication templates (press release, internal updates)
- ◈ Access to backup systems, storage, and runbooks
- ◈ Up-to-date architecture diagrams
- ◈ RTO/RPO matrix per workload

Team Involvement:

- **IT Ops**: Manages platform recovery.
- **Security Team**: Assesses risk and response to cyber incidents.
- **Compliance Officers**: Ensure alignment with regulatory obligations.
- **Executives**: Lead communication and stakeholder reassurance.

Real-World Example: Business Continuity for Healthcare App

Scenario: A critical patient management system must be online 24/7.

Architecture:

- Frontend in Azure App Service (Zone Redundant)
- Backend APIs in AKS (Multi-Zone Node Pools)

- Azure SQL with Failover Group
- Azure Front Door for global routing
- Azure Backup for nightly snapshots
- Site Recovery replicating critical VMs to secondary region

BCP Features:

- Health probes detect outages and fail traffic to the secondary region.
- "DR Runbook" in Azure Automation rebuilds core APIs in 30 minutes.
- Compliance with HIPAA via encrypted backups, role-based access, audit logs.

Summary

Business Continuity Planning in Azure goes beyond disaster recovery—it is about building a resilient culture, architecture, and process across the organization. Leveraging Azure's geo-redundant services, automation tools, and monitoring capabilities, you can ensure your systems remain available during adversity.

By clearly defining critical services, aligning with compliance, testing failover strategies regularly, and keeping documentation and training up to date, your organization can face any disruption with confidence. The goal is not just recovery, but graceful, rapid, and coordinated continuity.

Chapter 10: Hybrid and Multi-Cloud Scenarios

Azure Stack and Hybrid Architectures

In modern enterprise environments, the move to cloud computing is rarely an all-or-nothing decision. Most organizations face various constraints—be they technical, regulatory, or operational—that prevent full migration to the public cloud. Instead, they adopt a hybrid model that integrates on-premises infrastructure with cloud services. Microsoft Azure offers a comprehensive suite of tools and services to facilitate hybrid cloud deployments, with **Azure Stack** being a cornerstone of this strategy.

Understanding the Hybrid Cloud Model

The hybrid cloud model blends private (on-premises) and public cloud resources, allowing applications and data to move fluidly between the two. This offers several key benefits:

- **Regulatory Compliance**: Some data must remain on-premises due to legal requirements, particularly in finance, healthcare, and government sectors.

- **Latency and Performance**: Applications that require low latency may perform better when deployed closer to the user or device.

- **Gradual Migration**: Hybrid models enable gradual cloud adoption, reducing risk and easing transitions.

- **Business Continuity**: On-premises systems can serve as a backup or failover system in case of public cloud outages.

Introduction to Azure Stack

Azure Stack is a family of products that extend Azure services and capabilities to your environment of choice—from the data center to edge locations and remote branches. Azure Stack enables you to run Azure-consistent services on-premises, providing a unified development and operations experience.

There are three main offerings under the Azure Stack umbrella:

1. **Azure Stack Hub**: A fully integrated system for running IaaS and PaaS services on-premises.
2. **Azure Stack HCI**: A hyperconverged infrastructure solution for running virtualized workloads on-premises using Windows Server and Azure services.
3. **Azure Stack Edge**: A managed appliance for edge computing, supporting machine learning, IoT, and data processing at the edge.

Use Cases for Azure Stack

- **Disconnected Environments**: For scenarios with limited or no internet connectivity (e.g., oil rigs, military installations), Azure Stack Hub provides autonomous cloud capabilities.

- **Edge and IoT**: Azure Stack Edge allows real-time processing of data collected from edge devices, reducing the need to send large volumes to the cloud.

- **Cloud Bursting**: Applications can scale out to Azure public cloud when local capacity is exceeded.
- **Application Modernization**: Developers can build applications using Azure services on-premises and migrate them to the cloud later.

Deploying Azure Stack HCI

Azure Stack HCI (Hyperconverged Infrastructure) is built on validated hardware and Microsoft technologies like Windows Server 2022 and Azure Arc. It supports running Windows and Linux virtual machines and can be integrated with Azure for hybrid capabilities.

Here's a simplified example of deploying an Azure Stack HCI cluster:

```
# Install required PowerShell modules

Install-Module -Name Az -AllowClobber -Force

Install-Module -Name WindowsAdminCenter -Force

# Register the cluster with Azure Arc

Connect-AzAccount

$ResourceGroupName = "MyHCIGroup"

$Location = "eastus"

Register-AzStackHCI -ResourceGroupName $ResourceGroupName -Region $Location
```

Once connected to Azure, administrators can manage the cluster via the Azure Portal, apply updates, monitor usage, and deploy virtual machines through Windows Admin Center.

Azure Arc: Extending Azure Management

Azure Arc allows you to manage Windows and Linux servers, Kubernetes clusters, and data services across on-premises, multi-cloud, and edge environments. It brings services like Azure Policy, Azure Monitor, and Defender for Cloud to non-Azure environments.

Azure Arc-enabled servers can be onboarded using either the Azure Portal or a script:

```
# Download the onboarding script from Azure Portal

.\OnboardingScript.ps1
```

This registers your on-premises or third-party cloud machine with Azure Resource Manager (ARM), enabling it to be managed like any native Azure resource.

Identity and Security in Hybrid Environments

Identity and access management (IAM) is a critical aspect of hybrid architecture. Azure Active Directory (Azure AD) can be extended to on-premises environments using **Azure AD Connect**, enabling single sign-on (SSO), conditional access, and MFA across environments.

```
# Example: Synchronize users from on-prem AD to Azure AD

Start-ADSyncSyncCycle -PolicyType Delta
```

For security, tools like **Azure Security Center** and **Microsoft Defender for Cloud** can evaluate hybrid workloads and suggest security hardening recommendations.

Application Development in Hybrid Setups

Developers can use the same set of tools (e.g., Visual Studio, Azure DevOps, GitHub Actions) to build and deploy applications to both Azure and Azure Stack environments. Services like **Azure App Services**, **Functions**, and **Kubernetes** are available in Azure Stack Hub, enabling a truly consistent experience.

Here's a basic example using Azure CLI to deploy a web app to Azure App Service on Azure Stack:

az login—endpoint-resource-manager "https://management.local.azurestack.external/"

az webapp up—name myhybridwebapp—resource-group MyHybridRG—plan MyAppServicePlan

Data Considerations in Hybrid Environments

Data residency, governance, and sovereignty are key drivers for hybrid architectures. Azure Stack allows organizations to maintain sensitive data locally while integrating with Azure data services like:

- **Azure Backup**
- **Azure Site Recovery**
- **Azure Monitor**
- **Azure Blob Storage (via Edge)**

Organizations must classify data and define policies for how data is handled across environments, ensuring compliance with regulations such as GDPR or HIPAA.

Hybrid DevOps and CI/CD

Hybrid DevOps enables streamlined CI/CD pipelines that target both Azure and Azure Stack. Tools like **Azure DevOps** and **GitHub Actions** can deploy artifacts to either environment using environment-specific configuration.

Example GitHub Actions YAML snippet for a hybrid deployment:

```
jobs:

deploy:

runs-on: ubuntu-latest

steps:

- name: Checkout

uses: actions/checkout@v2

- name: Login to Azure Stack

run: az login—service-principal—username ${{ secrets.CLIENT_ID }}—password ${{ secrets.CLIENT_SECRET }}—tenant ${{ secrets.TENANT_ID }}—endpoint-resource-manager
https://management.local.azurestack.external/

- name: Deploy app

run: az webapp deploy—name myhybridwebapp—src-path ./app.zip—resource-group MyHybridRG
```

Challenges and Best Practices

While hybrid architectures are powerful, they come with complexity. Key challenges include:

- **Network latency and bandwidth** between on-prem and cloud
- **Identity federation** and synchronization
- **Unified monitoring** across environments
- **Consistent policy enforcement**

Best practices include:

- Use **Azure Arc** for centralized management.
- Adopt **Infrastructure as Code** (IaC) with Bicep or Terraform for consistent deployments.
- Ensure **RBAC and governance policies** are uniformly applied.
- Establish **monitoring baselines** and define SLAs for hybrid workloads.
- Regularly update and patch both cloud and on-prem components.

Conclusion

Hybrid cloud architecture is not just a transitional phase—it's a strategic choice for many organizations. With services like Azure Stack Hub, HCI, Edge, and Azure Arc, Microsoft enables enterprises to meet regulatory, performance, and operational requirements without sacrificing innovation. A well-architected hybrid solution offers the agility of the cloud while respecting the realities of enterprise IT. By mastering hybrid tools and best practices, organizations can confidently navigate complex environments and build resilient, scalable solutions for the future.

Integrating with AWS and GCP

As enterprises grow and diversify, many are choosing to adopt a **multi-cloud strategy**—leveraging services from more than one cloud provider, such as Microsoft Azure, Amazon Web Services (AWS), and Google Cloud Platform (GCP). This approach provides benefits such as avoiding vendor lock-in, enhancing resiliency, and taking advantage of best-in-class services from each provider.

In this section, we will explore the rationale behind multi-cloud architectures, challenges in integrating Azure with AWS and GCP, and real-world solutions to ensure smooth interoperation. We'll also dive into identity federation, cross-cloud networking, shared observability, and CI/CD pipelines that span multiple cloud environments.

Why Multi-Cloud?

Organizations may choose a multi-cloud strategy for several reasons:

- **Risk Mitigation**: Relying on one provider can lead to service disruptions; spreading workloads reduces risk.
- **Cost Optimization**: Providers offer different pricing models—multi-cloud allows selection based on cost efficiency.

- **Best-of-Breed Services**: GCP might offer the best data analytics tools, AWS may excel in compute performance, and Azure might provide enterprise-grade hybrid support.

- **Regulatory Requirements**: Some jurisdictions require data sovereignty that may only be achievable through multiple regional providers.

Foundational Concepts for Integration

Before integrating Azure with AWS and GCP, organizations must align on a few foundational areas:

- **Identity and Access Management (IAM)**

- **Networking and Connectivity**

- **Security and Compliance**

- **Resource Management and Monitoring**

- **Application Deployment Strategy**

Let's address each of these in detail.

Identity Federation Across Clouds

Maintaining separate identity systems across clouds leads to complexity and potential security gaps. Azure Active Directory (AAD) can act as a central identity provider across AWS and GCP, using **SAML 2.0** or **OpenID Connect** to federate identities.

Federating Azure AD with AWS IAM

Azure AD can be configured to enable single sign-on to AWS via SAML. The setup involves:

1. Creating an enterprise application in Azure AD.
2. Configuring SAML-based SSO.
3. Assigning roles via claim rules and mappings.

Example SAML claim for AWS:

```
<AttributeStatement>

<Attribute Name="https://aws.amazon.com/SAML/Attributes/Role">

<AttributeValue>arn:aws:iam::123456789012:role/AzureADRole,arn:aws:iam::123456789012:saml-provider/AzureAD</AttributeValue>

</Attribute>

</AttributeStatement>
```

This enables Azure AD users to access the AWS Management Console and CLI using their corporate credentials.

Federating Azure AD with GCP IAM

GCP supports federation via **Workforce Identity Federation**, allowing Azure AD users to access GCP resources without requiring a Google account.

Basic steps include:

1. Creating a Workforce Identity Pool in GCP.
2. Linking Azure AD as an OIDC provider.
3. Mapping Azure AD groups or claims to GCP roles.

This ensures a unified identity plane across all three platforms.

Networking Between Clouds

Networking is one of the more complex aspects of multi-cloud integration. The key challenge is securely connecting workloads across providers with minimal latency.

Options for Connectivity

- **IPsec VPNs**: Traditional method using site-to-site tunnels. Each cloud provides VPN gateways.
- **Transit Gateways**: AWS and Azure support transit hubs to centralize connectivity.
- **Third-Party SD-WAN Solutions**: Vendors like Cisco and Fortinet offer cross-cloud networking fabrics.
- **Private Interconnects**: Azure ExpressRoute, AWS Direct Connect, and GCP Cloud Interconnect offer private, low-latency links.

Azure to AWS VPN Example

```
# On Azure: Create local network gateway pointing to AWS VPN endpoint

az network local-gateway create \
```

```
—name AWSGateway \
—resource-group MultiCloudRG \
—gateway-ip-address <AWS_PUBLIC_IP> \
—local-address-prefixes <AWS_CIDR_BLOCK>
# Create VPN connection from Azure to AWS
az network vpn-connection create \
—name ToAWS \
—resource-group MultiCloudRG \
—vnet-gateway1 AzureGateway \
—local-gateway2 AWSGateway \
—shared-key "SecureSharedKey123"
```

This can be mirrored with similar configurations on the AWS side.

Unified Monitoring and Observability

Managing telemetry and observability across multiple clouds requires a platform-agnostic approach.

Strategies

- **Centralized Logging**: Export logs from AWS CloudWatch and GCP Stackdriver to Azure Monitor or a third-party system like Splunk or Datadog.

- **Metrics Aggregation**: Use Prometheus and Grafana to collect and visualize metrics across cloud environments.

- **Distributed Tracing**: Implement OpenTelemetry in applications to capture traces regardless of where the workload runs.

Azure Monitor Ingestion Example

{

"time": "2025-04-20T13:05:00Z",

"resourceId": "/subscriptions/xxxx/resourceGroups/MultiCloudRG/providers/Microsoft.Compute/virtualMachines/web-vm",

"category": "CustomLogs",

"operationName": "AppLogEvent",

"properties": {

"cloud": "AWS",

"message": "EC2 instance started",

"level": "Information"

}

}

This log, ingested via the Azure Monitor API, provides cross-cloud visibility.

CI/CD Across Clouds

DevOps workflows in a multi-cloud world must handle deployment pipelines targeting different clouds while maintaining consistency.

GitHub Actions with Multi-Cloud Targets

A single pipeline can deploy infrastructure and applications to Azure, AWS, and GCP:

```
jobs:

deploy-azure:

runs-on: ubuntu-latest

steps:

- uses: azure/login@v1

with:

creds: ${{ secrets.AZURE_CREDENTIALS }}

deploy-aws:

runs-on: ubuntu-latest

steps:

- uses: aws-actions/configure-aws-credentials@v1

with:

aws-access-key-id: ${{ secrets.AWS_ACCESS_KEY }}

aws-secret-access-key: ${{ secrets.AWS_SECRET_KEY }}
```

region: us-east-1

deploy-gcp:

runs-on: ubuntu-latest

steps:

- uses: google-github-actions/auth@v0

with:

credentials_json: ${{ secrets.GCP_CREDENTIALS }}

Each job handles deployment logic for its respective platform, enabling seamless multi-cloud delivery.

Resource Tagging and Governance

Maintaining governance across clouds is essential for cost control, security, and compliance.

Common Tagging Scheme

Adopt a uniform tagging taxonomy for all resources:

Tag Name	Description
env	Environment (prod, dev, test)
owner	Responsible team or individual
cost-center	Billing code or department
compliance	Regulatory requirement identifier

Ensure that tagging policies are enforced using tools like:

- Azure Policy
- AWS Organizations Service Control Policies (SCP)

- GCP Organization Policies

Cost Management Across Clouds

Tracking and optimizing cloud spend becomes increasingly difficult in multi-cloud environments.

Tools and Techniques

- **Azure Cost Management + Billing**: Now supports AWS integration.
- **CloudHealth by VMware**: Multi-cloud cost visibility and optimization.
- **Kubecost**: Tracks Kubernetes costs across clusters in any cloud.

Best practices:

- Define budgets per environment and enforce alerts.
- Monitor idle resources and right-size regularly.
- Use reserved instances or savings plans where applicable.

Security Considerations

Security should be holistic and not siloed by provider.

Common Practices

- Implement **Zero Trust** models across all platforms.

- Use **centralized secrets management** (e.g., HashiCorp Vault).
- Regularly run **vulnerability scans and compliance audits** on all assets.

Azure Sentinel for Multi-Cloud Security

Azure Sentinel can ingest logs from AWS and GCP to enable unified security operations.

Example data connector setup:

```
New-AzSentinelDataConnector -Name "AWSCloudTrail" -WorkspaceName "sentinel-workspace" -ConnectorType "AmazonWebServicesCloudTrail"
```

Challenges and Recommendations

Challenges

- Diverse APIs and SDKs increase complexity.
- Identity sprawl if not centrally managed.
- Difficulties in achieving consistent security policies.

Recommendations

- Standardize DevOps toolchains to abstract cloud differences.
- Favor open standards and containerized workloads.

- Use **cloud-agnostic IaC tools** like Terraform for infrastructure provisioning.
- Build internal **cloud broker layers** that abstract provider-specific logic.

Conclusion

Integrating Azure with AWS and GCP requires careful planning, robust architecture, and sound governance. However, the strategic advantages of flexibility, resilience, and innovation make multi-cloud an attractive option for modern enterprises. With services like Azure Arc, Identity Federation, centralized observability, and multi-cloud CI/CD pipelines, organizations can unlock the full potential of the cloud while maintaining control and compliance. The key lies in treating each cloud as a component of a larger system, not as isolated silos, and in establishing a unifying strategy that transcends platform boundaries.

Multi-Cloud Governance Strategies

As enterprises scale across cloud platforms like Azure, AWS, and GCP, maintaining governance becomes both critical and challenging. Without a robust multi-cloud governance strategy, organizations risk uncontrolled costs, compliance violations, and inconsistent security postures. Governance is the foundation for operational stability and risk management, especially in multi-cloud environments where services, billing models, and access controls differ between providers.

This section delves into comprehensive governance approaches tailored for multi-cloud ecosystems, emphasizing policy standardization, identity governance, financial controls, security and compliance, and architectural consistency.

Principles of Multi-Cloud Governance

Before diving into tooling and implementation, it's essential to understand the fundamental principles that should guide a multi-cloud governance strategy:

- **Unified Policy Enforcement**: Governance rules must apply consistently across all cloud providers.
- **Decentralized Execution with Central Oversight**: Teams can operate independently, but governance and audit must be centralized.
- **Visibility and Accountability**: Every resource, deployment, and identity should be tracked and attributable.
- **Security by Design**: Compliance and security controls should be embedded into workflows, not bolted on afterward.
- **Automation and Scale**: Governance mechanisms should scale via automation, not manual oversight.

Standardizing Policies Across Cloud Providers

Each cloud provider has its own method for enforcing policies:

- **Azure**: Azure Policy
- **AWS**: Service Control Policies (SCP) and AWS Config
- **GCP**: Organization Policy Service

To standardize governance across providers, organizations can define a **cloud policy baseline** that is translated into provider-specific implementations.

Example: Enforcing Region Restrictions

Business Policy: "All production resources must be deployed in approved regions only."

Azure Implementation (via Azure Policy):

```
{
"if": {
"not": {
"field": "location",
"in": ["eastus", "westeurope"]
}
},
"then": {
"effect": "deny"
}
}
```

AWS Implementation (via SCP):

```
{
"Version": "2012-10-17",
```

```
"Statement": [
{
"Effect": "Deny",
"Action": "*",
"Resource": "*",
"Condition": {
"StringNotEquals": {
"aws:RequestedRegion": ["us-east-1", "eu-west-1"]
}
}
}
]
}
```

GCP Implementation (via Organization Policy):

```
{
"constraint": "constraints/gcp.resourceLocations",
"listPolicy": {
"allowedValues": [
"in:us-east1",
"in:europe-west1"
```

```
]
}
}
```

The translation of a single business rule into three implementations illustrates why a governance strategy should start from abstract, provider-agnostic policies.

Identity and Access Governance

In a multi-cloud world, managing identity and access becomes exponentially more complex. Without tight controls, users may accumulate permissions across clouds, leading to overprivileged accounts and compliance gaps.

Best Practices

- **Centralize Identity with Azure AD**: Use Azure AD B2B or B2C to federate identities across platforms.
- **Adopt Role-Based Access Control (RBAC)**: Define roles by job function and enforce least privilege.
- **Review Access Regularly**: Set up access review policies in Azure AD and AWS IAM Access Analyzer.
- **Automate Identity Provisioning**: Use SCIM (System for Cross-domain Identity Management) to synchronize users across clouds.

Example: Azure AD Conditional Access Policy

```
New-AzureADMSConditionalAccessPolicy `
```

```
-DisplayName "Block Access from Unsupported Locations" `
-State "enabled" `
-Conditions @{
Locations = @{
IncludeLocations = @("All")
ExcludeLocations = @("TrustedLocationID")
}
} `
-GrantControls @{
BuiltInControls = @("Block")
}
```

This policy blocks access from untrusted locations, which can also be implemented using AWS IAM Conditions and GCP VPC Service Controls.

Cost and Budget Governance

Controlling and forecasting costs across multiple cloud platforms is a critical governance concern. Without proper tools and policies, cloud spend can spiral out of control due to overprovisioning, idle resources, or inconsistent procurement strategies.

Techniques for Financial Governance

1. **Set Budgets and Alerts per Project and Environment**
2. **Use Cost Tagging Standards**

3. **Implement Chargeback/Showback Models**
4. **Use Cloud Cost Management Tools**

Azure Example: Budget Setup

```
New-AzConsumptionBudget `

-ResourceGroupName "FinanceRG" `

-Name "ProdBudget" `

-Amount 10000 `

-Category "Cost" `

-TimeGrain "Monthly" `

-StartDate "2025-01-01" `

-EndDate "2025-12-31"
```

AWS Example: Budgets

AWS Budgets can be configured via the console or using the AWS Budgets API to alert when usage exceeds defined thresholds.

GCP Example: Budgets API

```
{

"budget": {

"displayName": "TeamA Monthly Budget",

"budgetFilter": {
```

```
"projects": ["projects/my-project-id"]
},
"amount": {
"specifiedAmount": {
"currencyCode": "USD",
"units": "5000"
}
}
}
}
```

Security and Compliance Governance

A core element of governance is ensuring security and compliance, particularly when dealing with sensitive data in regulated industries like healthcare or finance.

Unified Security Controls

- **Use Azure Security Center, AWS Security Hub, and GCP Security Command Center**
- **Automate Compliance Checks with CIS Benchmarks**
- **Integrate with SIEMs like Azure Sentinel or Splunk**

- **Run Regular Penetration Testing and Vulnerability Scans**

Azure Example: Built-In Initiative

Azure has built-in policy initiatives for standards like **ISO 27001** and **NIST 800-53**. Assigning them at the subscription or management group level ensures consistent enforcement.

```
New-AzPolicyAssignment `
-Name "NIST-Mandatory" `
-PolicyDefinitionId "/providers/Microsoft.Authorization/policySetDefinitions/NIST_SP_800-53_R4" `
-Scope "/subscriptions/xxxx"
```

Multi-Cloud Security Logging

To create a unified security view, forward logs from all platforms to a central location (Azure Sentinel, AWS OpenSearch, GCP Cloud Logging):

```
# Azure example: Log forwarding to Sentinel
az monitor diagnostic-settings create \
—name "ForwardToSentinel" \
—resource "/subscriptions/.../resourceGroups/.../providers/Microsoft.Compute/virtualMachines/myVM" \
—workspace "/subscriptions/.../resourceGroups/.../providers/Microsoft.OperationalInsights/workspaces/mySentinelWorkspace" \
```

—logs '[{"category": "AuditLogs","enabled": true}]'

Infrastructure as Code for Governance

A unified governance strategy should extend to **Infrastructure as Code (IaC)**. IaC tools like Terraform and Pulumi support multi-cloud deployments and governance by codifying standards.

Example Terraform Module: Enforce Tagging Across Clouds

```
variable "required_tags" {

type = map(string)

default = {

environment = "prod"

cost_center = "12345"

}

}

resource "azurerm_resource_group" "rg" {

name = "multi-cloud-rg"

location = "eastus"

tags = var.required_tags

}
```

This pattern can be replicated across AWS (aws_instance) and GCP (google_compute_instance), ensuring tagging policies are always enforced.

Organizational Structures and Guardrails

Larger organizations often implement **landing zones** and **guardrails** to enforce governance at scale.

Azure: Management Groups and Blueprints

- Use Management Groups to group subscriptions by environment or business unit.
- Assign policies and role assignments at the Management Group level.

AWS: Organizations and Control Tower

- AWS Organizations helps enforce Service Control Policies (SCP) across accounts.
- AWS Control Tower offers a prebuilt landing zone framework with governance baked in.

GCP: Folders and Organization Policies

- Use the Organization Node and Folders for policy inheritance.
- Define constraints at the folder or organization level for consistent application.

Audit and Reporting

Continuous audit trails are necessary to prove governance compliance to internal and external stakeholders.

- Enable **CloudTrail** in AWS, **Activity Logs** in Azure, and **Audit Logs** in GCP.

- Aggregate logs in a central data lake for forensic analysis.

- Use tools like Power BI, Looker, or Grafana for dashboarding compliance KPIs.

Conclusion

Governance in a multi-cloud world is not about replicating rules across platforms—it's about establishing a **cohesive framework** that abstracts complexity and enforces consistency. With proper identity federation, policy translation, cost controls, security postures, and automation through Infrastructure as Code, organizations can effectively govern their cloud environments. This governance provides the foundation for operational resilience, regulatory compliance, and strategic innovation across Azure, AWS, and GCP.

Unified Management with Azure Arc

Managing a dispersed ecosystem of workloads across Azure, on-premises data centers, edge locations, AWS, and GCP is a significant challenge for IT operations. Traditional cloud management tools often lack the extensibility to support multi-environment visibility, governance, and automation. This is where **Azure Arc** becomes a game-changer, enabling organizations to unify the management of diverse infrastructure under the Azure umbrella.

Azure Arc extends Azure management capabilities to any infrastructure. It brings services like **Azure Policy**, **Azure**

Monitor, **Azure Defender**, and **Azure Resource Graph** to resources hosted outside of Azure, delivering a truly consistent control plane across the cloud and on-premises environments.

Core Capabilities of Azure Arc

Azure Arc enables several key features:

- **Resource Organization**: Onboard non-Azure resources into Azure Resource Manager (ARM) for centralized visibility.

- **Governance and Compliance**: Apply Azure Policy and role-based access control (RBAC) to all Arc-enabled resources.

- **Monitoring and Insights**: Send logs and metrics to Azure Monitor regardless of resource location.

- **Security and Threat Protection**: Use Microsoft Defender for Cloud across hybrid and multi-cloud environments.

- **Configuration Management**: Apply guest configurations, script extensions, and VM policies from Azure.

- **Data Services Anywhere**: Deploy Azure SQL and PostgreSQL managed instances on any infrastructure.

Let's explore each of these in depth.

Onboarding Resources with Azure Arc

To manage a machine with Azure Arc, you first install the Azure Arc agent on that machine and register it with Azure.

Prerequisites

- Azure CLI
- Access to the target server (Windows or Linux)
- Contributor role in the target Azure subscription

Example: Onboarding a Linux VM

```
# Log in to Azure

az login

# Create a resource group

az group create—name ArcGroup—location eastus

# Onboard Linux server

az connectedmachine onboard \

—resource-group ArcGroup \

—location eastus \

—name arc-linux-vm \

—os-type Linux \

—client-token "$(az connectedmachine generate-token)"
```

The onboarded server now appears as a first-class citizen in the Azure portal with resource ID, tags, and policies.

Windows VM Onboarding via PowerShell

```
Connect-AzAccount

$resourceGroup = "ArcGroup"

$location = "eastus"

$machineName = "arc-win-vm"

Install-AzConnectedMachine `

-ResourceGroupName $resourceGroup `

-Location $location `

-Name $machineName
```

After onboarding, you can manage both VMs using the same tooling as native Azure VMs.

Governance with Azure Policy and RBAC

Once external resources are onboarded, Azure Arc enables the application of Azure-native policies and access controls.

Applying Policies

You can apply compliance policies to ensure all VMs—whether in Azure, AWS, or on-prem—adhere to standards.

```
az policy assignment create \

—name "EnforceMonitoringAgent" \
```

—scope "/subscriptions/<sub_id>/resourceGroups/ArcGroup" \

—policy "/providers/Microsoft.Authorization/policyDefinitions/<policy_id>"

This ensures that all Arc-enabled machines must have the Azure Monitor agent installed.

Role-Based Access Control

You can assign RBAC roles to Arc resources to maintain consistent access governance.

az role assignment create \

—assignee user@domain.com \

—role "Reader" \

—scope "/subscriptions/<sub_id>/resourceGroups/ArcGroup/providers/Microsoft.HybridCompute/machines/arc-linux-vm"

This gives the user read-only access to a Linux server hosted in AWS or on-premises, governed through Azure.

Unified Monitoring with Azure Monitor and Log Analytics

Azure Arc allows seamless integration with Azure Monitor, centralizing observability for all infrastructure.

Enabling Monitoring

Once Arc-enabled, you can install the Log Analytics agent on the VM to start collecting metrics and logs.

```
az monitor log-analytics workspace create \

—resource-group ArcGroup \

—workspace-name ArcWorkspace

az monitor diagnostics settings create \

—name "ArcVMMonitoring" \

—resource "/subscriptions/<sub_id>/resourceGroups/ArcGroup/providers/Microsoft.HybridCompute/machines/arc-linux-vm" \

—workspace "/subscriptions/<sub_id>/resourceGroups/ArcGroup/providers/Microsoft.OperationalInsights/workspaces/ArcWorkspace" \

—logs '[{"category": "Syslog","enabled": true}]'
```

Now, logs from an Arc-enabled VM in Google Cloud can appear alongside Azure VMs in the same Log Analytics workspace.

Security with Microsoft Defender for Cloud

Security posture management is simplified using Microsoft Defender for Cloud with Azure Arc. Arc enables Defender to assess, report, and respond to threats on hybrid and multi-cloud workloads.

Enabling Defender on Arc Resources

```
az security auto-provisioning-setting update \

—name "default" \

—auto-provision "On"
```

```
az security pricing create \
—name "VirtualMachines" \
—tier "Standard"
```

Once enabled, Defender performs continuous assessments of all onboarded resources, offering threat alerts and recommendations.

Guest Configuration and Desired State

Arc supports guest configuration policies, allowing you to enforce configurations such as time zone, security settings, or installed applications.

Example: Enforce Time Zone on Arc-Enabled Windows VMs

```
az policy assignment create \
—name "EnforceTimeZone" \
—policy "timeZonePolicyDefinition" \
—scope "/subscriptions/<sub_id>/resourceGroups/ArcGroup"
```

You can also push PowerShell or Bash scripts using **Custom Script Extension**, providing centralized management of automation tasks.

Deploying Azure Data Services Anywhere

Azure Arc is not just about management—it also brings platform services to your infrastructure. With **Azure Arc-enabled Data Services**, you can deploy Azure SQL Managed Instance or PostgreSQL Hyperscale on Kubernetes clusters in AWS, GCP, or on-prem.

Prerequisites

- Kubernetes cluster (e.g., Amazon EKS, Google GKE)
- Azure Arc Data Controller
- Azure subscription

Example Deployment

```
# Connect Kubernetes cluster
az connectedk8s connect \
—name arc-k8s-cluster \
—resource-group ArcGroup \
—location eastus
# Install data controller
az arcdata dc create \
—name arc-dc \
—k8s-namespace arc \
—resource-group ArcGroup \
—connectivity-mode indirect \
—location eastus
# Deploy SQL Managed Instance
az arcdata sql mi create \
```

—name arc-sqlmi \

—resource-group ArcGroup \

—k8s-namespace arc \

—location eastus

This deployment gives you the benefits of Azure SQL—including auto-patching, high availability, and Azure Monitor integration—without leaving your existing infrastructure.

Arc-Enabled Kubernetes for Multi-Cloud Containers

Azure Arc can manage Kubernetes clusters outside of Azure (e.g., EKS, GKE, OpenShift).

Onboarding a Kubernetes Cluster

az connectedk8s connect \

—name eks-prod-cluster \

—resource-group ArcGroup \

—location eastus

Now, Azure Policy, Monitor, Defender, and GitOps (via Flux) can be applied to the cluster, unifying its governance with Azure-native services.

GitOps Deployment with Arc

az k8sconfiguration create \

```
—name flux-config \

—cluster-name eks-prod-cluster \

—resource-group ArcGroup \

—cluster-type connectedClusters \

—operator-namespace cluster-config \

—operator-instance-name flux \

—repository-url https://github.com/org/repo \

—scope cluster
```

This applies GitOps configurations to your non-Azure clusters via Azure Arc, promoting DevOps consistency.

Centralized Inventory and Tagging

Arc-enabled resources can be inventoried and queried using **Azure Resource Graph**, and tagging can be applied for cost and governance purposes.

```
az resource tag \

—ids "/subscriptions/<sub_id>/resourceGroups/ArcGroup/providers/Microsoft.HybridCompute/machines/arc-linux-vm" \

—tags environment=production owner=devops
```

Querying Arc resources with Resource Graph:

```
Resources

| where type =~ "microsoft.hybridcompute/machines"

| project name, location, resourceGroup, tags
```

Challenges and Considerations

Despite its power, Azure Arc requires careful planning:

- **Network Access**: Ensure outbound connectivity to Azure is available.
- **Agent Overhead**: Some performance impact from telemetry and monitoring agents.
- **Pricing**: Azure Arc is free for resource registration, but additional services (Monitor, Defender, SQL MI) incur charges.
- **Skill Alignment**: Teams must become familiar with Azure-native tooling to effectively manage Arc resources.

Best Practices

- Use **Azure Management Groups** and **Tags** for logical organization.
- Group policies by **resource type** (VM, SQL, Kubernetes).
- Regularly audit Arc-enabled resources via Azure Resource Graph.
- Integrate **Azure Lighthouse** for MSP/multi-tenant visibility.
- Automate onboarding via ARM templates, Bicep, or Terraform.

Conclusion

Azure Arc bridges the gap between on-premises, edge, and multi-cloud infrastructure by bringing Azure's management layer everywhere. With its deep integration into Azure Policy, Defender, Monitor, and RBAC, Arc transforms how IT operations manage diverse infrastructure. Whether you're running legacy servers in a data center, containers on AWS, or databases at the edge, Azure Arc ensures they can all be governed, secured, and monitored from one unified platform. It's a vital enabler for organizations embracing a hybrid or multi-cloud future.

Chapter 11: Real-World Case Studies and Architectures

Enterprise Migration to Azure

Enterprise migration to Azure is a transformative journey that modernizes infrastructure, enhances agility, improves scalability, and enables cost optimization. Migrating large-scale legacy systems to Azure, however, is far more complex than simple lift-and-shift efforts. It requires careful planning, stakeholder alignment, workload assessment, governance structuring, and iterative modernization. This section offers a deep dive into a typical enterprise migration project, detailing tools, strategies, patterns, and a real-world architectural example to anchor the theory in practice.

Key Phases of Enterprise Cloud Migration

Azure's Cloud Adoption Framework (CAF) outlines a robust, phased approach that enterprises can use as a migration blueprint. The stages include:

1. **Strategy**
2. **Plan**
3. **Ready**
4. **Migrate**
5. **Innovate**
6. **Govern**
7. **Manage**

These phases ensure a holistic migration journey that aligns technology with business outcomes.

Strategy

The strategy phase defines business motivations and expected outcomes. Stakeholders identify financial goals, scalability objectives, innovation opportunities, and regulatory requirements. Outcomes from this stage include:

- Business justification and ROI models
- Executive sponsorship
- Migration KPIs
- Preliminary workload inventory

Plan

Planning revolves around workload assessment and readiness evaluation. Microsoft's **Azure Migrate** tool plays a critical role here.

```
# Deploy Azure Migrate project

az migrate project create \

—resource-group MigrationRG \

—location eastus \

—name EnterpriseMigrationProject
```

Assessment tools collect performance data, dependencies, OS compatibility, and licensing constraints. This phase includes:

- Application discovery and grouping

- TCO calculations and budget planning
- Migration wave definition

Ready

This phase prepares the Azure landing zone. It includes:

- Subscription and management group hierarchy
- Role-based access control (RBAC)
- Policy enforcement (via Azure Policy)
- Resource naming and tagging standards
- Network and identity integration (e.g., hybrid DNS, Azure AD Connect)

Migrate

Depending on the workload profile, organizations can opt for various migration strategies:

- **Rehost** (Lift and Shift)
- **Refactor** (Containerization, minimal code changes)
- **Rearchitect** (Decompose monoliths into microservices)
- **Rebuild** (Full rewrite using PaaS)

Azure offers tools such as:

- **Azure Migrate: Server Migration**
- **Database Migration Service (DMS)**
- **App Service Migration Assistant**
- **Azure Site Recovery (ASR)**

Example: Rehosting a VMware VM using Azure Migrate:

```
az migrate server replication create \
—project-name EnterpriseMigrationProject \
—resource-group MigrationRG \
—machine-name vm01 \
—target-resource-group VMsRG \
—target-vnet AzureVNet
```

Innovate

Post-migration, enterprises can modernize applications using Azure-native services:

- Replace IIS apps with **App Services**
- Break monoliths using **AKS** or **Azure Functions**
- Introduce **Event Grid** and **Service Bus** for event-driven architecture
- Integrate **Azure Cognitive Services** for enhanced user experiences

Govern

Establishing a governance foundation ensures control, compliance, and cost optimization.

- Enforce **resource consistency** via tagging policies
- Audit deployments using **Azure Policy**
- Apply **cost management alerts and budgets**
- Monitor with **Azure Security Center** and **Defender for Cloud**

Manage

Ongoing management uses Azure-native and integrated third-party tools for:

- Monitoring (Azure Monitor, Log Analytics)
- Backup (Azure Backup)
- Disaster recovery (Azure Site Recovery)
- Patch management (Update Management Center)

Real-World Migration Example: Financial Services Company

Let's walk through the architecture and process of migrating a mid-size financial services provider to Azure.

Business Context

The company operated three data centers hosting over 200 virtual machines, with SQL Server, Oracle, and custom Java applications. Goals included:

- Reducing on-prem data center footprint
- Improving disaster recovery capabilities
- Meeting GDPR and PCI-DSS compliance
- Enabling DevOps and automation

Architectural Decisions

Landing Zone Design:

- **Management Groups**: Organized by production, staging, and dev
- **Subscriptions**: Per environment and department
- **Networking**: Hub-and-spoke model with Azure Firewall and VPN Gateway
- **Identity**: Hybrid Azure AD with conditional access and PIM (Privileged Identity Management)

Migration Strategy:

- Phase 1: Lift-and-shift mission-critical VMs
- Phase 2: Modernize applications to PaaS

- Phase 3: Containerize backend services

Tools Used

- **Azure Migrate**: For discovery and replication
- **Database Migration Service**: To move SQL Server and Oracle databases
- **App Service Environment**: For secure, scalable PaaS hosting
- **Azure Monitor**: For post-migration observability

Azure Landing Zone Reference Implementation

```
module "hub_network" {

source = "Azure/hub-network/azurerm"

version = "~> 2.0"

location = "eastus"

vnet_address_space = ["10.0.0.0/16"]

subnets = {

firewall = { address_prefixes = ["10.0.1.0/24"] }

gateway = { address_prefixes = ["10.0.2.0/24"] }

}

}

module "vm_rg" {
```

```
source = "Azure/resource-group/azurerm"

name = "ProdVMs"

location = "eastus"

}
```

Results

- Reduced infrastructure costs by 32% in Year 1
- Achieved 99.99% uptime with Availability Zones
- Streamlined deployments with CI/CD pipelines in Azure DevOps
- Enabled real-time fraud detection using Azure Event Hub and Stream Analytics

Lessons Learned

1. **Pilot First**: Start with non-critical workloads to refine the migration process.
2. **Data Dependencies**: Application dependencies on shared databases often delay migration—map them early.
3. **Communication is Key**: Include business units in planning to prevent resistance and shadow IT.
4. **Automation is Critical**: Use IaC, pipelines, and runbooks to scale.
5. **Review Licensing**: Use Azure Hybrid Benefit and bring-your-own-license (BYOL) models where applicable.

Common Pitfalls to Avoid

- **Underestimating Network Complexity**: Plan for hybrid DNS, express routes, and subnetting strategies.

- **Ignoring Identity Early**: Azure AD strategy must be defined early to avoid ACL and RBAC chaos.

- **Inadequate Cost Monitoring**: Always implement tagging and cost controls at the start.

- **Lack of Governance**: Set guardrails before teams start deploying.

- **Skipping Training**: Ensure your ops and dev teams are trained in Azure services and automation tools.

Conclusion

Enterprise migration to Azure is a journey that goes far beyond simply moving VMs. It's an opportunity to rethink, refactor, and rebuild your IT operations into a more agile, secure, and cost-efficient framework. With proper planning, phased execution, and strategic use of Azure-native tools like Azure Migrate, Policy, Arc, and DevOps, even complex environments can be transformed. The real-world case presented shows how thoughtful migration drives measurable business value and paves the way for long-term digital transformation.

Cloud-Native Applications in Practice

Cloud-native applications represent a modern paradigm for building and deploying scalable, resilient, and agile software systems using cloud technologies. Unlike traditional monolithic applications, cloud-native solutions are built from the ground up to leverage the full potential of cloud platforms—embracing microservices, containerization, DevOps automation, managed services, and continuous delivery.

In this section, we explore what it means to design, build, deploy, and manage cloud-native applications in Azure. We break down architectural patterns, design principles, tooling choices, deployment practices, and common challenges—all illustrated through practical, production-grade examples.

What Makes an Application Cloud-Native?

Cloud-native applications typically exhibit the following characteristics:

- **Microservices Architecture**: Decomposed into loosely coupled, independently deployable services.
- **API-First Design**: Services expose well-defined APIs for interaction.
- **Containerization**: Each microservice is packaged with its dependencies.
- **DevOps Practices**: CI/CD pipelines, infrastructure as code, automated testing.
- **Elastic Scalability**: Able to scale horizontally across nodes or regions.
- **Observability**: Built-in telemetry, logging, tracing, and monitoring.

- **Resilience and Fault Tolerance**: Gracefully handle failures and self-heal.

Azure provides a comprehensive set of tools to support all these pillars.

Core Azure Services for Cloud-Native Applications

- **Azure Kubernetes Service (AKS)**: Managed Kubernetes for running containerized microservices.
- **Azure Container Apps**: Serverless containers for event-driven architectures.
- **Azure Functions**: Event-based, serverless computing.
- **Azure API Management (APIM)**: Secure, publish, and analyze APIs.
- **Azure Cosmos DB**: Globally distributed NoSQL database.
- **Azure Key Vault**: Secure secrets and certificate management.
- **Azure DevOps & GitHub Actions**: CI/CD and automation tooling.

Architectural Overview: A Sample Cloud-Native Application

Let's walk through the architecture of a real-world application—a ride-sharing platform built using cloud-native principles.

Key Components:

- **User Service** (AKS)
- **Ride Booking Service** (Azure Functions)
- **Payment Processor** (Container App)
- **Real-Time Location Tracking** (SignalR + Event Hubs)
- **API Gateway** (Azure APIM)
- **Database** (Cosmos DB for bookings, Azure SQL for payments)
- **CI/CD** (GitHub Actions)
- **Observability** (Azure Monitor, App Insights)

Microservices and Containerization with AKS

Each core domain (user, ride, payment) is deployed as a microservice inside AKS. Kubernetes manages service discovery, scaling, and rolling updates.

Example Kubernetes Deployment:

apiVersion: apps/v1

kind: Deployment

metadata:

name: user-service

spec:

replicas: 3

```
selector:
matchLabels:
app: user-service
template:
metadata:
labels:
app: user-service
spec:
containers:
- name: user-service
image: myregistry.azurecr.io/user-service:v1
ports:
- containerPort: 80
```

The deployment is exposed via an internal Kubernetes service and routed through APIM.

Event-Driven Serverless with Azure Functions

Ride bookings trigger workflows that don't require a constantly running backend. These are implemented as Azure Functions triggered by HTTP, queues, or Event Grid.

Example HTTP-triggered Azure Function (Python):

```
import logging
```

```
import azure.functions as func

def main(req: func.HttpRequest) -> func.HttpResponse:

user_id = req.params.get('userId')

if user_id:

return func.HttpResponse(f"Booking confirmed for user {user_id}")

else:

return func.HttpResponse("Missing userId", status_code=400)
```

Functions can scale to zero and handle spikes efficiently, which is ideal for sporadic but high-volume workloads like ride requests.

API Gateway Pattern with Azure APIM

APIM acts as the single entry point for all client applications. It abstracts and secures the microservices beneath it and supports rate limiting, caching, and logging.

Example: Rate Limiting Policy in APIM

```
<policies>

<inbound>

<rate-limit calls="100" renewal-period="60" />

<base />

</inbound>

</policies>
```

This prevents abuse of APIs by throttling requests per subscription key.

Managing Secrets with Azure Key Vault

Each microservice retrieves secrets (DB passwords, API keys) from Azure Key Vault during startup.

Example: Accessing Key Vault with a Managed Identity

```
az keyvault secret show \
—name PaymentServiceApiKey \
—vault-name MyKeyVault
```

In production, services use MSI and SDKs to fetch secrets securely without hardcoding credentials.

Data Layer: Choosing the Right Database

The platform uses a polyglot persistence strategy:

- **Cosmos DB**: Stores JSON documents for real-time ride tracking and user data.
- **Azure SQL**: Relational database for payment transactions and reporting.

Example Cosmos DB SDK Query (Node.js):

```
const querySpec = {
query: "SELECT * FROM c WHERE c.userId = @userId",
parameters: [{ name: "@userId", value: "abc123" }]
```

```
};

const { resources: results } = await
container.items.query(querySpec).fetchAll();
```

Using the right data store for the workload optimizes both performance and cost.

CI/CD Pipeline with GitHub Actions

All services follow GitOps principles. Every code change triggers a pipeline that builds, tests, and deploys containers to AKS or Container Apps.

Example GitHub Actions Workflow for AKS:

```
jobs:

build-and-deploy:

runs-on: ubuntu-latest

steps:

- uses: actions/checkout@v2

- name: Log in to Azure

uses: azure/login@v1

with:

creds: ${{ secrets.AZURE_CREDENTIALS }}

- name: Deploy to AKS

run: |

az aks get-credentials—resource-group myrg—name myaks
```

```
kubectl apply -f k8s/user-service.yaml
```

The same model applies to infrastructure updates via Bicep or Terraform, enabling consistent IaC.

Observability with Azure Monitor and App Insights

Microservices are instrumented using OpenTelemetry, emitting traces, metrics, and logs to Azure Monitor.

Key telemetry components:

- **Distributed Tracing**: Track requests across services
- **Custom Metrics**: Monitor business KPIs like bookings per minute
- **Live Metrics Stream**: Real-time troubleshooting

Query Example in Log Analytics:

```
requests
| where cloud_RoleName == "user-service"
| summarize count() by bin(timestamp, 5m)
```

This gives visibility into service behavior and can drive alerts or automated remediation workflows.

Resilience and Health Checks

Each service implements health endpoints and liveness probes:

```
livenessProbe:
httpGet:
```

path: /health

port: 80

initialDelaySeconds: 10

periodSeconds: 5

AKS uses this to restart failing pods. Azure Front Door or Traffic Manager can be layered for global failover.

Security Best Practices

- **Network Policies**: Enforce east-west traffic restrictions in AKS.
- **RBAC**: Scoped per service team and namespace.
- **TLS Everywhere**: Use Azure-managed certificates.
- **Authentication**: JWT via Azure AD B2C for mobile clients, API tokens for internal services.
- **WAF**: Protect APIs using Application Gateway or APIM with WAF policies.

Cost Optimization Tactics

- Use **spot instances** for non-critical workloads.
- Schedule dev/test environments to shut down after hours.
- Enable autoscaling on AKS and App Services.

- Analyze cost reports using Azure Cost Management + Power BI.

Real-World Implementation Summary

A retail company implemented a cloud-native e-commerce system using:

- **BFF pattern** (Backend-for-Frontend) for web and mobile channels
- **Service Mesh** (Istio on AKS) for secure service-to-service communication
- **Redis on Azure Cache** for low-latency shopping cart management
- **Feature flags** using Azure App Configuration
- **Container Scanning** with Defender for Containers

Their average deployment velocity increased from once every 3 weeks to 20+ times per day, reducing downtime and increasing customer engagement.

Challenges and Considerations

- **Complexity**: Microservices require rigorous design, strong ops discipline.
- **Skill Requirements**: Devs must understand Docker, k8s, CI/CD, and monitoring.
- **State Management**: Distributed systems make consistency difficult.

- **Debugging**: Requires tools like Jaeger, OpenTelemetry, and centralized logs.
- **Latency**: Network hops between microservices can degrade performance.

Conclusion

Cloud-native development on Azure enables organizations to deliver software faster, more reliably, and at scale. By embracing microservices, containers, serverless functions, DevOps, and managed services, teams can build systems that are not only cloud-ready but cloud-optimized. From architectural flexibility to automated observability and global resiliency, cloud-native applications lay the foundation for continuous innovation and digital transformation. With the right mindset and tooling, any enterprise can evolve its legacy systems into modern, cloud-native ecosystems.

Chapter 10: Hybrid and Multi-Cloud Scenarios

Azure Stack and Hybrid Architectures

In modern enterprise environments, the move to cloud computing is rarely an all-or-nothing decision. Most organizations face various constraints—be they technical, regulatory, or operational—that prevent full migration to the public cloud. Instead, they adopt a hybrid model that integrates on-premises infrastructure with cloud services. Microsoft Azure offers a comprehensive suite of tools and services to facilitate hybrid cloud deployments, with **Azure Stack** being a cornerstone of this strategy.

Understanding the Hybrid Cloud Model

The hybrid cloud model blends private (on-premises) and public cloud resources, allowing applications and data to move fluidly between the two. This offers several key benefits:

- **Regulatory Compliance**: Some data must remain on-premises due to legal requirements, particularly in finance, healthcare, and government sectors.

- **Latency and Performance**: Applications that require low latency may perform better when deployed closer to the user or device.

- **Gradual Migration**: Hybrid models enable gradual cloud adoption, reducing risk and easing transitions.

- **Business Continuity**: On-premises systems can serve as a backup or failover system in case of public cloud outages.

Introduction to Azure Stack

Azure Stack is a family of products that extend Azure services and capabilities to your environment of choice—from the data center to edge locations and remote branches. Azure Stack enables you to run Azure-consistent services on-premises, providing a unified development and operations experience.

There are three main offerings under the Azure Stack umbrella:

1. **Azure Stack Hub**: A fully integrated system for running IaaS and PaaS services on-premises.
2. **Azure Stack HCI**: A hyperconverged infrastructure solution for running virtualized workloads on-premises using Windows Server and Azure services.
3. **Azure Stack Edge**: A managed appliance for edge computing, supporting machine learning, IoT, and data processing at the edge.

Use Cases for Azure Stack

- **Disconnected Environments**: For scenarios with limited or no internet connectivity (e.g., oil rigs, military installations), Azure Stack Hub provides autonomous cloud capabilities.

- **Edge and IoT**: Azure Stack Edge allows real-time processing of data collected from edge devices, reducing the need to send large volumes to the cloud.

- **Cloud Bursting**: Applications can scale out to Azure public cloud when local capacity is exceeded.
- **Application Modernization**: Developers can build applications using Azure services on-premises and migrate them to the cloud later.

Deploying Azure Stack HCI

Azure Stack HCI (Hyperconverged Infrastructure) is built on validated hardware and Microsoft technologies like Windows Server 2022 and Azure Arc. It supports running Windows and Linux virtual machines and can be integrated with Azure for hybrid capabilities.

Here's a simplified example of deploying an Azure Stack HCI cluster:

```
# Install required PowerShell modules

Install-Module -Name Az -AllowClobber -Force

Install-Module -Name WindowsAdminCenter -Force

# Register the cluster with Azure Arc

Connect-AzAccount

$ResourceGroupName = "MyHCIGroup"

$Location = "eastus"

Register-AzStackHCI -ResourceGroupName
$ResourceGroupName -Region $Location
```

Once connected to Azure, administrators can manage the cluster via the Azure Portal, apply updates, monitor usage, and deploy virtual machines through Windows Admin Center.

Azure Arc: Extending Azure Management

Azure Arc allows you to manage Windows and Linux servers, Kubernetes clusters, and data services across on-premises, multi-cloud, and edge environments. It brings services like Azure Policy, Azure Monitor, and Defender for Cloud to non-Azure environments.

Azure Arc-enabled servers can be onboarded using either the Azure Portal or a script:

```
# Download the onboarding script from Azure Portal

.\OnboardingScript.ps1
```

This registers your on-premises or third-party cloud machine with Azure Resource Manager (ARM), enabling it to be managed like any native Azure resource.

Identity and Security in Hybrid Environments

Identity and access management (IAM) is a critical aspect of hybrid architecture. Azure Active Directory (Azure AD) can be extended to on-premises environments using **Azure AD Connect**, enabling single sign-on (SSO), conditional access, and MFA across environments.

```
# Example: Synchronize users from on-prem AD to Azure AD

Start-ADSyncSyncCycle -PolicyType Delta
```

For security, tools like **Azure Security Center** and **Microsoft Defender for Cloud** can evaluate hybrid workloads and suggest security hardening recommendations.

Application Development in Hybrid Setups

Developers can use the same set of tools (e.g., Visual Studio, Azure DevOps, GitHub Actions) to build and deploy applications to both Azure and Azure Stack environments. Services like **Azure App Services**, **Functions**, and **Kubernetes** are available in Azure Stack Hub, enabling a truly consistent experience.

Here's a basic example using Azure CLI to deploy a web app to Azure App Service on Azure Stack:

az login—endpoint-resource-manager "https://management.local.azurestack.external/"

az webapp up—name myhybridwebapp—resource-group MyHybridRG—plan MyAppServicePlan

Data Considerations in Hybrid Environments

Data residency, governance, and sovereignty are key drivers for hybrid architectures. Azure Stack allows organizations to maintain sensitive data locally while integrating with Azure data services like:

- **Azure Backup**
- **Azure Site Recovery**
- **Azure Monitor**
- **Azure Blob Storage (via Edge)**

Organizations must classify data and define policies for how data is handled across environments, ensuring compliance with regulations such as GDPR or HIPAA.

Hybrid DevOps and CI/CD

Hybrid DevOps enables streamlined CI/CD pipelines that target both Azure and Azure Stack. Tools like **Azure DevOps** and **GitHub Actions** can deploy artifacts to either environment using environment-specific configuration.

Example GitHub Actions YAML snippet for a hybrid deployment:

```
jobs:

deploy:

runs-on: ubuntu-latest

steps:

- name: Checkout

uses: actions/checkout@v2

- name: Login to Azure Stack

run: az login—service-principal—username ${{ secrets.CLIENT_ID }}—password ${{ secrets.CLIENT_SECRET }}—tenant ${{ secrets.TENANT_ID }}—endpoint-resource-manager https://management.local.azurestack.external/

- name: Deploy app

run: az webapp deploy—name myhybridwebapp—src-path ./app.zip—resource-group MyHybridRG
```

Challenges and Best Practices

While hybrid architectures are powerful, they come with complexity. Key challenges include:

- **Network latency and bandwidth** between on-prem and cloud
- **Identity federation** and synchronization
- **Unified monitoring** across environments
- **Consistent policy enforcement**

Best practices include:

- Use **Azure Arc** for centralized management.
- Adopt **Infrastructure as Code** (IaC) with Bicep or Terraform for consistent deployments.
- Ensure **RBAC and governance policies** are uniformly applied.
- Establish **monitoring baselines** and define SLAs for hybrid workloads.
- Regularly update and patch both cloud and on-prem components.

Conclusion

Hybrid cloud architecture is not just a transitional phase—it's a strategic choice for many organizations. With services like Azure Stack Hub, HCI, Edge, and Azure Arc, Microsoft enables enterprises to meet regulatory, performance, and operational requirements without sacrificing innovation. A well-architected hybrid solution offers the agility of the cloud while respecting the realities of enterprise IT. By mastering hybrid tools and best practices, organizations can confidently navigate complex environments and build resilient, scalable solutions for the future.

Integrating with AWS and GCP

As enterprises grow and diversify, many are choosing to adopt a **multi-cloud strategy**—leveraging services from more than one cloud provider, such as Microsoft Azure, Amazon Web Services (AWS), and Google Cloud Platform (GCP). This approach provides benefits such as avoiding vendor lock-in, enhancing resiliency, and taking advantage of best-in-class services from each provider.

In this section, we will explore the rationale behind multi-cloud architectures, challenges in integrating Azure with AWS and GCP, and real-world solutions to ensure smooth interoperation. We'll also dive into identity federation, cross-cloud networking, shared observability, and CI/CD pipelines that span multiple cloud environments.

Why Multi-Cloud?

Organizations may choose a multi-cloud strategy for several reasons:

- **Risk Mitigation**: Relying on one provider can lead to service disruptions; spreading workloads reduces risk.
- **Cost Optimization**: Providers offer different pricing models—multi-cloud allows selection based on cost efficiency.

- **Best-of-Breed Services**: GCP might offer the best data analytics tools, AWS may excel in compute performance, and Azure might provide enterprise-grade hybrid support.

- **Regulatory Requirements**: Some jurisdictions require data sovereignty that may only be achievable through multiple regional providers.

Foundational Concepts for Integration

Before integrating Azure with AWS and GCP, organizations must align on a few foundational areas:

- **Identity and Access Management (IAM)**

- **Networking and Connectivity**

- **Security and Compliance**

- **Resource Management and Monitoring**

- **Application Deployment Strategy**

Let's address each of these in detail.

Identity Federation Across Clouds

Maintaining separate identity systems across clouds leads to complexity and potential security gaps. Azure Active Directory (AAD) can act as a central identity provider across AWS and GCP, using **SAML 2.0** or **OpenID Connect** to federate identities.

Federating Azure AD with AWS IAM

Azure AD can be configured to enable single sign-on to AWS via SAML. The setup involves:

1. Creating an enterprise application in Azure AD.
2. Configuring SAML-based SSO.
3. Assigning roles via claim rules and mappings.

Example SAML claim for AWS:

<AttributeStatement>

<Attribute Name="https://aws.amazon.com/SAML/Attributes/Role">

<AttributeValue>arn:aws:iam::123456789012:role/AzureADRole,arn:aws:iam::123456789012:saml-provider/AzureAD</AttributeValue>

</Attribute>

</AttributeStatement>

This enables Azure AD users to access the AWS Management Console and CLI using their corporate credentials.

Federating Azure AD with GCP IAM

GCP supports federation via **Workforce Identity Federation**, allowing Azure AD users to access GCP resources without requiring a Google account.

Basic steps include:

1. Creating a Workforce Identity Pool in GCP.
2. Linking Azure AD as an OIDC provider.
3. Mapping Azure AD groups or claims to GCP roles.

This ensures a unified identity plane across all three platforms.

Networking Between Clouds

Networking is one of the more complex aspects of multi-cloud integration. The key challenge is securely connecting workloads across providers with minimal latency.

Options for Connectivity

- **IPsec VPNs**: Traditional method using site-to-site tunnels. Each cloud provides VPN gateways.

- **Transit Gateways**: AWS and Azure support transit hubs to centralize connectivity.

- **Third-Party SD-WAN Solutions**: Vendors like Cisco and Fortinet offer cross-cloud networking fabrics.

- **Private Interconnects**: Azure ExpressRoute, AWS Direct Connect, and GCP Cloud Interconnect offer private, low-latency links.

Azure to AWS VPN Example

```
# On Azure: Create local network gateway pointing to AWS VPN endpoint

az network local-gateway create \
```

```
—name AWSGateway \
—resource-group MultiCloudRG \
—gateway-ip-address <AWS_PUBLIC_IP> \
—local-address-prefixes <AWS_CIDR_BLOCK>
# Create VPN connection from Azure to AWS
az network vpn-connection create \
—name ToAWS \
—resource-group MultiCloudRG \
—vnet-gateway1 AzureGateway \
—local-gateway2 AWSGateway \
—shared-key "SecureSharedKey123"
```

This can be mirrored with similar configurations on the AWS side.

Unified Monitoring and Observability

Managing telemetry and observability across multiple clouds requires a platform-agnostic approach.

Strategies

- **Centralized Logging**: Export logs from AWS CloudWatch and GCP Stackdriver to Azure Monitor or a third-party system like Splunk or Datadog.

- **Metrics Aggregation**: Use Prometheus and Grafana to collect and visualize metrics across cloud environments.

- **Distributed Tracing**: Implement OpenTelemetry in applications to capture traces regardless of where the workload runs.

Azure Monitor Ingestion Example

{

"time": "2025-04-20T13:05:00Z",

"resourceId": "/subscriptions/xxxx/resourceGroups/MultiCloudRG/providers/Microsoft.Compute/virtualMachines/web-vm",

"category": "CustomLogs",

"operationName": "AppLogEvent",

"properties": {

"cloud": "AWS",

"message": "EC2 instance started",

"level": "Information"

}

}

This log, ingested via the Azure Monitor API, provides cross-cloud visibility.

CI/CD Across Clouds

DevOps workflows in a multi-cloud world must handle deployment pipelines targeting different clouds while maintaining consistency.

GitHub Actions with Multi-Cloud Targets

A single pipeline can deploy infrastructure and applications to Azure, AWS, and GCP:

```
jobs:
deploy-azure:
runs-on: ubuntu-latest
steps:
- uses: azure/login@v1
with:
creds: ${{ secrets.AZURE_CREDENTIALS }}
deploy-aws:
runs-on: ubuntu-latest
steps:
- uses: aws-actions/configure-aws-credentials@v1
with:
aws-access-key-id: ${{ secrets.AWS_ACCESS_KEY }}
aws-secret-access-key: ${{ secrets.AWS_SECRET_KEY }}
```

```
region: us-east-1
deploy-gcp:
runs-on: ubuntu-latest
steps:
- uses: google-github-actions/auth@v0
with:
credentials_json: ${{ secrets.GCP_CREDENTIALS }}
```

Each job handles deployment logic for its respective platform, enabling seamless multi-cloud delivery.

Resource Tagging and Governance

Maintaining governance across clouds is essential for cost control, security, and compliance.

Common Tagging Scheme

Adopt a uniform tagging taxonomy for all resources:

Tag Name	Description
env	Environment (prod, dev, test)
owner	Responsible team or individual
cost-center	Billing code or department
compliance	Regulatory requirement identifier

Ensure that tagging policies are enforced using tools like:

- Azure Policy
- AWS Organizations Service Control Policies (SCP)

- GCP Organization Policies

Cost Management Across Clouds

Tracking and optimizing cloud spend becomes increasingly difficult in multi-cloud environments.

Tools and Techniques

- **Azure Cost Management + Billing**: Now supports AWS integration.
- **CloudHealth by VMware**: Multi-cloud cost visibility and optimization.
- **Kubecost**: Tracks Kubernetes costs across clusters in any cloud.

Best practices:

- Define budgets per environment and enforce alerts.
- Monitor idle resources and right-size regularly.
- Use reserved instances or savings plans where applicable.

Security Considerations

Security should be holistic and not siloed by provider.

Common Practices

- Implement **Zero Trust** models across all platforms.

- Use **centralized secrets management** (e.g., HashiCorp Vault).
- Regularly run **vulnerability scans and compliance audits** on all assets.

Azure Sentinel for Multi-Cloud Security

Azure Sentinel can ingest logs from AWS and GCP to enable unified security operations.

Example data connector setup:

```
New-AzSentinelDataConnector -Name "AWSCloudTrail" -WorkspaceName "sentinel-workspace" -ConnectorType "AmazonWebServicesCloudTrail"
```

Challenges and Recommendations

Challenges

- Diverse APIs and SDKs increase complexity.
- Identity sprawl if not centrally managed.
- Difficulties in achieving consistent security policies.

Recommendations

- Standardize DevOps toolchains to abstract cloud differences.
- Favor open standards and containerized workloads.

- Use **cloud-agnostic IaC tools** like Terraform for infrastructure provisioning.
- Build internal **cloud broker layers** that abstract provider-specific logic.

Conclusion

Integrating Azure with AWS and GCP requires careful planning, robust architecture, and sound governance. However, the strategic advantages of flexibility, resilience, and innovation make multi-cloud an attractive option for modern enterprises. With services like Azure Arc, Identity Federation, centralized observability, and multi-cloud CI/CD pipelines, organizations can unlock the full potential of the cloud while maintaining control and compliance. The key lies in treating each cloud as a component of a larger system, not as isolated silos, and in establishing a unifying strategy that transcends platform boundaries.

Multi-Cloud Governance Strategies

As enterprises scale across cloud platforms like Azure, AWS, and GCP, maintaining governance becomes both critical and challenging. Without a robust multi-cloud governance strategy, organizations risk uncontrolled costs, compliance violations, and inconsistent security postures. Governance is the foundation for operational stability and risk management, especially in multi-cloud environments where services, billing models, and access controls differ between providers.

This section delves into comprehensive governance approaches tailored for multi-cloud ecosystems, emphasizing policy standardization, identity governance, financial controls, security and compliance, and architectural consistency.

Principles of Multi-Cloud Governance

Before diving into tooling and implementation, it's essential to understand the fundamental principles that should guide a multi-cloud governance strategy:

- **Unified Policy Enforcement**: Governance rules must apply consistently across all cloud providers.

- **Decentralized Execution with Central Oversight**: Teams can operate independently, but governance and audit must be centralized.

- **Visibility and Accountability**: Every resource, deployment, and identity should be tracked and attributable.

- **Security by Design**: Compliance and security controls should be embedded into workflows, not bolted on afterward.

- **Automation and Scale**: Governance mechanisms should scale via automation, not manual oversight.

Standardizing Policies Across Cloud Providers

Each cloud provider has its own method for enforcing policies:

- **Azure**: Azure Policy

- **AWS**: Service Control Policies (SCP) and AWS Config

- **GCP**: Organization Policy Service

To standardize governance across providers, organizations can define a **cloud policy baseline** that is translated into provider-specific implementations.

Example: Enforcing Region Restrictions

Business Policy: "All production resources must be deployed in approved regions only."

Azure Implementation (via Azure Policy):

```
{
"if": {
"not": {
"field": "location",
"in": ["eastus", "westeurope"]
}
},
"then": {
"effect": "deny"
}
}
```

AWS Implementation (via SCP):

```
{
"Version": "2012-10-17",
```

```
"Statement": [
{
"Effect": "Deny",
"Action": "*",
"Resource": "*",
"Condition": {
"StringNotEquals": {
"aws:RequestedRegion": ["us-east-1", "eu-west-1"]
}
}
}
]
}
```

GCP Implementation (via Organization Policy):

```
{
"constraint": "constraints/gcp.resourceLocations",
"listPolicy": {
"allowedValues": [
"in:us-east1",
"in:europe-west1"
```

```
]
}
}
```

The translation of a single business rule into three implementations illustrates why a governance strategy should start from abstract, provider-agnostic policies.

Identity and Access Governance

In a multi-cloud world, managing identity and access becomes exponentially more complex. Without tight controls, users may accumulate permissions across clouds, leading to overprivileged accounts and compliance gaps.

Best Practices

- **Centralize Identity with Azure AD**: Use Azure AD B2B or B2C to federate identities across platforms.
- **Adopt Role-Based Access Control (RBAC)**: Define roles by job function and enforce least privilege.
- **Review Access Regularly**: Set up access review policies in Azure AD and AWS IAM Access Analyzer.
- **Automate Identity Provisioning**: Use SCIM (System for Cross-domain Identity Management) to synchronize users across clouds.

Example: Azure AD Conditional Access Policy

```
New-AzureADMSConditionalAccessPolicy `
```

```
-DisplayName "Block Access from Unsupported Locations" `
-State "enabled" `
-Conditions @{
Locations = @{
IncludeLocations = @("All")
ExcludeLocations = @("TrustedLocationID")
}
} `
-GrantControls @{
BuiltInControls = @("Block")
}
```

This policy blocks access from untrusted locations, which can also be implemented using AWS IAM Conditions and GCP VPC Service Controls.

Cost and Budget Governance

Controlling and forecasting costs across multiple cloud platforms is a critical governance concern. Without proper tools and policies, cloud spend can spiral out of control due to overprovisioning, idle resources, or inconsistent procurement strategies.

Techniques for Financial Governance

1. **Set Budgets and Alerts per Project and Environment**
2. **Use Cost Tagging Standards**

3. **Implement Chargeback/Showback Models**
4. **Use Cloud Cost Management Tools**

Azure Example: Budget Setup

```
New-AzConsumptionBudget `
-ResourceGroupName "FinanceRG" `
-Name "ProdBudget" `
-Amount 10000 `
-Category "Cost" `
-TimeGrain "Monthly" `
-StartDate "2025-01-01" `
-EndDate "2025-12-31"
```

AWS Example: Budgets

AWS Budgets can be configured via the console or using the AWS Budgets API to alert when usage exceeds defined thresholds.

GCP Example: Budgets API

```
{
"budget": {
"displayName": "TeamA Monthly Budget",
"budgetFilter": {
```

"projects": ["projects/my-project-id"]

},

"amount": {

"specifiedAmount": {

"currencyCode": "USD",

"units": "5000"

}

}

}

}

Security and Compliance Governance

A core element of governance is ensuring security and compliance, particularly when dealing with sensitive data in regulated industries like healthcare or finance.

Unified Security Controls

- **Use Azure Security Center, AWS Security Hub, and GCP Security Command Center**
- **Automate Compliance Checks with CIS Benchmarks**
- **Integrate with SIEMs like Azure Sentinel or Splunk**

- **Run Regular Penetration Testing and Vulnerability Scans**

Azure Example: Built-In Initiative

Azure has built-in policy initiatives for standards like **ISO 27001** and **NIST 800-53**. Assigning them at the subscription or management group level ensures consistent enforcement.

```
New-AzPolicyAssignment `

-Name "NIST-Mandatory" `

-PolicyDefinitionId "/providers/Microsoft.Authorization/policySetDefinitions/NIST_SP_800-53_R4" `

-Scope "/subscriptions/xxxx"
```

Multi-Cloud Security Logging

To create a unified security view, forward logs from all platforms to a central location (Azure Sentinel, AWS OpenSearch, GCP Cloud Logging):

```
# Azure example: Log forwarding to Sentinel

az monitor diagnostic-settings create \

—name "ForwardToSentinel" \

—resource "/subscriptions/.../resourceGroups/.../providers/Microsoft.Compute/virtualMachines/myVM" \

—workspace "/subscriptions/.../resourceGroups/.../providers/Microsoft.OperationalInsights/workspaces/mySentinelWorkspace" \
```

```
—logs '[{"category": "AuditLogs","enabled": true}]'
```

Infrastructure as Code for Governance

A unified governance strategy should extend to **Infrastructure as Code (IaC)**. IaC tools like Terraform and Pulumi support multi-cloud deployments and governance by codifying standards.

Example Terraform Module: Enforce Tagging Across Clouds

```
variable "required_tags" {

type = map(string)

default = {

environment = "prod"

cost_center = "12345"

}

}

resource "azurerm_resource_group" "rg" {

name = "multi-cloud-rg"

location = "eastus"

tags = var.required_tags

}
```

This pattern can be replicated across AWS (aws_instance) and GCP (google_compute_instance), ensuring tagging policies are always enforced.

Organizational Structures and Guardrails

Larger organizations often implement **landing zones** and **guardrails** to enforce governance at scale.

Azure: Management Groups and Blueprints

- Use Management Groups to group subscriptions by environment or business unit.
- Assign policies and role assignments at the Management Group level.

AWS: Organizations and Control Tower

- AWS Organizations helps enforce Service Control Policies (SCP) across accounts.
- AWS Control Tower offers a prebuilt landing zone framework with governance baked in.

GCP: Folders and Organization Policies

- Use the Organization Node and Folders for policy inheritance.
- Define constraints at the folder or organization level for consistent application.

Audit and Reporting

Continuous audit trails are necessary to prove governance compliance to internal and external stakeholders.

- Enable **CloudTrail** in AWS, **Activity Logs** in Azure, and **Audit Logs** in GCP.
- Aggregate logs in a central data lake for forensic analysis.
- Use tools like Power BI, Looker, or Grafana for dashboarding compliance KPIs.

Conclusion

Governance in a multi-cloud world is not about replicating rules across platforms—it's about establishing a **cohesive framework** that abstracts complexity and enforces consistency. With proper identity federation, policy translation, cost controls, security postures, and automation through Infrastructure as Code, organizations can effectively govern their cloud environments. This governance provides the foundation for operational resilience, regulatory compliance, and strategic innovation across Azure, AWS, and GCP.

Unified Management with Azure Arc

Managing a dispersed ecosystem of workloads across Azure, on-premises data centers, edge locations, AWS, and GCP is a significant challenge for IT operations. Traditional cloud management tools often lack the extensibility to support multi-environment visibility, governance, and automation. This is where **Azure Arc** becomes a game-changer, enabling organizations to unify the management of diverse infrastructure under the Azure umbrella.

Azure Arc extends Azure management capabilities to any infrastructure. It brings services like **Azure Policy**, **Azure**

Monitor, **Azure Defender**, and **Azure Resource Graph** to resources hosted outside of Azure, delivering a truly consistent control plane across the cloud and on-premises environments.

Core Capabilities of Azure Arc

Azure Arc enables several key features:

- **Resource Organization**: Onboard non-Azure resources into Azure Resource Manager (ARM) for centralized visibility.

- **Governance and Compliance**: Apply Azure Policy and role-based access control (RBAC) to all Arc-enabled resources.

- **Monitoring and Insights**: Send logs and metrics to Azure Monitor regardless of resource location.

- **Security and Threat Protection**: Use Microsoft Defender for Cloud across hybrid and multi-cloud environments.

- **Configuration Management**: Apply guest configurations, script extensions, and VM policies from Azure.

- **Data Services Anywhere**: Deploy Azure SQL and PostgreSQL managed instances on any infrastructure.

Let's explore each of these in depth.

Onboarding Resources with Azure Arc

To manage a machine with Azure Arc, you first install the Azure Arc agent on that machine and register it with Azure.

Prerequisites

- Azure CLI
- Access to the target server (Windows or Linux)
- Contributor role in the target Azure subscription

Example: Onboarding a Linux VM

```
# Log in to Azure

az login

# Create a resource group

az group create—name ArcGroup—location eastus

# Onboard Linux server

az connectedmachine onboard \

—resource-group ArcGroup \

—location eastus \

—name arc-linux-vm \

—os-type Linux \

—client-token "$(az connectedmachine generate-token)"
```

The onboarded server now appears as a first-class citizen in the Azure portal with resource ID, tags, and policies.

Windows VM Onboarding via PowerShell

```
Connect-AzAccount

$resourceGroup = "ArcGroup"

$location = "eastus"

$machineName = "arc-win-vm"

Install-AzConnectedMachine `

-ResourceGroupName $resourceGroup `

-Location $location `

-Name $machineName
```

After onboarding, you can manage both VMs using the same tooling as native Azure VMs.

Governance with Azure Policy and RBAC

Once external resources are onboarded, Azure Arc enables the application of Azure-native policies and access controls.

Applying Policies

You can apply compliance policies to ensure all VMs—whether in Azure, AWS, or on-prem—adhere to standards.

```
az policy assignment create \

—name "EnforceMonitoringAgent" \
```

```
—scope "/subscriptions/<sub_id>/resourceGroups/ArcGroup" \

—policy "/providers/Microsoft.Authorization/policyDefinitions/<policy_id>"
```

This ensures that all Arc-enabled machines must have the Azure Monitor agent installed.

Role-Based Access Control

You can assign RBAC roles to Arc resources to maintain consistent access governance.

```
az role assignment create \

—assignee user@domain.com \

—role "Reader" \

—scope "/subscriptions/<sub_id>/resourceGroups/ArcGroup/providers/Microsoft.HybridCompute/machines/arc-linux-vm"
```

This gives the user read-only access to a Linux server hosted in AWS or on-premises, governed through Azure.

Unified Monitoring with Azure Monitor and Log Analytics

Azure Arc allows seamless integration with Azure Monitor, centralizing observability for all infrastructure.

Enabling Monitoring

Once Arc-enabled, you can install the Log Analytics agent on the VM to start collecting metrics and logs.

```
az monitor log-analytics workspace create \

—resource-group ArcGroup \

—workspace-name ArcWorkspace

az monitor diagnostics settings create \

—name "ArcVMMonitoring" \

—resource "/subscriptions/<sub_id>/resourceGroups/ArcGroup/providers/Microsoft.HybridCompute/machines/arc-linux-vm" \

—workspace "/subscriptions/<sub_id>/resourceGroups/ArcGroup/providers/Microsoft.OperationalInsights/workspaces/ArcWorkspace" \

—logs '[{"category": "Syslog","enabled": true}]'
```

Now, logs from an Arc-enabled VM in Google Cloud can appear alongside Azure VMs in the same Log Analytics workspace.

Security with Microsoft Defender for Cloud

Security posture management is simplified using Microsoft Defender for Cloud with Azure Arc. Arc enables Defender to assess, report, and respond to threats on hybrid and multi-cloud workloads.

Enabling Defender on Arc Resources

```
az security auto-provisioning-setting update \

—name "default" \

—auto-provision "On"
```

```
az security pricing create \
—name "VirtualMachines" \
—tier "Standard"
```

Once enabled, Defender performs continuous assessments of all onboarded resources, offering threat alerts and recommendations.

Guest Configuration and Desired State

Arc supports guest configuration policies, allowing you to enforce configurations such as time zone, security settings, or installed applications.

Example: Enforce Time Zone on Arc-Enabled Windows VMs

```
az policy assignment create \
—name "EnforceTimeZone" \
—policy "timeZonePolicyDefinition" \
—scope "/subscriptions/<sub_id>/resourceGroups/ArcGroup"
```

You can also push PowerShell or Bash scripts using **Custom Script Extension**, providing centralized management of automation tasks.

Deploying Azure Data Services Anywhere

Azure Arc is not just about management—it also brings platform services to your infrastructure. With **Azure Arc-enabled Data Services**, you can deploy Azure SQL Managed Instance or PostgreSQL Hyperscale on Kubernetes clusters in AWS, GCP, or on-prem.

Prerequisites

- Kubernetes cluster (e.g., Amazon EKS, Google GKE)
- Azure Arc Data Controller
- Azure subscription

Example Deployment

```
# Connect Kubernetes cluster
az connectedk8s connect \
—name arc-k8s-cluster \
—resource-group ArcGroup \
—location eastus
# Install data controller
az arcdata dc create \
—name arc-dc \
—k8s-namespace arc \
—resource-group ArcGroup \
—connectivity-mode indirect \
—location eastus
# Deploy SQL Managed Instance
az arcdata sql mi create \
```

```
—name arc-sqlmi \
—resource-group ArcGroup \
—k8s-namespace arc \
—location eastus
```

This deployment gives you the benefits of Azure SQL—including auto-patching, high availability, and Azure Monitor integration—without leaving your existing infrastructure.

Arc-Enabled Kubernetes for Multi-Cloud Containers

Azure Arc can manage Kubernetes clusters outside of Azure (e.g., EKS, GKE, OpenShift).

Onboarding a Kubernetes Cluster

```
az connectedk8s connect \
—name eks-prod-cluster \
—resource-group ArcGroup \
—location eastus
```

Now, Azure Policy, Monitor, Defender, and GitOps (via Flux) can be applied to the cluster, unifying its governance with Azure-native services.

GitOps Deployment with Arc

```
az k8sconfiguration create \
```

—name flux-config \

—cluster-name eks-prod-cluster \

—resource-group ArcGroup \

—cluster-type connectedClusters \

—operator-namespace cluster-config \

—operator-instance-name flux \

—repository-url https://github.com/org/repo \

—scope cluster

This applies GitOps configurations to your non-Azure clusters via Azure Arc, promoting DevOps consistency.

Centralized Inventory and Tagging

Arc-enabled resources can be inventoried and queried using **Azure Resource Graph**, and tagging can be applied for cost and governance purposes.

az resource tag \

—ids "/subscriptions/<sub_id>/resourceGroups/ArcGroup/providers/Microsoft.HybridCompute/machines/arc-linux-vm" \

—tags environment=production owner=devops

Querying Arc resources with Resource Graph:

Resources

| where type =~ "microsoft.hybridcompute/machines"

| project name, location, resourceGroup, tags

Challenges and Considerations

Despite its power, Azure Arc requires careful planning:

- **Network Access**: Ensure outbound connectivity to Azure is available.

- **Agent Overhead**: Some performance impact from telemetry and monitoring agents.

- **Pricing**: Azure Arc is free for resource registration, but additional services (Monitor, Defender, SQL MI) incur charges.

- **Skill Alignment**: Teams must become familiar with Azure-native tooling to effectively manage Arc resources.

Best Practices

- Use **Azure Management Groups** and **Tags** for logical organization.

- Group policies by **resource type** (VM, SQL, Kubernetes).

- Regularly audit Arc-enabled resources via Azure Resource Graph.

- Integrate **Azure Lighthouse** for MSP/multi-tenant visibility.

- Automate onboarding via ARM templates, Bicep, or Terraform.

Conclusion

Azure Arc bridges the gap between on-premises, edge, and multi-cloud infrastructure by bringing Azure's management layer everywhere. With its deep integration into Azure Policy, Defender, Monitor, and RBAC, Arc transforms how IT operations manage diverse infrastructure. Whether you're running legacy servers in a data center, containers on AWS, or databases at the edge, Azure Arc ensures they can all be governed, secured, and monitored from one unified platform. It's a vital enabler for organizations embracing a hybrid or multi-cloud future.

Chapter 11: Real-World Case Studies and Architectures

Enterprise Migration to Azure

Enterprise migration to Azure is a transformative journey that modernizes infrastructure, enhances agility, improves scalability, and enables cost optimization. Migrating large-scale legacy systems to Azure, however, is far more complex than simple lift-and-shift efforts. It requires careful planning, stakeholder alignment, workload assessment, governance structuring, and iterative modernization. This section offers a deep dive into a typical enterprise migration project, detailing tools, strategies, patterns, and a real-world architectural example to anchor the theory in practice.

Key Phases of Enterprise Cloud Migration

Azure's Cloud Adoption Framework (CAF) outlines a robust, phased approach that enterprises can use as a migration blueprint. The stages include:

1. **Strategy**
2. **Plan**
3. **Ready**
4. **Migrate**
5. **Innovate**
6. **Govern**
7. **Manage**

These phases ensure a holistic migration journey that aligns technology with business outcomes.

Strategy

The strategy phase defines business motivations and expected outcomes. Stakeholders identify financial goals, scalability objectives, innovation opportunities, and regulatory requirements. Outcomes from this stage include:

- Business justification and ROI models
- Executive sponsorship
- Migration KPIs
- Preliminary workload inventory

Plan

Planning revolves around workload assessment and readiness evaluation. Microsoft's **Azure Migrate** tool plays a critical role here.

```
# Deploy Azure Migrate project

az migrate project create \

—resource-group MigrationRG \

—location eastus \

—name EnterpriseMigrationProject
```

Assessment tools collect performance data, dependencies, OS compatibility, and licensing constraints. This phase includes:

- Application discovery and grouping

- TCO calculations and budget planning
- Migration wave definition

Ready

This phase prepares the Azure landing zone. It includes:

- Subscription and management group hierarchy
- Role-based access control (RBAC)
- Policy enforcement (via Azure Policy)
- Resource naming and tagging standards
- Network and identity integration (e.g., hybrid DNS, Azure AD Connect)

Migrate

Depending on the workload profile, organizations can opt for various migration strategies:

- **Rehost** (Lift and Shift)
- **Refactor** (Containerization, minimal code changes)
- **Rearchitect** (Decompose monoliths into microservices)
- **Rebuild** (Full rewrite using PaaS)

Azure offers tools such as:

- **Azure Migrate: Server Migration**
- **Database Migration Service (DMS)**
- **App Service Migration Assistant**
- **Azure Site Recovery (ASR)**

Example: Rehosting a VMware VM using Azure Migrate:

```
az migrate server replication create \
—project-name EnterpriseMigrationProject \
—resource-group MigrationRG \
—machine-name vm01 \
—target-resource-group VMsRG \
—target-vnet AzureVNet
```

Innovate

Post-migration, enterprises can modernize applications using Azure-native services:

- Replace IIS apps with **App Services**
- Break monoliths using **AKS** or **Azure Functions**
- Introduce **Event Grid** and **Service Bus** for event-driven architecture
- Integrate **Azure Cognitive Services** for enhanced user experiences

Govern

Establishing a governance foundation ensures control, compliance, and cost optimization.

- Enforce **resource consistency** via tagging policies
- Audit deployments using **Azure Policy**
- Apply **cost management alerts and budgets**
- Monitor with **Azure Security Center** and **Defender for Cloud**

Manage

Ongoing management uses Azure-native and integrated third-party tools for:

- Monitoring (Azure Monitor, Log Analytics)
- Backup (Azure Backup)
- Disaster recovery (Azure Site Recovery)
- Patch management (Update Management Center)

Real-World Migration Example: Financial Services Company

Let's walk through the architecture and process of migrating a mid-size financial services provider to Azure.

Business Context

The company operated three data centers hosting over 200 virtual machines, with SQL Server, Oracle, and custom Java applications. Goals included:

- Reducing on-prem data center footprint
- Improving disaster recovery capabilities
- Meeting GDPR and PCI-DSS compliance
- Enabling DevOps and automation

Architectural Decisions

Landing Zone Design:

- **Management Groups**: Organized by production, staging, and dev
- **Subscriptions**: Per environment and department
- **Networking**: Hub-and-spoke model with Azure Firewall and VPN Gateway
- **Identity**: Hybrid Azure AD with conditional access and PIM (Privileged Identity Management)

Migration Strategy:

- Phase 1: Lift-and-shift mission-critical VMs
- Phase 2: Modernize applications to PaaS

- Phase 3: Containerize backend services

Tools Used

- **Azure Migrate**: For discovery and replication
- **Database Migration Service**: To move SQL Server and Oracle databases
- **App Service Environment**: For secure, scalable PaaS hosting
- **Azure Monitor**: For post-migration observability

Azure Landing Zone Reference Implementation

```
module "hub_network" {
source = "Azure/hub-network/azurerm"
version = "~> 2.0"
location = "eastus"
vnet_address_space = ["10.0.0.0/16"]
subnets = {
firewall = { address_prefixes = ["10.0.1.0/24"] }
gateway = { address_prefixes = ["10.0.2.0/24"] }
}
}
module "vm_rg" {
```

```
source = "Azure/resource-group/azurerm"

name = "ProdVMs"

location = "eastus"

}
```

Results

- Reduced infrastructure costs by 32% in Year 1
- Achieved 99.99% uptime with Availability Zones
- Streamlined deployments with CI/CD pipelines in Azure DevOps
- Enabled real-time fraud detection using Azure Event Hub and Stream Analytics

Lessons Learned

1. **Pilot First**: Start with non-critical workloads to refine the migration process.
2. **Data Dependencies**: Application dependencies on shared databases often delay migration—map them early.
3. **Communication is Key**: Include business units in planning to prevent resistance and shadow IT.
4. **Automation is Critical**: Use IaC, pipelines, and runbooks to scale.
5. **Review Licensing**: Use Azure Hybrid Benefit and bring-your-own-license (BYOL) models where applicable.

Common Pitfalls to Avoid

- **Underestimating Network Complexity**: Plan for hybrid DNS, express routes, and subnetting strategies.
- **Ignoring Identity Early**: Azure AD strategy must be defined early to avoid ACL and RBAC chaos.
- **Inadequate Cost Monitoring**: Always implement tagging and cost controls at the start.
- **Lack of Governance**: Set guardrails before teams start deploying.
- **Skipping Training**: Ensure your ops and dev teams are trained in Azure services and automation tools.

Conclusion

Enterprise migration to Azure is a journey that goes far beyond simply moving VMs. It's an opportunity to rethink, refactor, and rebuild your IT operations into a more agile, secure, and cost-efficient framework. With proper planning, phased execution, and strategic use of Azure-native tools like Azure Migrate, Policy, Arc, and DevOps, even complex environments can be transformed. The real-world case presented shows how thoughtful migration drives measurable business value and paves the way for long-term digital transformation.

Cloud-Native Applications in Practice

Cloud-native applications represent a modern paradigm for building and deploying scalable, resilient, and agile software systems using cloud technologies. Unlike traditional monolithic applications, cloud-native solutions are built from the ground up to leverage the full potential of cloud platforms—embracing microservices, containerization, DevOps automation, managed services, and continuous delivery.

In this section, we explore what it means to design, build, deploy, and manage cloud-native applications in Azure. We break down architectural patterns, design principles, tooling choices, deployment practices, and common challenges—all illustrated through practical, production-grade examples.

What Makes an Application Cloud-Native?

Cloud-native applications typically exhibit the following characteristics:

- **Microservices Architecture**: Decomposed into loosely coupled, independently deployable services.
- **API-First Design**: Services expose well-defined APIs for interaction.
- **Containerization**: Each microservice is packaged with its dependencies.
- **DevOps Practices**: CI/CD pipelines, infrastructure as code, automated testing.
- **Elastic Scalability**: Able to scale horizontally across nodes or regions.
- **Observability**: Built-in telemetry, logging, tracing, and monitoring.

- **Resilience and Fault Tolerance**: Gracefully handle failures and self-heal.

Azure provides a comprehensive set of tools to support all these pillars.

Core Azure Services for Cloud-Native Applications

- **Azure Kubernetes Service (AKS)**: Managed Kubernetes for running containerized microservices.
- **Azure Container Apps**: Serverless containers for event-driven architectures.
- **Azure Functions**: Event-based, serverless computing.
- **Azure API Management (APIM)**: Secure, publish, and analyze APIs.
- **Azure Cosmos DB**: Globally distributed NoSQL database.
- **Azure Key Vault**: Secure secrets and certificate management.
- **Azure DevOps & GitHub Actions**: CI/CD and automation tooling.

Architectural Overview: A Sample Cloud-Native Application

Let's walk through the architecture of a real-world application—a ride-sharing platform built using cloud-native principles.

Key Components:

- **User Service** (AKS)
- **Ride Booking Service** (Azure Functions)
- **Payment Processor** (Container App)
- **Real-Time Location Tracking** (SignalR + Event Hubs)
- **API Gateway** (Azure APIM)
- **Database** (Cosmos DB for bookings, Azure SQL for payments)
- **CI/CD** (GitHub Actions)
- **Observability** (Azure Monitor, App Insights)

Microservices and Containerization with AKS

Each core domain (user, ride, payment) is deployed as a microservice inside AKS. Kubernetes manages service discovery, scaling, and rolling updates.

Example Kubernetes Deployment:

```
apiVersion: apps/v1

kind: Deployment

metadata:

name: user-service

spec:

replicas: 3
```

```
selector:
matchLabels:
app: user-service
template:
metadata:
labels:
app: user-service
spec:
containers:
- name: user-service
image: myregistry.azurecr.io/user-service:v1
ports:
- containerPort: 80
```

The deployment is exposed via an internal Kubernetes service and routed through APIM.

Event-Driven Serverless with Azure Functions

Ride bookings trigger workflows that don't require a constantly running backend. These are implemented as Azure Functions triggered by HTTP, queues, or Event Grid.

Example HTTP-triggered Azure Function (Python):

```
import logging
```

```
import azure.functions as func

def main(req: func.HttpRequest) -> func.HttpResponse:

user_id = req.params.get('userId')

if user_id:

return func.HttpResponse(f"Booking confirmed for user {user_id}")

else:

return func.HttpResponse("Missing userId", status_code=400)
```

Functions can scale to zero and handle spikes efficiently, which is ideal for sporadic but high-volume workloads like ride requests.

API Gateway Pattern with Azure APIM

APIM acts as the single entry point for all client applications. It abstracts and secures the microservices beneath it and supports rate limiting, caching, and logging.

Example: Rate Limiting Policy in APIM

```
<policies>

<inbound>

<rate-limit calls="100" renewal-period="60" />

<base />

</inbound>

</policies>
```

This prevents abuse of APIs by throttling requests per subscription key.

Managing Secrets with Azure Key Vault

Each microservice retrieves secrets (DB passwords, API keys) from Azure Key Vault during startup.

Example: Accessing Key Vault with a Managed Identity

```
az keyvault secret show \
—name PaymentServiceApiKey \
—vault-name MyKeyVault
```

In production, services use MSI and SDKs to fetch secrets securely without hardcoding credentials.

Data Layer: Choosing the Right Database

The platform uses a polyglot persistence strategy:

- **Cosmos DB**: Stores JSON documents for real-time ride tracking and user data.
- **Azure SQL**: Relational database for payment transactions and reporting.

Example Cosmos DB SDK Query (Node.js):

```
const querySpec = {
query: "SELECT * FROM c WHERE c.userId = @userId",
parameters: [{ name: "@userId", value: "abc123" }]
```

```
};

const { resources: results } = await container.items.query(querySpec).fetchAll();
```

Using the right data store for the workload optimizes both performance and cost.

CI/CD Pipeline with GitHub Actions

All services follow GitOps principles. Every code change triggers a pipeline that builds, tests, and deploys containers to AKS or Container Apps.

Example GitHub Actions Workflow for AKS:

```
jobs:

build-and-deploy:

runs-on: ubuntu-latest

steps:

- uses: actions/checkout@v2

- name: Log in to Azure

uses: azure/login@v1

with:

creds: ${{ secrets.AZURE_CREDENTIALS }}

- name: Deploy to AKS

run: |

az aks get-credentials—resource-group myrg—name myaks
```

kubectl apply -f k8s/user-service.yaml

The same model applies to infrastructure updates via Bicep or Terraform, enabling consistent IaC.

Observability with Azure Monitor and App Insights

Microservices are instrumented using OpenTelemetry, emitting traces, metrics, and logs to Azure Monitor.

Key telemetry components:

- **Distributed Tracing**: Track requests across services
- **Custom Metrics**: Monitor business KPIs like bookings per minute
- **Live Metrics Stream**: Real-time troubleshooting

Query Example in Log Analytics:

requests

| where cloud_RoleName == "user-service"

| summarize count() by bin(timestamp, 5m)

This gives visibility into service behavior and can drive alerts or automated remediation workflows.

Resilience and Health Checks

Each service implements health endpoints and liveness probes:

livenessProbe:

httpGet:

path: /health

port: 80

initialDelaySeconds: 10

periodSeconds: 5

AKS uses this to restart failing pods. Azure Front Door or Traffic Manager can be layered for global failover.

Security Best Practices

- **Network Policies**: Enforce east-west traffic restrictions in AKS.
- **RBAC**: Scoped per service team and namespace.
- **TLS Everywhere**: Use Azure-managed certificates.
- **Authentication**: JWT via Azure AD B2C for mobile clients, API tokens for internal services.
- **WAF**: Protect APIs using Application Gateway or APIM with WAF policies.

Cost Optimization Tactics

- Use **spot instances** for non-critical workloads.
- Schedule dev/test environments to shut down after hours.
- Enable autoscaling on AKS and App Services.

- Analyze cost reports using Azure Cost Management + Power BI.

Real-World Implementation Summary

A retail company implemented a cloud-native e-commerce system using:

- **BFF pattern** (Backend-for-Frontend) for web and mobile channels
- **Service Mesh** (Istio on AKS) for secure service-to-service communication
- **Redis on Azure Cache** for low-latency shopping cart management
- **Feature flags** using Azure App Configuration
- **Container Scanning** with Defender for Containers

Their average deployment velocity increased from once every 3 weeks to 20+ times per day, reducing downtime and increasing customer engagement.

Challenges and Considerations

- **Complexity**: Microservices require rigorous design, strong ops discipline.
- **Skill Requirements**: Devs must understand Docker, k8s, CI/CD, and monitoring.
- **State Management**: Distributed systems make consistency difficult.

- **Debugging**: Requires tools like Jaeger, OpenTelemetry, and centralized logs.
- **Latency**: Network hops between microservices can degrade performance.

Conclusion

Cloud-native development on Azure enables organizations to deliver software faster, more reliably, and at scale. By embracing microservices, containers, serverless functions, DevOps, and managed services, teams can build systems that are not only cloud-ready but cloud-optimized. From architectural flexibility to automated observability and global resiliency, cloud-native applications lay the foundation for continuous innovation and digital transformation. With the right mindset and tooling, any enterprise can evolve its legacy systems into modern, cloud-native ecosystems.

IoT and Big Data Workloads in Azure

The rise of the Internet of Things (IoT) and the exponential growth of data has transformed industries across the globe. From manufacturing to agriculture, healthcare to energy, connected devices and data-driven insights now play a vital role in operational efficiency, predictive maintenance, customer engagement, and strategic decision-making. Azure provides an enterprise-grade platform to handle the full lifecycle of IoT and big data workloads, from device connectivity to real-time analytics and machine learning.

This section explores the architecture, services, and implementation strategies for building secure, scalable, and intelligent IoT and big data systems in Azure. We'll walk through common components, deployment patterns, storage approaches, analytics workflows, and integration with artificial intelligence to build real-world-ready solutions.

Key Principles of IoT and Big Data Design

IoT and big data workloads share several architectural principles:

- **Scalability**: Systems must handle millions of devices and events per second.
- **Resilience**: Failures in hardware or software should be isolated and recoverable.
- **Real-time Processing**: Some use cases require sub-second decision-making.
- **Batch and Historical Analysis**: Long-term trends, forecasts, and ML training.
- **Security by Design**: End-to-end encryption, identity, and access control.
- **Data Governance**: Compliant storage, classification, and retention policies.

Azure enables all of these through a modular, integrated services approach.

End-to-End Architecture Overview

A typical IoT and big data solution in Azure includes:

1. **Device Layer**

Sensors, edge devices, industrial machines generating telemetry.

2. **Connectivity Layer**

○ Azure IoT Hub or IoT Central for secure, scalable device communication.

○ Azure IoT Edge for local processing.

3. **Ingestion Layer**

○ Azure Event Hubs for high-throughput streaming.

○ Azure Functions for reactive processing.

○ Azure Stream Analytics for real-time querying.

4. **Storage Layer**

○ Azure Data Lake Storage Gen2 for raw and transformed data.

○ Cosmos DB for low-latency document access.

○ Time Series Insights for time-based visual exploration.

5. **Processing & Analytics Layer**

○ Azure Synapse Analytics for big data querying.

○ Azure Databricks for distributed Spark-based processing.

○ Azure Machine Learning for model training and inference.

6. **Visualization Layer**

○ Power BI for dashboards.

○ Azure Monitor and Application Insights for observability.

Device Connectivity and Management

Azure IoT Hub acts as a central broker between devices and the cloud. It supports:

- Bi-directional communication (device-to-cloud and cloud-to-device).
- Device identity and per-device credentials.
- Integration with Azure Defender for IoT for security.
- Device provisioning with the IoT Hub Device Provisioning Service (DPS).

Example: Registering a Device with DPS

```
az iot dps enrollment create \
—dps-name "myDPS" \
—resource-group "iot-rg" \
—enrollment-id "device001" \
—attestation-type "symmetricKey" \
—primary-key "base64primarykey" \
```

—secondary-key "base64secondarykey" \

—iot-hubs "my-iot-hub"

Real-Time Ingestion and Event Processing

Once devices are connected, telemetry data is ingested using Azure Event Hubs or routed via IoT Hub's Event Grid integration. Event Hubs supports millions of events per second and integrates with downstream services.

Use **Azure Stream Analytics** for filtering, aggregation, and transformation in real time.

Example: Detect High Temperature Events

```
SELECT
deviceId,
temperature,
System.Timestamp AS eventTime
INTO
alertOutput
FROM
iotInput
WHERE
temperature > 80
```

The result can trigger Azure Functions, write to storage, or push to a Power BI dashboard.

Serverless Transformation with Azure Functions

Azure Functions can process events from Event Hubs or IoT Hub using triggers. Functions are cost-effective and auto-scale on demand.

Example: Event Hub Trigger for JSON Telemetry

```
import json

def main(event: func.EventHubEvent):

data = json.loads(event.get_body().decode('utf-8'))

if data["vibration"] > 1.2:

# call alerting system

send_alert(data["deviceId"], data["vibration"])
```

This architecture decouples ingestion from processing and enables microservice-style event handlers.

Data Lake and Time-Based Storage

Azure Data Lake Storage Gen2 is optimized for hierarchical file access, fine-grained security, and massive parallelism. It's the foundation for batch processing and ML training.

Best practices:

- Use partitioned folders (e.g., year/month/day/hour).

- Use Parquet or Avro format for efficiency.
- Integrate with Synapse or Databricks.

Folder structure example:

/raw/telemetry/year=2025/month=04/day=20/hour=13/

/processed/anomalies/year=2025/month=04/

Time Series and Observability

Azure Time Series Insights provides a purpose-built environment for analyzing time-ordered sensor data. It integrates directly with IoT Hub and supports:

- Event visualization.
- Querying across billions of events.
- Heatmaps, anomalies, and drill-downs.

For broader observability, use **Azure Monitor**, **Log Analytics**, and **Application Insights** to track processing latency, error rates, and system health.

Big Data Analytics with Synapse and Databricks

Azure Synapse Analytics enables SQL-based exploration of data in Data Lake and integration with pipelines.

Example: Querying Sensor Averages in Synapse

SELECT

deviceId,

```
AVG(temperature) AS avg_temp,

COUNT(*) AS count_readings

FROM

OPENROWSET(

BULK 'https://datalake.blob.core.windows.net/telemetry/*.parquet',

FORMAT='PARQUET'

) AS data

GROUP BY deviceId
```

Azure Databricks supports Apache Spark for distributed machine learning, stream processing, and ETL at scale.

```
from pyspark.sql import SparkSession

spark = SparkSession.builder.appName("IoTAnalysis").getOrCreate()

df = spark.read.parquet("abfss://telemetry@datalake.dfs.core.windows.net/raw/")

df.filter(df.temperature > 80).groupBy("deviceId").count().show()
```

Machine Learning and Predictive Models

IoT workloads benefit greatly from predictive analytics—forecasting demand, predicting failure, or optimizing operations.

Use **Azure Machine Learning** to build and deploy models:

- Train with historical telemetry in Data Lake.
- Deploy to real-time scoring endpoints.
- Run inference at the edge using IoT Edge modules.

Model Deployment Example

```
az ml model deploy \
—name anomaly-detector \
—model-id mymodel:1 \
—inference-config inference.json \
—deployment-config aci.json
```

Models can also be integrated into Stream Analytics jobs using the PREDICT function or called from Azure Functions.

Security Architecture

Security spans device to cloud and must address:

- **Device Authentication**: Unique keys or certificates per device.
- **Data Encryption**: TLS for in-transit, AES for at-rest.
- **RBAC and Policies**: Apply to IoT Hub, storage accounts, Synapse.
- **Azure Defender for IoT**: Monitors threat patterns and alerts.

- **Private Endpoints**: Secure access to Event Hubs, Functions, and storage.

Real-World Case Study: Smart Agriculture System

A global agricultural company deployed Azure-based IoT systems across 10,000+ farms:

- Soil moisture, temperature, and weather sensors stream to IoT Hub.
- Data is enriched and stored in Data Lake.
- Stream Analytics triggers alerts for irrigation.
- Synapse provides seasonal yield forecasting.
- Azure ML predicts pest outbreaks using environmental patterns.
- Farmers access Power BI dashboards and get alerts via mobile apps.

Results:

- 30% improvement in crop yield.
- 25% reduction in water usage.
- Unified view of operations across regions and farms.

Challenges and Best Practices

Challenges:

- **Data Overload**: Implement filtering and aggregation early.

- **Edge Connectivity**: Use IoT Edge for local decision-making.

- **Latency Sensitivity**: Real-time vs batch workloads must be clearly separated.

- **Device Diversity**: Standardize protocols (MQTT, AMQP) and SDKs.

- **Data Governance**: Implement tagging, classification, and retention policies.

Best Practices:

- Use **Device Twins** for metadata and configuration.

- Leverage **IoT Central** for rapid prototyping.

- Enforce **naming conventions** and **n-tier architecture** in pipelines.

- Adopt **Infrastructure as Code** (e.g., Bicep, Terraform) for reproducibility.

- Integrate **GitOps and CI/CD** for processing components.

Conclusion

IoT and big data workloads in Azure represent one of the most impactful ways for organizations to gain operational insights, automate responses, and create predictive, intelligent systems.

With tools like IoT Hub, Event Hubs, Stream Analytics, Synapse, Data Lake, Azure Machine Learning, and Power BI, Azure offers a complete stack to implement scalable, secure, and insightful solutions. Enterprises embracing this architecture position themselves for significant innovation, efficiency, and competitive advantage in a data-driven world.

FinTech, Healthcare, and Government Deployments

Deploying cloud-based solutions in highly regulated industries like FinTech, healthcare, and government presents unique challenges. These sectors must navigate complex compliance frameworks, ensure strict data security, and meet performance and reliability standards while still delivering innovation, scale, and user-centric digital experiences. Azure's broad set of services—along with its robust compliance portfolio—makes it a compelling platform for building mission-critical applications in these verticals.

This section explores how Azure enables tailored cloud deployments in FinTech, healthcare, and public sector environments. It outlines design patterns, compliance considerations, secure deployment strategies, and real-world architecture examples that illustrate best practices across each domain.

Shared Requirements Across Regulated Industries

Despite their differences, FinTech, healthcare, and government workloads often share the following core requirements:

- **High Availability and Resilience**
- **Data Sovereignty and Residency**

- **Identity Federation and Role-Based Access Control**
- **Zero Trust Security Posture**
- **Regulatory Compliance (e.g., PCI-DSS, HIPAA, FedRAMP)**
- **Auditability and Logging**
- **Encryption in Transit and at Rest**
- **Secure DevOps (DevSecOps)**

Azure services are aligned with these needs through tools like Azure Policy, Azure Blueprints, Microsoft Defender for Cloud, and regulatory-specific compliance offerings.

FinTech Deployments in Azure

The financial services industry demands robust performance, low latency, and adherence to regulatory standards such as **PCI-DSS**, **SOX**, and **GDPR**. Azure supports FinTech organizations with:

- **High-throughput compute** via Azure Kubernetes Service (AKS) or Azure Functions
- **Real-time analytics** with Azure Synapse and Event Hubs
- **Secure payments infrastructure** using Azure Confidential Ledger
- **Compliance with financial standards** via Azure Policy and Compliance Manager

FinTech Architecture Example: Digital Payments Platform

Scenario: A FinTech startup wants to build a secure, real-time payment processing platform using microservices.

Architecture:

- **Frontend**: React + Azure Static Web Apps
- **API Gateway**: Azure API Management
- **Backend Services**: AKS-hosted microservices for payments, fraud detection, account management
- **Event Processing**: Azure Event Grid for transaction events
- **Data Layer**: Azure SQL for transactions, Cosmos DB for session and identity data
- **Compliance & Monitoring**: Azure Policy, Azure Monitor, Key Vault, and Defender for Cloud

Code Snippet: Event Grid Subscription for Transaction Events

```
az eventgrid event-subscription create \

—name payment-events \

—source-resource-id "/subscriptions/xxx/resourceGroups/rg/providers/Microsoft.EventGrid/topics/transactionTopic" \

—endpoint https://fraud-detection-service/api/process \

—endpoint-type webhook
```

Compliance Tip: Use Azure Blueprints with predefined artifacts to deploy a PCI-DSS compliant environment.

Healthcare Deployments in Azure

Healthcare organizations handle **Protected Health Information (PHI)** and must comply with frameworks such as **HIPAA**, **HITECH**, **ISO 27799**, and **GDPR**. Azure enables secure, scalable health tech solutions that improve patient care, enable interoperability, and accelerate clinical research.

Key Azure services for healthcare:

- **FHIR Server for Azure**: Standards-compliant API for healthcare data exchange
- **Azure Health Data Services**: Unified platform for clinical data ingestion and normalization
- **Azure Machine Learning**: Predictive modeling for patient outcomes
- **Azure API for FHIR + Azure Logic Apps**: Automating workflows between EMRs and external systems

Healthcare Architecture Example: Remote Patient Monitoring (RPM)

Scenario: A healthcare provider wants to build an RPM solution that collects vitals from wearable devices and alerts care teams in real-time.

Architecture:

- **Device Integration**: Azure IoT Hub receives data from wearables
- **Event Processing**: Azure Stream Analytics to flag abnormal readings
- **Data Normalization**: Azure API for FHIR
- **Visualization**: Power BI dashboards for care teams
- **Data Storage**: Azure Data Lake Gen2 (historical), Cosmos DB (real-time)
- **AI/ML**: Azure ML for risk scoring models
- **Security**: Azure AD B2C for patient access, Key Vault, Private Endpoints

Code Snippet: Stream Analytics Rule for Detecting Abnormal Heart Rate

```
SELECT

deviceId,

AVG(heartRate) AS avg_heartRate

INTO

alertOutput

FROM

iotInput TIMESTAMP BY eventTime

GROUP BY deviceId, TumblingWindow(minute, 1)
```

HAVING AVG(heartRate) > 120

Compliance Tip: Enable Diagnostic Settings and export logs to a secure Log Analytics workspace for HIPAA audit trails.

Government Deployments in Azure

Public sector agencies are often bound by stringent security and compliance mandates such as **FedRAMP High**, **CJIS**, **ITAR**, and **DoD IL5**. Azure Government and Azure Government Secret offer dedicated cloud environments with isolated hardware and restricted personnel access.

Key considerations:

- **Sovereign Data Environments**: US-only data centers with US-only support staff
- **Role-based Access Control (RBAC)** integrated with Microsoft Entra ID (Azure AD)
- **High availability and DR** for mission-critical workloads
- **Offline capabilities** using Azure Stack Hub

Government Architecture Example: Citizen Services Portal

Scenario: A local government wants to modernize its citizen services portal for tax filings, licensing, and support requests.

Architecture:

- **Frontend**: Blazor app hosted in Azure App Services

- **Authentication**: Azure AD B2C with multi-factor authentication
- **Backend APIs**: Azure Functions
- **Data**: Azure SQL Database for records; Blob Storage for documents
- **Workflow**: Azure Logic Apps for application approvals
- **Logging**: Azure Monitor with custom dashboards for performance metrics
- **Compliance**: Azure Blueprints for FedRAMP High configuration

Code Snippet: Azure Function for License Renewal Submission

```
[FunctionName("SubmitLicenseRenewal")]

public static async Task<IActionResult> Run(

[HttpTrigger(AuthorizationLevel.Function, "post", Route = null)] HttpRequest req,

ILogger log)

{

string requestBody = await new StreamReader(req.Body).ReadToEndAsync();

var data = JsonConvert.DeserializeObject<LicenseRequest>(requestBody);

await _databaseService.SaveAsync(data);
```

```
return new OkObjectResult("Renewal Submitted");
}
```

Security Tip: Implement Azure Security Center recommendations and use Just-In-Time VM access to reduce attack surface.

Common Strategies for Regulated Cloud Deployments

1. Zero Trust Architecture

- **Identity-Centric Access**: All users and devices must authenticate.
- **Microsegmentation**: Use NSGs, ASGs, and Azure Firewall to restrict lateral movement.
- **Conditional Access**: Enforce access policies based on risk level and location.

2. Policy-Driven Enforcement

- Define custom policies in Azure Policy (e.g., enforce tag compliance, prevent public IPs).
- Use **initiative definitions** to group multiple policies and track compliance posture.

3. Encryption and Key Management

- Use **customer-managed keys** (CMKs) via Azure Key Vault.

- Enable **Double Encryption** where required.
- Secure storage accounts and databases with **Always Encrypted** or **TDE**.

4. Secure DevOps (DevSecOps)

- Integrate static analysis, container scanning, and secrets management into CI/CD pipelines.
- Use tools like GitHub Advanced Security or Microsoft Defender for DevOps.
- Define IaC standards with Terraform/Bicep and enforce reviews and scans.

5. Data Loss Prevention (DLP) and Governance

- Use Microsoft Purview to classify, catalog, and govern sensitive data.
- Set DLP policies and monitor policy violations.
- Apply role-based permissions on Purview assets.

Real-World Impact

FinTech: A European neobank built its entire infrastructure on Azure, achieving PSD2 compliance using Azure AD, Key Vault, and Azure SQL. It scaled to 2M users and reduced fraud by 38% through AI-driven risk scoring.

Healthcare: A US-based hospital network deployed a telehealth platform using Azure API for FHIR, integrated with their Epic EMR. They achieved HIPAA compliance and scaled to 5,000 virtual visits per day.

Government: A city in Australia migrated its entire permit processing system to Azure Government. Using Azure Logic Apps and Power Platform, they reduced application time by 60% and increased citizen satisfaction.

Conclusion

Azure provides a secure, compliant, and scalable foundation for mission-critical applications in FinTech, healthcare, and government. By leveraging purpose-built services, adopting a Zero Trust approach, and applying automation across governance and deployment, organizations in regulated industries can transform with confidence. Whether it's securing financial transactions, improving patient outcomes, or delivering efficient public services, Azure enables innovation without compromising trust or compliance.

Chapter 12: Appendices

Glossary of Terms

Understanding the terminology used throughout this book is essential for successfully navigating the Azure ecosystem. This glossary provides definitions and context for a wide range of foundational terms, covering infrastructure, services, architecture patterns, security, governance, and development practices in the Azure cloud. Whether you're a beginner building your first cloud solution or an experienced architect working on complex enterprise systems, these terms will serve as a valuable reference.

Availability Zone

A physically separate zone within an Azure region designed to provide high availability. Each zone is made up of one or more data centers equipped with independent power, cooling, and networking. Applications deployed across multiple zones are protected against datacenter-level failures.

Azure Active Directory (Azure AD)

Microsoft's cloud-based identity and access management service. It allows employees to sign in and access resources in external and internal services securely. Azure AD supports features like SSO, MFA, conditional access, B2B/B2C identity federation, and integration with on-premises directories.

Azure Arc

A set of technologies that allows Azure services to be extended to environments outside of Azure, including on-premises data centers, edge devices, and other cloud providers. It enables centralized management and governance of hybrid and multi-cloud infrastructure.

Azure CLI

The Azure Command-Line Interface is a cross-platform tool used to create and manage Azure resources via the terminal or shell. It's scriptable and supports automation scenarios.

Example:

az vm create—name myVM—resource-group myRG—image UbuntuLTS

Azure DevOps

A suite of development tools for software teams, including Azure Repos, Azure Pipelines, Azure Boards, and Azure Test Plans. It enables CI/CD, version control, backlog tracking, and test automation, and integrates tightly with GitHub and Visual Studio.

Azure Functions

A serverless compute service that enables you to run code on-demand without provisioning or managing infrastructure. Ideal for event-driven workloads and microservices.

Azure Kubernetes Service (AKS)

A fully managed Kubernetes service that simplifies deploying, managing, and operating containerized applications. It offers features like auto-scaling, integrated monitoring, and security hardening.

Azure Monitor

A service that collects and analyzes telemetry data (metrics, logs, traces) from applications and infrastructure, helping you understand performance and detect issues. It integrates with Log Analytics, Application Insights, and custom dashboards.

Azure Policy

A service for enforcing organizational standards and assessing compliance at scale. It allows you to create policies that govern resource creation and configurations, ensuring security and cost efficiency.

Example policy: Deny virtual machines in unapproved regions.

Azure Resource Manager (ARM)

The deployment and management service for Azure. It provides a consistent management layer to create, update, and delete resources using declarative templates (ARM templates), CLI, PowerShell, REST API, or SDKs.

Bicep

A domain-specific language (DSL) for deploying Azure resources declaratively. Bicep simplifies the syntax of ARM templates and improves developer productivity.

Example:

resource storage 'Microsoft.Storage/storageAccounts@2022-09-01' = {

name: 'mystorageacct'

```
location: resourceGroup().location
sku: {
name: 'Standard_LRS'
}
kind: 'StorageV2'
}
```

Blob Storage

An Azure service for storing unstructured data such as images, documents, videos, and logs. It offers different tiers (hot, cool, archive) for managing cost and access performance.

Cloud Adoption Framework (CAF)

A Microsoft framework that provides guidance and best practices for adopting Azure in a structured, strategic way. It includes phases like strategy, plan, ready, adopt, govern, and manage.

Cloud-Native Application

An application built specifically to run and scale in a cloud environment. Typically consists of microservices, containerization, DevOps practices, and use of managed services.

Conditional Access

A feature of Azure AD that provides policy-based controls to enforce access restrictions based on conditions like user location, device state, and risk levels.

Container

A lightweight, standalone executable package of software that includes everything needed to run it: code, runtime, libraries, and dependencies. Containers are managed using tools like Docker and orchestrated in Azure via AKS or Azure Container Apps.

Data Lake

A storage repository that holds vast amounts of raw data in its native format until needed. Azure Data Lake Storage Gen2 integrates with analytics services like Synapse and Databricks.

Defender for Cloud

A unified infrastructure security management system that strengthens the security posture of your Azure environment and provides advanced threat protection for workloads across Azure, hybrid, and other clouds.

Disaster Recovery (DR)

The process of restoring application functionality and data access after an outage. Azure Site Recovery enables automated DR for virtual machines and physical servers.

Elasticity

The cloud's ability to automatically allocate and de-allocate resources to match workload demands. Azure offers services like VM Scale Sets and App Service autoscaling for elastic resource management.

Event Grid

An event routing service that allows services to publish and subscribe to events in a reactive architecture. Commonly used with Azure Functions, Logic Apps, and custom event sources.

ExpressRoute

A service that provides a private connection between on-premises networks and Azure data centers, bypassing the public internet. Ideal for performance-sensitive and secure workloads.

High Availability (HA)

A design approach ensuring that a system or application remains operational for a high percentage of time. Azure supports HA via availability zones, sets, and geographically redundant services.

Hybrid Cloud

A computing model that combines on-premises infrastructure (private cloud) with public cloud services, allowing data and applications to move between environments. Azure Stack and Azure Arc support hybrid scenarios.

Infrastructure as Code (IaC)

The practice of managing and provisioning infrastructure using code templates rather than manual processes. Azure supports IaC through ARM templates, Bicep, Terraform, and Pulumi.

Key Vault

A secure service for managing secrets, keys, and certificates used by cloud applications and services. Access is tightly controlled using RBAC and managed identities.

Load Balancer

A service that distributes network traffic across multiple servers or services. Azure Load Balancer operates at layer 4 (TCP/UDP), while Application Gateway operates at layer 7 (HTTP/HTTPS).

Managed Identity

An identity managed by Azure AD that can authenticate to Azure services without storing credentials in code. Useful for securing API calls from Azure VMs, Functions, and Logic Apps.

Microservices

An architectural style where an application is composed of small, independent services that communicate over APIs. Azure supports microservices through AKS, Service Fabric, and Azure Container Apps.

Network Security Group (NSG)

A security filter that controls traffic to and from Azure resources at the network interface or subnet level. Rules can be inbound or outbound and are based on IP, port, and protocol.

PaaS (Platform as a Service)

A cloud computing model that delivers application development and deployment platforms as a managed service. Azure App

Services, Azure Functions, and Azure SQL Database are PaaS offerings.

RBAC (Role-Based Access Control)

A mechanism for assigning permissions to users, groups, and services based on their role in the organization. Azure RBAC enables fine-grained access control to resources.

Resource Group

A logical container that holds related Azure resources. Resource groups help manage and organize resources for deployment, access control, and billing.

Serverless

A computing model where you write and deploy code without managing infrastructure. Azure Functions and Azure Logic Apps are key serverless services.

Site-to-Site VPN

A secure connection between an on-premises network and Azure virtual networks. Enables hybrid connectivity using VPN Gateway.

Virtual Network (VNet)

An isolated, private network within Azure where resources such as VMs and databases communicate securely. Supports subnets, route tables, NSGs, and peering.

Virtual Machine Scale Sets (VMSS)

An Azure service that lets you deploy and manage a set of auto-scaling virtual machines. Useful for stateless applications that require elasticity.

Zero Trust

A security model that assumes no implicit trust and verifies every access request. Azure supports Zero Trust through identity protection, conditional access, device compliance, and segmented networks.

This glossary serves as a foundational reference for understanding and navigating the Azure ecosystem effectively. Keep it handy as you explore and build with Azure to ensure clarity and consistency across your projects.

Resources for Further Learning

Learning Azure is an ongoing journey. The platform evolves continuously, with new services, integrations, and best practices introduced at a rapid pace. To stay current, reinforce foundational knowledge, and explore specialized domains, it's essential to build a habit of continuous learning. This section provides an extensive list of high-quality resources for deepening your Azure expertise, from official documentation and certification guides to community blogs, forums, open-source repositories, and hands-on labs.

These resources are organized by learning modality and depth—from introductory overviews to advanced architectures—covering various formats such as written guides, video tutorials, interactive labs, certifications, and communities of practice.

Microsoft Official Documentation

The officialMicrosoft Learn[2] platform is the definitive source for Azure learning. It includes interactive, role-based learning paths and is regularly updated to reflect the latest changes in the platform.

Recommended modules:

- **Azure Fundamentals**: Ideal for beginners
- **Architecting Cloud Solutions**: Mid-level content for aspiring cloud architects
- **Manage Resources with Azure CLI and ARM Templates**: DevOps and infrastructure automation
- **Azure for Developers**: Focuses on App Services, Functions, SDKs
- **Security, Compliance, and Identity Fundamentals**

Each module contains interactive code labs, quizzes, and guided walkthroughs.

Microsoft Learn Sandbox

Microsoft provides a **free sandbox** environment where you can complete labs without needing your own subscription. The sandbox resets after use and is perfect for testing:

az login

az group create—name learn-rg—location eastus

---

2. https://learn.microsoft.com/en-us/training/azure/

az vm create—resource-group learn-rg—name learn-vm—image UbuntuLTS

The sandbox is included in many Learn modules and allows you to safely test features in a controlled environment.

Azure Certifications

Microsoft offers a series of role-based certifications that validate your knowledge of Azure services and your ability to design, build, secure, and optimize cloud-based solutions.

Foundational:

- **AZ-900**: Microsoft Azure Fundamentals

  Topics: Cloud concepts, core services, pricing, and support

Associate Level:

- **AZ-104**: Azure Administrator

  Topics: VM provisioning, network setup, storage, identities

- **AZ-204**: Azure Developer

  Topics: PaaS solutions, APIs, storage, monitoring

Expert Level:

- **AZ-305**: Azure Solutions Architect

  Topics: Hybrid networking, governance, identity, BCDR

- **AZ-400**: Azure DevOps Engineer

  Topics: CI/CD, IaC, testing strategies, security

Each exam has an associated learning path, available for free on Microsoft Learn.

Books and eBooks

A selection of curated reading materials for deep dives:

- **"Exam Ref AZ-104 Microsoft Azure Administrator"** – Microsoft Press

  Structured study material for the certification.

- **"Azure Architecture Explained"** – Packt Publishing

  Real-world design patterns and reference architectures.

- **"Azure for Architects" by Ritesh Modi** – Packt

  A practical guide covering hybrid setups, security, and scalability.

- **"Microsoft Azure Security Infrastructure"** – Yuri Diogenes, Tom Shinder

  Detailed focus on securing infrastructure and compliance.

- **"Serverless computing in Azure with .NET"** – Microsoft Docs

  A focused ebook for developers using Functions and Logic Apps.

These books are available in print, PDF, and Kindle editions, and are often updated to include new features.

Video Learning Platforms

Microsoft Learn TV

- Live and on-demand videos from Azure engineers.
- Covers new service releases, best practices, and case studies.

Pluralsight (Partnered with Microsoft)

- Curated paths for certifications.
- Labs and assessments included.
- Free access for Microsoft-certified students or Azure learners via sponsored programs.

LinkedIn Learning

- Offers courses like "Azure Essential Training," "Designing for Resiliency," and "Monitoring Azure Workloads."

YouTube Channels

- Microsoft Azure (Official): News, tutorials, case studies
- John Savill's Technical Training: Deep technical dives, whiteboarding

- Azure Friday: Bite-sized service introductions and walkthroughs

---

Open-Source and GitHub Repositories

The open-source ecosystem around Azure is vibrant. Microsoft and the community maintain numerous GitHub repos with templates, tools, and patterns.

Key repositories:

- https://github.com/Azure/azure-quickstart-templates

  Thousands of ARM/Bicep templates to deploy real-world scenarios.

- https://github.com/Azure/azure-architecture-center

  Reference architectures, decision trees, and implementation guides.

- https://github.com/Azure/terraform

  Terraform modules for deploying and managing Azure infrastructure.

- https://github.com/Azure/azure-cli

  CLI development and contributions.

Example deployment using a quickstart template:

az deployment group create \

—resource-group demo-rg \

—template-uri "https://raw.githubusercontent.com/Azure/azure-quickstart-templates/master/101-vm-simple-linux/azuredeploy.json"

Interactive Labs and Sandboxes

Microsoft Hands-on Labs

- Scenario-based challenges in a live Azure environment.
- Includes guided and unguided options.

Katacoda (Archived)

- Still hosts Azure CLI and Azure Functions walkthroughs.

Cloud Skills Challenge (Microsoft Events)

- Time-bound competitions with labs and quizzes.
- Often tied to free exam vouchers and swag.

Whizlabs and A Cloud Guru

- Hands-on labs, quizzes, and practice exams tailored to Azure certs.

Communities, Forums, and Blogs

Engaging with the community can rapidly accelerate learning and keep you informed of real-world applications.

Tech Community:

https://techcommunity.microsoft.com/t5/azure

- Blog posts, webinars, and discussions from Microsoft staff and MVPs.

Stack Overflow

- A treasure trove of Azure-related Q&A, often referenced by Microsoft Docs.

Reddit:

- r/AZURE: Community discussions, r/AzureDevOps for pipeline-specific topics.

Azure Weekly:

- A curated newsletter with latest news, articles, and community contributions.

Bloggers to follow:

- Thomas Maurer (Microsoft): Azure Hybrid and Infra
- Scott Hanselman: Developer productivity, Azure App Services
- Sarah Lean: Hybrid cloud, migration, IT Ops

Azure Architecture Center

One of the most powerful resources for cloud architects is theAzure Architecture Center[3].

3. https://learn.microsoft.com/en-us/azure/architecture/

What you'll find:

- Reference architectures
- Design patterns (e.g., CQRS, Event Sourcing, Retry)
- Cloud design principles (scalability, reliability, security)
- Decision guides and checklists
- Industry-specific designs (e.g., FinTech, Healthcare)

These architectures are illustrated with diagrams, component breakdowns, trade-offs, and GitHub samples.

Staying Current: News and Releases

To keep up with Azure's rapid evolution:

- **Azure Updates**:https://azure.microsoft.com/en-us/updates/

  Official announcements of new features and deprecations.

- **Azure Roadmap**:

  Future service improvements and upcoming regional availability.

- **Azure Blog**:https://azure.microsoft.com/en-us/blog/

  Technical deep dives, service launches, and case studies.

- **Build and Ignite Conferences:**

Microsoft's flagship events showcasing innovation and roadmap previews.

Learning Paths by Role

Developers

- Azure App Services
- Serverless with Azure Functions
- API Management and Logic Apps
- Azure SDKs (.NET, JavaScript, Python)

Admins / Ops

- Identity and Access Management
- Virtual Networking and NSGs
- Resource Management and Governance
- BCDR (Backup and Site Recovery)

Architects

- Hybrid Networking
- Monitoring and Telemetry
- Scaling and High Availability

- Secure DevOps Patterns

Security Professionals

- Defender for Cloud
- Azure Sentinel
- Azure Key Vault and Secrets
- Policy and Compliance Enforcement

Conclusion

The Azure learning ecosystem is vast and ever-growing. Whether you're studying for a certification, architecting a production system, or simply exploring cloud computing for the first time, there are resources tailored to your learning style and experience level. Bookmark the documentation, subscribe to newsletters, attend community events, and build projects. With persistent curiosity and the right resources, mastering Azure is entirely within reach.

Sample Projects and Code Snippets

To truly understand and retain Azure concepts, hands-on experience is essential. This section provides a curated collection of sample projects and reusable code snippets that span key services and architectural patterns discussed throughout the book. These projects are intended to reinforce your understanding, accelerate learning, and provide a reference for building real-world solutions.

Each project includes a description of the use case, the Azure services involved, deployment guidance, and code where appropriate. You can run these projects in your own Azure subscription using the Azure CLI, Bicep, or ARM templates.

Project 1: Serverless Contact Form API

Objective: Create a serverless backend for a website's contact form using Azure Functions, Azure Storage, and SendGrid.

Services Used:

- Azure Functions (HTTP Trigger)
- Azure Blob Storage
- SendGrid Email API
- Azure Key Vault (optional, for securing the API key)

Steps:

1. **Create a Resource Group**:

az group create—name contactapi-rg—location eastus

1. **Deploy the Function App**:

az functionapp create \

—resource-group contactapi-rg \

—consumption-plan-location eastus \

—runtime node \

—functions-version 4 \

—name contactform-fn \

—storage-account contactstorageacct

1. **Function Code (JavaScript):**

```
module.exports = async function (context, req) {

const sgMail = require('@sendgrid/mail');

sgMail.setApiKey(process.env.SENDGRID_API_KEY);

const msg = {

to: 'support@example.com',

from: 'no-reply@example.com',

subject: `New Contact: ${req.body.name}`,

text: req.body.message

};

await sgMail.send(msg);

context.res = {

status: 200,

body: 'Message sent successfully'

};

};
```

This is an excellent starting point for anyone exploring serverless architectures or email-based workflows.

Project 2: Static Website with CDN and Custom

Domain

Objective: Host a performant, globally distributed static website using Azure Storage, Azure CDN, and a custom domain with HTTPS.

Services Used:

- Azure Storage (Static Website feature)
- Azure CDN (Microsoft or Verizon profile)
- Azure DNS or external domain registrar

Steps:

1. **Create a storage account and enable static website hosting**:

```
az storage account create \
—name staticwebdemo \
—resource-group webdemo-rg \
—location westus \
—sku Standard_LRS \
—kind StorageV2
az storage blob service-properties update \
—account-name staticwebdemo \
—static-website \
—index-document index.html \
```

—error-document 404.html

1. **Upload content:**

az storage blob upload-batch \

—account-name staticwebdemo \

—source ./site \

—destination '$web'

1. **Configure CDN and link it to the storage endpoint.**

This project helps reinforce foundational knowledge of storage, DNS, and performance optimization.

Project 3: IoT Telemetry Pipeline

Objective: Simulate an IoT scenario where devices stream telemetry to Azure IoT Hub, process the data with Stream Analytics, and persist it to a SQL Database.

Services Used:

- Azure IoT Hub
- Azure Stream Analytics
- Azure SQL Database
- Azure Monitor

Steps:

1. **Create the IoT Hub:**

az iot hub create—name iotpipelinehub—resource-group iot-rg—sku S1

1. **Simulate device messages** (Python):

```
import time

import json

from azure.iot.device import IoTHubDeviceClient, Message

conn_str = "HostName=iotpipelinehub.azure-devices.net;DeviceId=dev01;SharedA

client = IoTHubDeviceClient.create_from_connection_string(conn_str)

while True:

telemetry = {

"temperature": 68 + (5 * random.random()),

"humidity": 30 + (10 * random.random())

}

message = Message(json.dumps(telemetry))

client.send_message(message)

time.sleep(10)
```

1. **Set up Stream Analytics job to write to SQL**:

```
SELECT

temperature,
```

humidity,

System.Timestamp AS recorded_at

INTO

sqloutput

FROM

iothubinput

This project demonstrates end-to-end streaming and data persistence using fully managed services.

Project 4: Scalable Web API with AKS and Cosmos DB

Objective: Deploy a RESTful API on Azure Kubernetes Service (AKS) with Cosmos DB as the backend database.

Services Used:

- Azure Kubernetes Service
- Azure Container Registry
- Azure Cosmos DB (MongoDB API)
- Azure Key Vault
- Azure Monitor for containers

Steps:

1. **Create AKS cluster and container registry**:

az acr create—name apidemoacr—resource-group apirg—sku Basic

az aks create—resource-group apirg—name apidemoaks—node-count 3—enable-addons monitoring—generate-ssh-keys—attach-acr apidemoacr

1. **Create Cosmos DB with Mongo API**:

az cosmosdb create—name apicosmos—resource-group apirg—kind MongoDB

1. **Sample Express.js API**:

```
const express = require('express');

const mongoose = require('mongoose');

mongoose.connect(process.env.MONGO_URL);

const Reading = mongoose.model('Reading', {

temperature: Number,

timestamp: Date

});

const app = express();

app.use(express.json());

app.post('/reading', async (req, res) => {

const reading = new Reading(req.body);

await reading.save();
```

```
res.status(201).send(reading);
});
app.listen(3000, () => console.log('Server running'));
```

1. **Build, push, and deploy using Helm or kubectl.**

This project is ideal for learning containers, NoSQL databases, and full-stack cloud development.

Project 5: Secure B2C-Enabled Portal

Objective: Build a web app that allows external users to register and log in using Azure AD B2C, securely calling a protected API.

Services Used:

- Azure AD B2C
- Azure App Service
- Azure API Management
- Azure Key Vault

Steps:

1. **Create an Azure AD B2C tenant** and configure user flows for sign-up and sign-in.
2. **Register SPA and API applications** in B2C.
3. **Frontend (React with MSAL.js)**:

```
const msalConfig = {
auth: {
```

```
clientId: "your-client-id",

authority:
"https://<tenant>.b2clogin.com/<tenant>.onmicrosoft.com/
B2C_1_signup_signin"

}

};

const msalInstance = new PublicClientApplication(msalConfig);
```

1. **Backend (Node.js API protected by JWT)**:

```
const jwt = require('express-jwt');

const jwks = require('jwks-rsa');

app.use(jwt({

secret: jwks.expressJwtSecret({

jwksUri:
'https://<tenant>.b2clogin.com/<tenant>.onmicrosoft.com/
discovery/v2.0/keys',

cache: true,

rateLimit: true

}),

algorithms: ['RS256']

}));
```

This project demonstrates secure authentication, JWT validation, and protecting APIs in a real-world scenario.

Utility Snippets and Templates

Bicep: Quick Virtual Network

```
resource vnet 'Microsoft.Network/virtualNetworks@2022-01-01'
= {
name: 'myVnet'
location: resourceGroup().location
properties: {
addressSpace: {
addressPrefixes: ['10.0.0.0/16']
}
subnets: [
{
name: 'default'
properties: {
addressPrefix: '10.0.1.0/24'
}
}
]
}
}
```

ARM Template: Storage Account

```
{
"$schema": "https://schema.management.azure.com/schemas/2019-04-01/deploymentTemplate.json#",
"resources": [
{
"type": "Microsoft.Storage/storageAccounts",
"apiVersion": "2022-09-01",
"name": "[parameters('storageAccountName')]",
"location": "[resourceGroup().location]",
"sku": { "name": "Standard_LRS" },
"kind": "StorageV2",
"properties": {}
}
]
}
```

Conclusion

These sample projects and snippets provide a practical foundation for applying Azure concepts in real-world scenarios. By building and deploying these hands-on examples, you'll gain experience with key Azure services, development practices, and architectural patterns. Use them as learning exercises, portfolio pieces, or even the foundation for production applications. With time and iteration, they will help turn theory into mastery.

API Reference Guide

A strong understanding of Azure's APIs empowers developers and DevOps engineers to automate, integrate, and extend the platform's capabilities. Azure exposes a broad set of REST APIs, client SDKs, and CLI commands to enable interaction with nearly every resource. This section serves as a practical reference for using the Azure API landscape—covering the REST API structure, authentication, key endpoints across major services, and example scenarios. It also includes code samples in multiple languages and discusses advanced usage, such as pagination, filtering, and automation.

Azure REST API Structure

Azure's REST API is based on a predictable pattern that allows consistent access to resources. All Azure APIs follow the format:

https://management.azure.com/{resource-path}?api-version={version}

Example: To list all resource groups in a subscription:

GET https://management.azure.com/subscriptions/{subscriptionId}/resourcegroups?api-version=2021-04-01

Common Elements:

- subscriptionId: Azure subscription identifier
- resourcegroups: Resource type

- api-version: Version of the API to use (each resource type has its own version history)

Authentication via Azure AD

All Azure REST APIs require an OAuth 2.0 access token issued by Azure Active Directory.

Steps to Authenticate:

1. Register an app in Azure AD
2. Grant it permissions to access Azure management APIs
3. Acquire a token using a client credential flow

Token Acquisition Example (Node.js):

```
const axios = require('axios');

const qs = require('qs');

const tokenEndpoint = `https://login.microsoftonline.com/${tenantId}/oauth2/token`;

const requestBody = qs.stringify({

grant_type: 'client_credentials',

client_id: clientId,

client_secret: clientSecret,

resource: 'https://management.azure.com/'

});
```

const { data } = await axios.post(tokenEndpoint, requestBody);

const accessToken = data.access_token;

Resource Management API Examples

Below are common use cases using REST endpoints.

Create a Resource Group

PUT https://management.azure.com/subscriptions/{subscriptionId}/resourcegroups/{rgName}?api-version=2

Request body:

```
{
"location": "eastus",
"tags": {
"environment": "dev"
}
}
```

List Virtual Machines

GET https://management.azure.com/subscriptions/{subscriptionId}/providers/Microsoft.Compute/virtualMachines?api-version=2021-07-01

Delete a Storage Account

DELETE https://management.azure.com/subscriptions/{subscriptionId}/resourceGroups/{rg}/providers/Microsoft.Storage/storageAccounts/{account}?api-version=2022-09-01

Advanced Querying and Filtering

Azure supports OData-like filtering and pagination.

Filter Resource Groups by Tag:

GET https://management.azure.com/subscriptions/{subscriptionId}/resourcegroups?$filter=tagName eq 'environment' and tagValue eq 'prod'&api-version=2021-04-01

Paginated Results

Some endpoints return a nextLink in the response:

{

"value": [...],

"nextLink": "https://management.azure.com/nextPageLink"

}

Continue calling nextLink until there are no more results.

Using the Azure CLI as an API Layer

The Azure CLI is built on top of REST APIs and is script-friendly.

Examples:

- List VMs:

az vm list—output table

- Get a specific VM:

az vm show—resource-group myrg—name myvm

- Create a storage account:

az storage account create—name mystorageacct—resource-group rg—location eastus—sku Standard_LRS

You can use—debug to see the raw HTTP request made by the CLI.

SDK Usage Across Languages

Azure provides SDKs for .NET, Java, Python, Go, JavaScript, and more.

Python SDK Example

```
from azure.identity import DefaultAzureCredential

from azure.mgmt.resource import ResourceManagementClient

credential = DefaultAzureCredential()

client = ResourceManagementClient(credential, subscription_id)

for rg in client.resource_groups.list():

print(rg.name)
```

.NET SDK Example

```
var credential = new DefaultAzureCredential();

var client = new ArmClient(credential);

SubscriptionResource subscription = await client.GetDefaultSubscriptionAsync();

await foreach (ResourceGroupResource rg in subscription.GetResourceGroups().GetAllAsync())

{

Console.WriteLine(rg.Data.Name);

}
```

JavaScript SDK Example (REST)

```
const axios = require('axios');

const res = await axios.get('https://management.azure.com/subscriptions/xxx/resourcegroups?api-version=2021-04-01', {

headers: {

Authorization: `Bearer ${accessToken}`

}

});

console.log(res.data.value);
```

Automating with REST and CI/CD

REST APIs can be used in GitHub Actions, Azure DevOps pipelines, or other CI/CD systems to:

- Deploy infrastructure
- Run compliance checks
- Automate tag enforcement
- Trigger remediation scripts

GitHub Actions Example: Call REST API

```
jobs:
call-api:
runs-on: ubuntu-latest
steps:
- name: Get Token and Call Azure API
run: |
TOKEN=$(az account get-access-token—query accessToken -o tsv)
curl -X GET \
-H "Authorization: Bearer $TOKEN" \
-H "Content-Type: application/json" \
```

"https://management.azure.com/subscriptions/$SUB_ID/resourcegroups?api-version=2021-04-01"

API Management for Custom APIs

Azure API Management (APIM) allows you to expose your own APIs securely, monitor usage, apply rate limits, and manage versions.

Basic Setup via CLI:

```
az apim create—name myapi—resource-group apimgroup—publisher-email admin@example.com—location eastus
```

Example API Policy (Rate Limit):

```
<inbound>

<rate-limit calls="100" renewal-period="60" />

</inbound>
```

Logging, Monitoring, and Throttling

Azure tracks API requests and provides diagnostic logs via Azure Monitor and Activity Logs.

Key points:

- Use x-ms-request-id for debugging.
- Most APIs are throttled; respect 429 Retry-After headers.

- Enable diagnostic settings to forward API logs to Log Analytics.

Querying API Usage Logs in Log Analytics:

```
AzureActivity
| where OperationNameValue startswith "Microsoft.Compute/virtualMachines"
| summarize count() by OperationNameValue, bin(TimeGenerated, 1h)
```

Useful API Endpoints Summary

Resource Type	Verb	Endpoint Snippet
Resource Groups	GET	/subscriptions/{sub}/resourcegroups
VMs	POST	/resourceGroups/{rg}/providers/Microsoft.Compute/virtualMachines/{vm}/start
Storage Accounts	PUT	/resourceGroups/{rg}/providers/Microsoft.Storage/storageAccounts/{name}
Policy Assignments	GET	/subscriptions/{sub}/providers/Microsoft.Authorization/policyAssignments
RBAC Roles	GET	/subscriptions/{sub}/providers/Microsoft.Authorization/roleDefinitions

Conclusion

The Azure API surface is extensive, powerful, and highly automatable. Whether you're building tools, writing scripts, managing deployments, or integrating with external platforms, understanding how to interact with Azure's REST APIs unlocks the full potential of the cloud. Coupled with SDKs, CLI tools, and security practices, this reference equips you to confidently work at the API level with real-world efficiency and flexibility.

Frequently Asked Questions

This section provides comprehensive answers to the most frequently asked questions about Azure, its services, and the broader cloud ecosystem. It's designed as a quick-reference guide for beginners and experienced users alike. Whether you're studying for a certification, troubleshooting a deployment, or looking for architectural guidance, this FAQ consolidates essential insights, best practices, and actionable tips to accelerate your Azure journey.

What is Microsoft Azure?

Microsoft Azure is a public cloud computing platform that offers over 200 services spanning compute, storage, networking, AI, IoT, DevOps, and security. It supports Infrastructure as a Service (IaaS), Platform as a Service (PaaS), and Software as a Service (SaaS), allowing organizations to build, deploy, and manage applications at global scale.

Is Azure suitable for small businesses and startups?

Yes. Azure provides a **free tier**, scalable pricing, and services tailored for small businesses and startups. Examples include:

- Azure App Service (free and shared tiers)
- Azure Functions (monthly free executions)

- Azure Static Web Apps
- GitHub integration for free CI/CD pipelines

Startups can also apply for the **Microsoft for Startups Founders Hub**, which offers free Azure credits, mentorship, and access to OpenAI services.

What's the difference between Azure App Service, Azure Functions, and AKS?

Feature	Azure App Service	Azure Functions	Azure Kubernetes Service (AKS)
Type	PaaS	Serverless (FaaS)	Container Orchestration
Use Case	Web apps, APIs	Event-driven apps	Microservices, large apps
Scalability	Auto-scaling	Dynamic, per-request	Manual or horizontal pod scaling
DevOps Integration	Good	Excellent	Excellent
Pricing	Per instance	Per execution	Per node/hour

How do I choose the right region for my resources?

Consider the following when choosing a region:

1. **Data Sovereignty**: Regulatory requirements may restrict where data can be stored.
2. **Latency**: Choose regions closest to your users for better performance.
3. **Service Availability**: Not all services are available in all regions.

4. **Redundancy**: For DR, choose paired regions (e.g., East US + West US).

You can check the regional availability of services here:

https://azure.microsoft.com/en-us/global-infrastructure/services/

What's the best way to manage Azure costs?

1. **Set Budgets** in Azure Cost Management.
2. **Use Tags** to allocate and filter costs.
3. **Right-size resources** using Azure Advisor.
4. **Use Reservations** for VMs, databases, and storage (1 or 3-year terms).
5. **Turn off non-prod resources** with automation (e.g., Logic Apps or Functions).
6. **Export cost data** to Storage or Power BI for detailed reporting.

Example CLI command to view spend:

az consumption usage list—start-date 2024-04-01—end-date 2024-04-30

What's the difference between a Subscription, Resource Group, and Management Group?

- **Management Group**: Groups multiple subscriptions for governance.

- **Subscription**: Billing boundary; contains all resources and policies.

- **Resource Group**: Logical container for related resources.

Use **Management Groups** to apply policies at scale, **Subscriptions** to separate billing or environments, and **Resource Groups** to logically organize deployments.

How does Azure support high availability?

Azure offers multiple layers of high availability:

- **Availability Sets**: Spread VMs across fault and update domains.
- **Availability Zones**: Physically separate datacenters within a region.
- **Geo-Redundancy**: Replicate storage/data to paired regions.
- **Load Balancers**: Distribute traffic across healthy endpoints.
- **Auto-Scaling**: Scale out services automatically based on load.

Example: Load-balanced VM with a zone-redundant Application Gateway ensures uptime even if a data center goes down.

What are Managed Identities?

Managed Identities allow Azure resources (e.g., VMs, Functions) to access other resources securely without storing credentials.

Two types:

- **System-assigned**: One identity tied to the resource lifecycle.
- **User-assigned**: Can be used by multiple resources.

Use them with Key Vault, Azure SQL, Storage, etc.

Example: Assigning a managed identity to a VM:

az vm identity assign—name myVM—resource-group myRG

How do I automate Azure deployments?

Use **Infrastructure as Code (IaC)** tools:

- **Bicep**: Native ARM template abstraction.
- **Terraform**: Popular third-party IaC with multi-cloud support.
- **Pulumi**: Code-first approach (TypeScript, Python, Go).
- **ARM Templates**: JSON-based, low-level.

Automate with CI/CD pipelines using **GitHub Actions**, **Azure DevOps**, or **Jenkins**.

What is Azure Blueprints?

Azure Blueprints let you **define, apply, and audit governance controls** across subscriptions. A blueprint includes:

- Role Assignments
- Policy Assignments

- ARM Templates
- Resource Groups

It ensures that new subscriptions or environments comply with enterprise standards from the start.

What is the difference between Azure Monitor, Log Analytics, and Application Insights?

- **Azure Monitor**: Umbrella service for collecting and analyzing telemetry.
- **Log Analytics**: Central query engine for logs using KQL.
- **Application Insights**: Focused on application performance monitoring.

Use them together to track infrastructure health, application performance, and custom business metrics.

How does Azure handle compliance and regulatory requirements?

Azure maintains one of the largest portfolios of compliance offerings:

- **Global**: ISO 27001, SOC 1/2/3, CSA STAR
- **Industry-Specific**: PCI-DSS, HIPAA, HITRUST
- **Regional**: GDPR (EU), FedRAMP (US), IRAP (AU)

You can view and download compliance reports in the **Microsoft Service Trust Portal**:

https://servicetrust.microsoft.com/

How do I protect secrets and keys in Azure?

Use **Azure Key Vault** to securely store and access:

- API keys
- Passwords
- Certificates
- Encryption keys (with HSM support)

Enable **RBAC**, **logging**, **soft delete**, and **purge protection**.

Example: Storing a secret via CLI:

az keyvault secret set—vault-name myvault—name "dbPassword"—value "SuperSecret!"

How does Azure handle disaster recovery?

Options include:

- **Azure Site Recovery (ASR)**: Replicate VMs or physical servers to Azure.
- **Geo-Redundant Storage (GRS)**: Automatically replicates data to paired regions.
- **Azure Backup**: Centralized backup solution for VMs, files, SQL databases.

- **Zone/Region Failover**: Built-in support for services like Azure SQL, Cosmos DB.

Use **BCDR plans** with automation scripts and test regularly.

How do I secure APIs in Azure?

1. **Host APIs** in App Services or Functions.
2. **Protect with Azure API Management (APIM)**.
3. **Use OAuth 2.0 or API keys** for authentication.
4. **Rate limit** and **validate headers** with APIM policies.
5. **Expose APIs via Private Link** when needed.

Example: Rate-limiting in APIM:

```
<inbound>

<rate-limit calls="100" renewal-period="60" />

</inbound>
```

What is the Azure Free Tier?

The Azure Free Account offers:

- 12 months of popular services (e.g., B1S VM, SQL, Blob Storage)

- 25+ services always free (e.g., Functions, Cosmos DB, Event Grid)

- $200 credit for 30 days

Great for learning, prototyping, and certifications.

Can I use Azure offline or on-premises?

Yes, through **hybrid solutions**:

- **Azure Stack HCI**: Run Azure workloads on-premises.
- **Azure Arc**: Manage on-prem and multi-cloud servers, VMs, Kubernetes.
- **Azure Stack Hub**: Full Azure services in disconnected environments.

These solutions are ideal for regulated industries, edge computing, and low-latency requirements.

Conclusion

These frequently asked questions serve as a launchpad for both new and experienced users to deepen their Azure knowledge. Azure's flexibility, scalability, and breadth of services offer solutions for nearly every workload and industry—but understanding best practices, service boundaries, and architectural trade-offs is essential to making the most of the platform. Keep this FAQ as a go-to reference during your daily work, learning sessions, or certification prep.

www.ingramcontent.com/pod-product-compliance
Lightning Source LLC
LaVergne TN
LVHW090254210926
848480LV00001B/16